Pledges of Jewish Allegiance

STANFORD STUDIES IN JEWISH HISTORY AND CULTURE

EDITED BY *Aron Rodrigue and Steven J. Zipperstein*

Pledges of Jewish Allegiance

Conversion, Law, and Policymaking in Nineteenth- and Twentieth-Century Orthodox Responsa

David Ellenson and Daniel Gordis

STANFORD UNIVERSITY PRESS

STANFORD, CALIFORNIA

Stanford University Press
Stanford, California

Parts of chapter 2 are based on material that appeared in Daniel Gordis,
"David Zevi Hoffmann on Civil Marriage: Evidence of a Traditional
Community under Siege," *Modern Judaism* 9, no. 1 (February 1990):
85–103. Parts of chapters 2 and 4 were originally published in an ear-
lier form in David Ellenson, "Representative Orthodox Responsa on
Conversion and Intermarriage in the Contemporary Period," *Jewish
Social Studies* 48, nos. 3–4 (1985): 209–20; and in David Ellenson, "The
Development of Orthodox Attitudes to Conversion in the Modern
Period," *Conservative Judaism* 36, no. 4 (1983): 57–73. Parts of chap-
ter 3 were originally published in David Ellenson, "On Conversion
and Intermarriage: The Evidence of Nineteenth Century Hungarian
Orthodox Rabbinic Writings," in *Text and Context: Essays in Modern
Jewish History and Historiography in Honor of Ismar Schorsch*, ed. Eli
Lederhendler and Jack Wertheimer (New York: Jewish Theological
Seminary, 2005), 321–46. Reprinted with permission.

Printed in the United States of America on acid-free, archival-quality paper

Library of Congress Cataloging-in-Publication Data

Ellenson, David Harry, 1947– author.
  Pledges of Jewish allegiance : conversion, law, and policymaking in
nineteenth- and twentieth-century Orthodox responsa / David Ellenson and
Daniel Gordis.
    p.   cm.—(Stanford studies in Jewish history and culture)
  Includes bibliographical references and index.
  ISBN 978-0-8047-7805-3 (cloth : alk. paper)
    1. Conversion—Judaism. 2. Responsa—History and criticism. 3. Jewish
law. 4. Jews—Identity. 5. Orthodox Judaism. 6. Judaism—History—
Modern period, 1750– I. Gordis, Daniel, author. II. Title. III. Series:
Stanford studies in Jewish history and culture.
BM645.C6E45 2012
296.1'85–dc23

                                                    2011021346

To our children

Ruth Ellenson
Micah and Sara Ellenson
Hannah Ellenson
Naomi Ellenson
Raphael Ellenson
Talia and Avishay Ben Sasson-Gordis
Aviel Gordis
Micha Gordis

Whose Jewish commitments
are as varied, and as passionate,
as those represented in this volume

Contents

Acknowledgments

In the more than a decade and a half during which we wrote this book, each of us has been privileged to be associated with institutions committed to both scholarship and the future of Jewish life. David Ellenson has served as the I. H. and Anna Grancell Professor of Jewish Religious Thought at the Hebrew Union College and, since 2001, as its president. When we began this book, Daniel Gordis was at the University of Judaism (now the American Jewish University), serving as vice president and founding dean of the Ziegler School of Rabbinic Studies, and subsequent to moving to Israel he has been vice president at the Mandel Foundation and senior vice president and senior fellow at the Shalem Center. Since 2011, he has also been president of the Shalem Foundation. All these institutions have encouraged this project and have afforded us stimulating colleagues who have enriched our work. We are grateful to all.

Our thanks, as well, to three people who did extensive work on the manuscript. Elisheva Urbas brought great insight to shaping the volume in its early stages, years ago, a task made appreciably more difficult by the fact that the book was written by two people on two continents. Zahava Stadler, then a student at Princeton University, did extensive editing of an early draft of the complete manuscript and improved it greatly. Janice Meyerson brought consummate professional abilities to the final editing of the book and to the preparation of the bibliography. We are grateful to all three for their significant contributions to the quality of this volume. Our thanks to Leslie Rubin for her thorough and thoughtful work on the index. Finally, Peter Joseph and Rob Bildner read an early draft of our conclusion and suggested significant changes in tone and direction that we incorporated and for which we are grateful.

To Steven Zipperstein and Norris Pope, of the Stanford University Press, our thanks for all they have done to shepherd this book through the process of review, acceptance, and publication, always acting with warmth and professionalism.

To our wives, Rabbi Jacqueline Koch Ellenson and Elisheva Waxman Gordis, our thanks for their forbearance and their belief that we would one day celebrate the completion of this project. Our gratitude to them can never be adequately expressed.

We began work on this volume when some of our children were still quite young, and now they are all adults. Even as they wondered aloud whether this volume would ever see the light of day, they celebrated with us the milestones of our progress and now can avidly participate in the larger conversation of which this book is a small part. We are enormously proud of what they have each accomplished and are delighted that their own Jewish commitments are as varied as the many opinions that we discuss in this volume, and no less passionate. Parents dare not wish for more.

New York and Jerusalem
Tu Bi-Shevat 5771
January 2011

Introduction Who Is a Jew? What Is a Jew?

Jewish Identity, Jewish Status, and the Challenge of Conversion

Lev Paschov certainly could never have imagined that he would be buried twice. An Israeli soldier who had immigrated to Israel from the former Soviet Union through the Law of Return, Paschov was killed along with another soldier while on active duty in southern Lebanon in 1993. Because Paschov's mother was not Jewish, the Israeli army's rabbi insisted that Paschov be buried outside the official military cemetery, which was consecrated exclusively for Jewish burial. After a public outcry, Paschov's corpse was exhumed, and he was buried a second time—this time, inside the Jewish military cemetery, though at its edge.[1]

Classical Jewish law defines a Jew as someone who either is born of a Jewish mother or has converted to Judaism before a valid court. As Paschov satisfied neither criterion, Israel's Orthodox religious authorities did not regard him as a Jew and ruled that he could not be buried in a Jewish cemetery. Many Israeli citizens were appalled by this decision. They were outraged that a man who had died defending the Jewish State and his fellow citizens, and who had immigrated to Israel under the Law of Return as a "Jew," could be denied the dignity of burial in a Jewish cemetery.

To many, Paschov and his life signaled that the classic criteria for defining and identifying a Jew were simply too narrow for the modern setting. Paschov exemplified a new and expansive model of how the Jewish community ought to be defined and how membership in the Jewish community ought to be determined today. Under Israel's Law of Return, which permits people with even one Jewish grandparent to immigrate to Israel as Jews, Paschov had been granted Israeli citizenship immediately. He died while defending his country, the Jewish

State, as a Jew. His fate and destiny were unquestionably and inextricably bound up with the fate of the Jewish people and a sovereign Jewish nation. Were these factors not sufficient to count him as a Jew?

In the ensuing debates surrounding his burial and reburial, many Israelis who were disturbed by what had transpired could not articulate the central questions that his case brought to light. Against the backdrop of the powerful social, political, religious, and demographic changes that have gripped the Jewish people since the onset of the modern period, this event demonstrated the complexity of the issues that surround the determination of Jewish status and the parameters of Jewish identity and community in the modern world.

Issues of how Jewish status should be resolved and what it means to be a Jew have hovered over Jewish legal discourse throughout Jewish history. Positions on these issues have never been universally held, and the assumptions upon which they rest have largely remained unarticulated. However, with the collapse of the Jewish community as a semi-autonomous political entity in Western Europe and the United States from the late 1700s on, and with the concomitant entry of the Jew as an individual citizen in the modern political arena, the modern period of Jewish history has seen the rise of these issues—as the Paschov case demonstrates—in a novel and intense fashion.

In this book, we will focus on the modern period of Jewish history and provide an analysis of nineteenth- and twentieth-century legal opinions and other writings by Orthodox rabbis regarding conversion. We will preface the analysis of these opinions with a discussion of these modern writings as parts of an ongoing legal tradition draw upon classical Jewish sources. We will employ these works as the lens through which we can understand the overlapping but distinct ways in which traditionalist religious authorities have gone about the task of defining the core of Jewishness—Jewish identity, status, and community—in the modern situation. In so doing, we hope to illuminate the larger phenomenon of how Jews and Judaism have responded to the challenges of the modern world regarding the continuity and borders of the Jewish people.

In order to reflect upon why modernity has so complicated and heightened the stakes of the debate surrounding the questions of "who is a Jew" and "what is the nature of the Jewish community," it is instructive to employ the contrasts that historians and sociologists routinely draw between the notion of "status" and the concept of "identity." While these two terms often overlap, they are two distinct referents that are not necessarily identical.

"Status," stemming from a Latin word meaning "standing," refers to the condition of a person in the eyes of the law. When employed with regard to a person's relationship to a group, the person's own conception of that relationship may be irrelevant. Authorities external to the group or within the group itself may well make status designations with no regard for the individual's sense of self-definition. For example, there were self-defined Christians who, living in Nazi Germany, were defined as Jews under the Nuremberg Laws of 1935. Similarly (though with very different implications), a person born of a Jewish mother who has sworn allegiance to another religious faith would still be considered Jewish by nearly all traditional Jewish legal authorities.

Conversely, despite an individual's own sense of identification and belonging, a group might well deny him legal status as one of their own. For example, the child of a woman converted to Judaism under non-Orthodox auspices would be denied Jewish status by Orthodox rabbinical authorities in virtually every case and would be refused the right to marry as a Jew within the Jewish State. Along the same lines, a Conservative rabbi would likely not perform the wedding of a patrilineally descended child (the child of a Jewish father and a non-Jewish mother) raised in Reform or Reconstructionist circles without a ceremony of formal conversion to Judaism. Other examples could be provided, but these should suffice to indicate that "status" is a legal designation indifferent to the subjective judgments or self-definitions of the individual.

"Identity," in contrast, embraces a more specific and personal component. Its etymological root, derived from the Greek *idios*, means "private" or "individual." When the term "identity," as opposed to "status," is employed to refer to a person's relationship to a group, it may simply signify the psychological orientation of the individual toward that group. It reflects the individual's autonomous understanding of who he or she is. Individuals who participate in the life of a given Jewish community might well identify as Jews despite not having undergone any formal rite of conversion to Judaism. Identity, in this instance, would not address the Jewish legal relationship that obtains between a person and the Jewish community. It would, rather, reflect a personal definition of self in reference to a group and might even be affirmed by one or more sectors of that group, though not necessarily—as we saw in the case of Paschov—the one with any legal authority to determine status.

The issue of "who is a Jew," along with the determination of membership in the Jewish people, grows particularly complex in the modern situation precisely because it involves considerations of both status and identity, which are no longer coterminous, as shown in the cases cited above. Many factors—the individual, the group, certain sectors of the group, and bodies external to the group that possess authority over it—may be involved in determining a given person's status as a Jew. These factors deserve special attention when we contrast the nature of Jewish existence in the premodern world with Jewish life in the modern world in settings such as the United States or the State of Israel.

Within the framework of a premodern political order, status was corporate. Individual citizenship in a modern nation-state, as present in many contemporary political models, did not exist. To compound matters, the Jewish community was politically autonomous or semiautonomous in governing the lives of its members, and it informed their sense of self-identity even as they internalized the cultural norms and teachings of the community. There was little or no dissonance between public and private spheres, or between individual and collective realms, with regard to Jewish status and identity. In a world where pluralism was controlled politically in such matters and where individualism and voluntarism had not yet arisen as they have in a modern setting, being Jewish was more than an expression of religious affiliation; it defined a person's political status, informed his culture, and determined his identity. Only in rare instances did conflict arise between individuals and public political bodies as to who was a Jew. Status and identity were virtually one and the same in almost every case. Individuals who defined themselves as Jews would have done so with the assent of a politically self-governing Jewish community that knew nothing of denominationalism as well as the assent of Gentile authorities who permitted Jews to enjoy semiautonomous political status.

Modernity has dissolved the "synonymity" of status and identity and has thrust upon Judaism a number of lasting changes that have redefined the terms under which Jews live. As Peter Berger, speaking of "Jewishness" in the premodern world, has observed, to be Jewish was "a taken-for-granted given of the individual's existence, ongoingly reaffirmed with ringing certainty by everyone in the individual's milieu."[2] Being a member of the Jewish collective was not a matter that was subject to an individual's own beliefs or desires but was dictated by the rules of Jewish law and the communal structures that enforced them. The lines between Jew and non-Jew were clearly drawn.

In today's world, the ever-changing contours of modern Judaism complicate the process of defining who is Jewish, as seen in the instance of Lev Paschov. These developments are evident not only in individual cases, but also more broadly. For example, in 2008, Rabbi Avraham Sherman, an ultraorthodox (*ḥaredi*) rabbi on the Israeli High Rabbinical Court, decided to invalidate thousands of conversions conducted by the Conversion Authority of the chief rabbinate under the supervision of Orthodox Rabbi Haim Druckman because of serious disagreements with Druckman as to the obligations of belief and practice that prospective converts were required to take upon themselves. We shall return to this episode in later chapters, but we mention it here because it highlights the intricacy of determining Jewish status and identity in the modern setting.

Of course, modernity did not descend on the Jewish community in one fell swoop. When we speak of the profoundly altered state of the Jewish community in modernity, we are actually referring to a number of factors that have coalesced during the last three hundred years. First, the Enlightenment of the late eighteenth century, along with its Jewish complement, the Haskalah, encouraged Jews to integrate into secular society and raised questions about personal autonomy, the theological origins of Jewish law, and the authority of the Jewish community that would have been virtually unthinkable just a few years earlier.

Second, particularly in Western Europe, Jews enjoyed a political emancipation that granted them rights of citizenship on par with their non-Jewish counterparts. This political emancipation ultimately destroyed the legal borders of the Jewish community and transformed the community from a legal corporation into a voluntary association of individual members.

This change provided individual Jews the option of abandoning the Jewish community and led to a third major factor: the waning influence of the rabbinate on its constituents. When Jews did not possess the legal option of leaving the communities that their rabbis controlled, and when the community functioned as a semiautonomous legal corporation, the rabbis possessed what scholars of law and culture have called "coercive legal authority." They were essentially civil magistrates. As soon as the legal power of the community as a distinct political entity dissolved or became severely limited, the rabbis faced unprecedented challenges and could, at best, exercise what these same scholars of law and culture label "influential authority." As rabbis were now religious authorities who could no longer function as civil magistrates with police powers, they could exert authority only among those whom they could persuade to obey and "command" only those Jews who had internalized the norms that they had promulgated. Yet, in an era in which traditional religious observance and belief among vast numbers of Jews had either severely attenuated or even dissolved, the rabbis were compelled to recognize that large numbers of Jews would not affirm their authority or their teachings in crucial areas of life.[3]

Primary among these areas was the social arena. It is vital to emphasize that, in the wake of the cultural, religious, and political changes that marked the transformation of Jewish life as Jews entered the modern world, a fourth change took place in the sphere of social relations: Jews and non-Jews came to intermingle regularly as social equals. The pace of Jewish exogamy soared to high levels in the generations following Emancipation and Enlightenment as Jews acculturated and as Gentiles saw Jews as desirable marriage partners.

As Jewish religious leaders struggled to evolve and to cope with these sweeping changes, the creation of Israel as the Jewish nation-state in 1948 only reinforced the urgency of addressing these changes. In offering a novel setting for considerations of Jewish status and identity in the modern world, the State forced a reconceptualization of what it meant both to be Jewish and to belong to a Jewish polity. Yet, even in Israel, the rabbinate, by and large, has never had control over civil law. It is true that the state-supported chief rabbinate and its arms possess sovereignty over matters of personal status, such as marriage, divorce, and burial, for its Jewish citizenry. Here the powers accorded the rabbinate are parallel to what they were in premodern times, and the Israeli rabbinate is called upon to adjudicate and determine questions of Jewish status for all who seek to be married, divorced, or buried as Jews within the Jewish State. These factors that mark the Israeli situation will receive special consideration in the analysis that we will provide in this book. However, even within Israel, the presence of a large number of secular Jews, as well as the emigration to Israel of hundreds of thousands of persons who identify themselves and are identified by others culturally and politically as Jews but lack halakhic (religious-legal) status as Jews, has made the issues of conversion and Jewish identity paramount and controversial topics on the Israeli scene.

In order to understand the issues of Jewish status and identity as well as the nature and framework of the Jewish community, this book will analyze a broad range of representative Orthodox rabbinic legal writings—principally responsa—on conversion, status, and identity against the backdrop of the changes that we have mentioned above. Responsa are elite, technical documents—case discussions and their holdings in modern Western jurisprudential nomenclature—and rabbis throughout the centuries have used them as opportunities to apply the insights, meanings, norms, and precedents provided by the literary and legal texts of the Jewish past (Bible, Talmud, codes, and other responsa) to the pressing and often novel issues of the present age. Consequently, a single responsum can be seen as part of a vast body of Jewish case law that stretches over the centuries. Responsa are the crossroads at which text and context meet in the ongoing tradition of Jewish legal hermeneutics. Each responsum is an autonomous text, written by a specific author; each should also be viewed as an individual reflection of a continuous body of Jewish literature with its own style, language, and logic. These idiomatic expressions of Jewish thought provide an excellent lens though which to witness the role of the classical Jewish literary tradition (Bible, Talmud, and, less often, midrash) and later rabbinic texts (codes, responsa, and occasionally commentaries and philosophical literature—for example, Maimonides), as well as the input of contemporary social, psychological, and ethical factors in the development of Judaism.[4]

In each era, *posekim* (authorities in the Jewish legal tradition; sing., *posek*) have had to determine how they stand with respect to all that comes down from the past, but they must do so as persons who are embedded in a present moment. Throughout history, these religious leaders have been compelled to mediate between a received religious tradition, on the one hand, and the inescapable demands of a contemporary cultural, social, and political context combined with influences of personality and personal values, on the other. In this sense, the history of the Jewish legal tradition, like other legal traditions, is fundamentally a history of diverse interpretations. Each interpretation and *posek* is linked to the past while offering opinions that open various portals to the future. This is not to say that *posekim* substitute their own values for those embedded in the legal materials and traditions that they have inherited and revere; they are expected to adhere to established principles and rules. They are not expected to create ideas out of thin air but to follow precedent as contained in the legal texts of Jewish tradition. Precedent, *stare decisis* in legal terminology, places constraints upon the *posek*, and *posekim* are never permitted to break self-consciously from the past because their authority rests upon their fidelity to original texts and prior holdings. A traditional account of Jewish legal adjudication emphasizes the faithful application of precedent to novel situations.

However, this straightforward description of the legal process is too narrow to capture or to explain the full range of factors that mark the adjudicatory process. A responsum functions on an immediate level as a ruling that is binding upon the questioner; but on a broader level, a responsum enters as a single precedent, an individual voice, in the larger body of Jewish legal discourse. In this broader sense, we would emphasize—and this is crucial for our book—that legal decision-making is analogical and always requires an interpretive performance on the part of those charged with rendering judgment. As David Hume pointed out over two centuries ago in his *Enquiry Concerning the Principles of Morals*, juridical reasoning must optimally be characterized by its dependence upon "imagination."⁵ The rationale that determines whether and how the rule contained in a precedent can be applied does not lie exclusively in the merits of the rule or the case itself. Rather, the question is how the jurist understands the rule and how he then extends the rule and its logical entailments to the case at hand, and this determination depends upon a host of logical, contextual, and personal factors. Consequently, case law is supple. Legal decision-making and the rationales and causes that support the holdings that emerge from the adjudicatory process are best treated as highly persuasive rather than absolutely incontestable.

Our book treats the responsa of exclusively Orthodox rabbis because they share an unremitting commitment to the authority of Jewish law. Halakhah is unquestionably binding on all of them and—in theory, at least—on their congregants. It also serves as a control for determining a common framework from which their rulings derive. Yet, despite this common framework, these responsa will display widely varied understandings of what constitutes the essential core of Jewish belonging and identity. They also reveal the diverse approaches of these rabbis as to how they believe that the resources of the Jewish legal tradition can best be applied to guide the Jewish community in a modern world beset by what they would regard as threatening social and demographic trends. Some of these rabbis were keenly aware of the weakened power of the rabbinate in the face of an ever more open civil society, which significantly influenced the decisions that they rendered. Others were indifferent to such changes. Some responsa that these rabbis issued were focused on stringently maintaining the boundaries of the traditional community; others demonstrated a wide-open flexibility that permitted them to adopt a policy of "constituency retention"⁶ in keeping with their understanding of how Jewish law could be applied in the modern context. In order to illuminate and grasp the dynamics at play in the works of the *posekim* we analyze in this volume, we will employ the philosophical writings of different philosophers and conceptions of secular law ranging from classically positivist notions of law to images of law as public policy.

Our book is divided into five substantive chapters. The first presents the classical sources of Jewish law and legend upon which all the rabbis we study in this volume—as persons committed to the authority of Jewish law—drew upon in issuing their own opinions. These texts constitute the raw material with which all these authorities had to grapple.

In the second chapter, we move to Germany, and in the third chapter to rabbis in central Europe during the nineteenth century, for it was in these places that these rabbis were first compelled to confront a world in which Jewish exogamy was common and in which the concomitant demand for conversion and the expansion of communal borders first arose in the Jewish encounter with modernity.

In the fourth chapter, we turn to the twentieth century and consider the setting of America and Germany to see the multifaceted responses that this time and these places elicited from leading Orthodox legal writers on these matters. Finally, Israel itself will occupy our attention: chapter 5 attempts to define the impact that reconstituted Jewish sovereignty has had upon Orthodox jurists as they have struggled with the problems of defining Jewish status and identity for a diverse population of secular and religious Jews who have returned to the Jewish homeland after two millennia.

We then offer a concluding chapter, summarizing what we have learned from this analysis of the various decisions that Orthodox *posekim* have rendered in their legal rulings on this topic during the past two hundred years.

A plethora of books that tackle the topic of conversion to Judaism in the modern era—including some that look specifically at responsa literature—have appeared in recent years. Foremost among them are *The Boundaries of Judaism*, by Donniel Hartman; and *Transforming Identity: The Ritual Transition from Gentile to Jew*, by Avi Sagi and Zvi Zohar.[7] In the former book, Hartman investigates a much smaller range of modern decisors and notes how the factionalism of modern Jewish life makes it difficult to define the collective identity of the Jewish people. In the latter, rather encyclopedic, work, Sagi and Zohar explore the totality of Jewish legal history and the disagreements that arise among interpreters of Jewish law throughout the centuries as experts assign diverse valence to religion, nationality, kinship, and autonomy in offering their conceptions of membership in the Jewish community. Most encyclopedic of all is Menachem Finkelstein's *Conversion:*

Halakhah and Practice,[8] a translation of Finkelstein's original work in Hebrew, which offers an unparalleled amalgam of traditional and modern sources from the earliest rabbinic sources through contemporary responsa.

What distinguishes our book from others is that our intent is not to be encyclopedic; our focus is limited to the work of nineteenth- and twentieth-century Orthodox rabbis. Nor have we sought to cover every authority in that more narrowly defined category. Our aim is much more constrained, focusing on the ways in which conversion responsa speak to the challenge of making Jewish public policy in our postmodern world, in which issues of identity have become more complex than ever. We seek to understand the legal opinions of the scholars we examine regarding the diverse ways in which Orthodox authorities understand what ought to be the kernel of commitment for those who seek to join the Jewish community, and how Orthodox authorities, who are essentially making public policy for the Jewish world, ought to navigate the uncharted waters of a rapidly changing and permeable Jewish world.

What is unique about our focus is the claim that these *posekim* should not be understood as legal arbiters in a narrow sense. Rather, as judges in their decisions, these men must be understood principally as framers of public policy directions. These *posekim* have struggled to address the overarching issues of what constitutes Jewish identity, status, and conversion for a Jewish community that exists in an era rife with intermarriage and religious nonobservance. Through the legal decisions they render, these rabbis strive to be faithful to the integrity of a tradition that they honor and revere. At the same time, they attempt to direct the community they serve in the present while preparing that community for the future.

While the attention of this book is devoted to writings taken solely from representatives of the Orthodox denomination of Judaism, our aim is to employ a presentation and analysis of their writings to illuminate the large and increasingly complex task that all contemporary Jewish leaders undertake as they seek to establish borders and define commitments and obligations for Jews and the Jewish community in the modern period. In this sense, our book moves beyond the specific denominational focus of the material to speak to the larger dynamics marking the contemporary Jewish situation as Jews of all persuasions respond to the challenges of the modern world. Even though we concentrate on the issue of conversion, we will essentially be examining the larger issue of the place of Jewish legal interpretation in Jewish public discourse and the dimensions of Jewish identity and status as the Jewish community and its leaders attempt to understand and define what it means to be a Jew in the modern world.

One Conversion in Jewish Tradition
An Introduction to the Classical Sources

To most modern Jews, the institution of conversion seems a natural part of Judaism. Conversion and converts are found in virtually all segments of Jewish society. Most Jewish communities welcome converts. In the United States alone, thousands of Gentiles convert to Judaism each year. The tradition itself seems to welcome converts, declaring that a convert is an Israelite in all respects[1] and warning that one who derides the convert violates as many as forty-six negative commandments.[2] The Mishnah in tractate Bava Metzia even forbids a Jew from reminding a convert that his ancestors were Gentiles.[3]

Despite these positive views of conversion and converts, no formal institution of conversion or ceremony for such a purpose is mentioned in the Torah. Indeed, a careful reading of Jewish texts reveals that Jewish tradition has always been conflicted about conversion as a possibility and about converts as members of the Jewish community. This ambivalence stems, in all likelihood, from the fact that the Jewish people is not simply a theological community but a historical and ethnic one as well. One can adopt a theology, but it is much more difficult (and perhaps even impossible) to fully adopt a history or an ethnicity.

An interesting reflection of this ambivalence is found in the Mishnah, the statutory collection of Jewish laws compiled by Rabbi Judah the Prince from the second century C.E. In its discussion of first-fruit offerings at the Temple, the Mishnah says that though a convert must bring first-fruit offerings, he may not say the words "which the Lord has sworn to our fathers, to give unto us" as part of his liturgical declaration because his ancestors were not part of that historical experience.[4] Apparently, the convert can become Jewish enough to be obligated to bring the offering but not Jewish enough to claim to have the same history as other Jews.

The convert thus occupies a strange and somewhat conflicted role in Jewish life. Jewish tradition permits the convert to join the Jewish people but often makes it difficult for him to do so. Even the Bible's word for "convert," *geir*, reflects this conflict, for *geir* means not only "convert" but "stranger" as well. The Bible refers to the convert as a *geir* even after he has joined the Jewish people. In some sense, therefore, he remains a stranger forever. At the same time, reminding him of his past as a Gentile is forbidden.

This ambivalence about conversion is palpable even today. Contentious debates over the Law of Return in Israel, the status of non-Orthodox conversions performed in Israel and in the Diaspora, high-profile decisions of a few American Jewish communities to disallow conversions, and harrowing accounts of immigrants to Israel who can find no place to bury their children[5]—all these might seem to point to crass politics but can be traced to conflicting undercurrents regarding what defines a person as Jewish. By implication, these disagreements as to what makes a person Jewish are actually debates over what Judaism is—and those discussions date back almost three thousand years. Any attempt to appreciate the confluence of conversion, law, and politics in the modern Jewish world must therefore begin with an examination of the ancient sources that reflect these competing attitudes.

In Orthodox Judaism, the arena in which conversion, law, and politics meet in modern Jewish life is halakhah, or Jewish law. Like all Jewish communities, the world of Orthodoxy grapples with issues of Jewish identity, social policy, and boundary maintenance. But it does so primarily through the halakhic, or Jewish legal, process and by engaging in legal discourse, because Orthodox Judaism in general and the Orthodox rabbinate in particular are theologically committed to the belief that God's will finds expression within the classical texts of the Jewish legal tradition and their ongoing interpretation. And because halakhah (like many other legal systems) is precedent-based, it is impossible to appreciate the subtleties of contemporary arguments without reference to the legal texts and cases to which they allude, whether explicitly or implicitly.

In the following pages, we lay the foundation for our discussion of conversion in the world of contemporary Jewish Orthodoxy by introducing the major texts, trends, and conflicts that have long undergirded Jewish legal discussions of this pivotal issue, particularly as they relate to the motivations of the convert.[6] As we will see, when it comes to conversion, the conflicts of modernity have their roots in the ambivalences of antiquity.

The Biblical Period

As we suggested above, the mere notion that Judaism once had no institution of conversion seems unthinkable, but this is indeed the case. The conversion ceremony is essentially rabbinic, not biblical, in origin and apparently has its roots in postexilic Jewish history, sometime after the destruction of the First Temple in 586 B.C.E.

The English word "conversion" comes from the Latin *convertere*, which connotes a spiritual orientation. In most religious conversions, converts are those who come to see their way of life as fundamentally spiritually inadequate and who consciously choose a new system of spiritual belief and behavior.[7] But the Hebrew Bible does not describe any process to promote such transformation and says nothing about the fundamental spiritual transformation that conversion ought to be reflecting.

At times, conversion in the Bible seems to be accomplished simply through marriage. By virtue of marrying an Israelite, at least in some instances, a wife joined her husband's community. Judah married a Canaanite, Joseph married an Egyptian, and Moses married both a Midianite and an Ethiopian. David wed a Philistine, and his son, Solomon, married numerous foreign women.[8] Though figures in later rabbinic tradition struggled with (and, in some cases, sought to deny) these facts, nowhere does the Bible even hint at a ceremony in which the originally non-Israelite biblical figures become personally or religiously transformed in order to enter into these unions. Even Ruth, the paradigmatic symbol of conversion in later Jewish tradition, never actually converts. Her famous statement, "Wherever you go, I will go; wherever you lodge, I will lodge; your people shall be my people, and your God my God. Where you die, I will die, and there I will be buried,"[9] is obviously a statement of loyalty to her mother-in-law, Naomi, not to some new theological system. Like others in the Bible who become part of the Israelite people through marriage or some other declaration, Ruth is adopting a family, not a religion. Shaye J. D. Cohen puts the matter succinctly: "The foreign woman who married an Israelite husband was supposed to leave her gods in her father's house, but even if she did not, it never occurred to anyone to argue that her children were not Israelites. Since the idea of conversion to Judaism did not yet exist . . . it never occurred to anyone to demand that the foreign woman undergo some ritual to indicate her acceptance into the religion of Israel."[10]

The same was apparently true in reverse. If an Israelite woman married a foreign man, it was she who was effectively joining his community, and the assumption was that her children would not be Israelites. In this, the biblical tradition echoes assumptions pervasive in the ancient world. People commonly switched their religious allegiances, but devoting their energies to a new god did not typically require their having to consciously repudiate their past religious attachments. To the extent that the Tanakh (Hebrew Bible) shares this characteristic of the ancient Near East, it differs radically from the rabbinic Jewish tradition that would later emerge.

Biblical tradition differs from contemporary Jewish practice in yet another significant way. For as we will shortly see, not only does the Bible not introduce a ritual for conversion or a theological construct that would accommodate it (whereas later Jewish tradition developed both), biblical terminology even suggests that the transformation from Gentile to Israelite could never eradicate all vestiges of the person's origins as a non-Israelite. This is radically different from the rabbinic tradition's claim that a convert is like a newborn child[11] and from the Mishnah's reminder that "if he was a child of converts, one may not say to him, 'Remember the deeds of your ancestors [when they were Gentiles],' for it is said, 'You shall not wrong a stranger or oppress him.' "[12]

The most obvious evidence that the convert retains some of his or her status as at least a quasi-outsider to the Jewish community is that the Bible uses the same word, *geir*, for both "stranger" and "convert."

Even after joining the Israelite community, the *geir* is still a stranger, an outsider, quintessentially "other" in some sense. That the *geir* remains a foreigner is clear from a variety of passages. Numerous verses in the Torah warn the Israelite not to oppress the stranger. The frequency of such warnings suggests that such oppression must have been a serious issue. The Torah warns: "There shall be one law for the citizen and for the stranger who dwells among you";[13] "You shall not wrong a *geir* or oppress him, for you were strangers in the land of Egypt";[14] and "You and the *geir* shall be alike before the Lord."[15] Indeed, the classic language of Deuteronomy associates the stranger with those most in need of protection: "You shall not subvert the rights of the *geir* or the fatherless; you shall not take a widow's garment in pawn."[16]

These warnings against oppressing the *geir* should not be construed to mean that the Torah believes that the stranger can ever be wholly incorporated into Israelite society. These warnings attest to what must have been an abiding sense of "otherness" for people such as these. Indeed, the Torah occasionally employs the "otherness" of the *geir* as an image of threat, a potential tool of God's wrath. In its famous section cursing the Israelite community, Deuteronomy warns: "The *geir* in your midst shall rise above you higher and higher, while you sink lower and lower: he shall be your creditor, but you shall not be his; he shall be the head and you the tail."[17]

Numerous legal structures also pointed to the "convert's" abiding difference. The command regarding the Sabbath points to the marginal status of the *geir*, as the Torah admonishes: "Six days shall you do your work, but on the seventh day you shall cease from labor, in order that your ox and your ass may rest, and that your bondman and the stranger may be refreshed."[18]

Despite the *geir*'s otherness, he is no mere trespasser. The Torah permits the *geir*'s participation in a variety of rituals that were clearly religious in nature—rituals in which someone with no relationship to the community would not have been permitted to participate. Consider the following passage on the paschal sacrifice from Exodus 12:

> The Lord said to Moses and Aaron: This is the law of the Passover offering: No foreigner shall eat of it. But any slave a man has bought may eat of it once he has been circumcised. No bound or hired laborer

shall eat of it. It shall be eaten in one house: you shall not take any of the flesh outside the house; nor shall you break a bone of it. The whole community of Israel shall offer it. If a stranger who dwells with you would offer the Passover to the Lord, all his males must be circumcised; then he shall be admitted to offer it; he shall then be as a citizen of the country. But no uncircumcised person may eat of it. There shall be one law for the citizen and for the stranger who dwells among you.[19]

The reference to the *geir* as distinct highlights his otherness. Permitting him to participate in the ritual suggests a degree of inclusiveness. The fact that the *geir* belonged to no tribe and did not own land rendered him socioeconomically vulnerable, leading the Torah to stipulate his treatment in the realm of charity[20] and his eligibility for the gleanings of the farmer's fields.[21] Requiring circumcision seems to be some form of what later generations might have called a conversion ceremony, but it is important to note that the *geir* was not required to renounce any religious attachments of his past or to make any declaration of fealty to Israel or its God. The combination of these factors suggests an ambivalence that, as we shall see in future chapters, endures to this day.

The biblical tradition thus describes no formal means of joining the Israelite community, and it employs a term for the person who does join this community that continues to point to his otherness. In a tradition deeply rooted in land, territory, and tribal affiliation, this was quite natural. But the destruction of the Bible's land-based, tribal Judaism in 586 B.C.E., combined with the emergence of a tradition in which religious practice was the chief defining characteristic of belonging to the Jewish community, altered this approach permanently. In its creation of a formal process of conversion, rabbinic Judaism was doing more than naturally developing its biblical antecedents; it was engaging in a powerful shift, perhaps even rebellion, in the way that it saw the whole notion of religious-ethnic identity and in the way that it construed what it meant to be a Jew.

The Emergence of a Rabbinic Conception of Conversion: The Tannaitic Period

Scholars seem to agree that what ultimately emerged as the rabbinic conversion ceremony had begun to take shape by the time that Ezra and Nehemiah led the return to Zion after several decades of Babylonian exile.[22] However, there is no indication that Ezra even considered conversion as a possibility for the problem of foreign women having married into Israelite society.[23] His decision to expel them without consideration of an alternative suggests that even if conversion as an institution had begun to emerge, it was still not fully accepted or developed at that point.

Yet it is understandable that the experience of exile would have opened the possibility of conversion. Dispersion and the destruction of the Temple marked a shift from Israelite religion to Judaism. Surrounded by foreign people, living as a small minority in Babylon with the Temple devastated and their tribal structure gone, the people formerly known as Israelites could no longer be defined exclusively by the place where they resided. Inevitably, the geographic basis of their self-definition had to subside (despite the enduring importance of Zion in their self-conceptions), while a series of new commitments would come to the fore, commitments that others could theoretically adopt. Gentiles could not have become Israelites; but now, they could become Jews.

The dispersion of the Jews from their land not only made conversion a possibility but also created a necessity for a ritual. The biblical system of a *geir* simply joining the community by residing in it now bore the potential for marked chaos and disorder. No longer, therefore, could conversion remain a personal and private affair. A Gentile could no longer join the community simply by claiming to be a convert and could no longer convert to Judaism on his own.[24]

By the time the Mishnah was codified in 220 C.E., conversion as a concept and the details of its ritual had taken hold in Jewish life. The Mishnah itself does not mention the requirement of immersion in a *mikveh* (ritual bath) as part of conversion, but immersion figures prominently in several other rabbinic texts (called *baraitot*; sing., *baraita*)[25] that were written during the same period as the texts of the Mishnah.[26] The most commonly cited text on the subject is a *baraita* from the tractate Yevamot:

> Our Rabbis taught: If at the present time a man desires to become a proselyte, he is to be addressed as follows: "What reason have you for desiring to become a proselyte? Do you not know that Israel at the present time is persecuted and oppressed, despised, harassed, and overcome by afflictions?"
>
> If he replies, "I know and yet I am unworthy," he is accepted immediately and is given instruction in some of the minor and some of the major commandments. He is informed of the sin [of the neglect of the agricultural commandments of] Gleanings, the Forgotten Sheaf, the Corner, and the Poor Man's Tithe. He is also told of the punishment for the transgression of the commandments. Furthermore, he is addressed thus: "Be it known to you that before you came to this condition, if you had eaten forbidden fat, you would not have been punishable with *kareit* [excision]; if you had profaned the Sabbath, you would not have been punishable with stoning; but now were you to eat suet you would be punished with *kareit*; were you to profane the Sabbath, you would be punished with stoning."
>
> And as he is informed of the punishment for the transgression of the commandments, so is he informed of the reward granted for their fulfillment. He is told: "Be it known to you that the world to come was made only for the righteous, and that Israel at the present time is unable to bear either too much prosperity or too much suffering." He is not, however, to be persuaded or dissuaded too much. If he accepted, he is circumcised forthwith. Should any shreds that render the circumcision invalid remain, he is to be circumcised a second time. As soon as he is healed, arrangements are made for his immediate immersion, when two learned men must stand by his side and acquaint him with some of the minor commandments and with some of the major ones. When he comes up after his immersion, he is deemed to be an Israelite in all respects.[27]

This famous passage, which is repeated almost verbatim in later codes, establishes the basic ritual of conversion. The first element is a discussion of the commandments and of the system of reward and punishment predicated on their observance. It is not clear what, exactly, the convert must commit to doing or to believing, but some commitment to ritual observance is demanded. Some later authorities hold that the prospective convert must agree to observe every detail of Jewish law.[28] While that assertion is faithful to a variety of talmudic and post-talmudic texts, it is important to note that it is not at all clear that this was the intent of the *baraita* here in Yevamot.

The multiple interpretations to which this passage lends itself will become linchpins of the later debate in nineteenth- and twentieth-century Orthodox policy on conversion. In the modern period, one of the most divisive elements of the conversion debate is the legitimacy of a conversion in which it is clear that the convert will not become a fully observant Jew. The social environment of post-Emancipation Europe and the United States was radically altered, and they witnessed a proliferation of models of active and public Jews who were not fully observant. Thus, the question of whether absolute commitment to observance is required for conversion has become relevant.

What does the *baraita* in Yevamot imply? That depends, of course, upon which interpretation of that passage one prefers, but certain elements ought to be noted. First, not all talmudic sources skirt the issue of acceptance of commandments in quite the way that this passage does. Indeed, soon after this discussion in Yevamot, the tractate asserts: "For it was indeed taught, 'Both a proselyte and a slave bought from an idolater must make a declaration [of acceptance of the commandments].' "[29] Similarly, in a talmudic discussion in Bekhorot,[30] Rabbi Yossi ben Yehudah says that a convert who rejects even one detail of Jewish law is not to be accepted, but that view is nowhere mentioned in Yevamot.

Second, the choreographed conversation that the court has with the prospective convert focuses much more on the historical experience of the Jew than on any theological issues. Note that the questions that he is asked are not intended to be impossible to answer. He is not being interrogated rigorously; if anything, the questions are an opportunity for the presiding rabbinic court to engage in a conversation about Jewish life and identity. Indeed, the court may be checking only whether the prospective convert is willing to endure the sufferings of the Jewish people. Shaye Cohen suggests that "the authors of the *baraita* . . . were not interested in discovering reasons to reject the convert. Their primary concern was not to verify that the convert accepted all the commandments but that he knew what awaited him, and for this purpose instruction in a 'few' (representative) commandments would suffice. The rest he would learn later."[31]

Just as the prospective convert's ritual practice was not subjected to intensive analysis, so, too, was the tradition relatively flexible regarding the convert's theological commitments. In a particularly astute observation, Cohen continues: "[The ritual] is not primarily an initiation ritual. It is not concerned with the spiritual state of the convert or with making him a member of the Jewish community. In this ceremony, by which a gentile converts to Judaism, there is no mention of God or of the eternality of the Torah. There is no denial of paganism or the pagan gods, no repentance for the sins of a life lived under the sway of foreign deities, no abjuration of evil, no language of rebirth and renewal. There is no review of the sacred history of the holy people, nor is there any prayer."[32]

Finally, the above-mentioned passage from Yevamot communicates an interesting sense of what it means to be a Jew. Because the acceptance of the commandments is not as central here as it is in other texts, the essence of Jewishness does not seem to be theological or covenantal. To a degree, it is historical, but to be more precise, the Jew here is described as essentially the "other." To be a Jew means to be "persecuted and oppressed, despised, harassed, and overcome by afflictions." A prospective convert has to accept that conception of Jewishness and even deem himself inadequate to it. He is to be "other" among the "others." Note the specific commandments to which the convert is introduced as he is instructed in Judaism. Aside from a rudimentary introduction to the Sabbath and rules of forbidden fat, "he is informed of the sin [of the neglect of the agricultural commandments of] Gleanings, the Forgotten Sheaf, the Corner, and the Poor Man's Tithe." These commandments are those that protect the poor, the disenfranchised, the landless. To become a Jew means to join a people at the fringes of humanity and then to dedicate oneself to defending and protecting those who are even more marginalized.

Though our passage from Yevamot concludes with the assertion that after the immersion stage of conversion, the applicant is "deemed to be an Israelite in all respects," other evidence from the tannaitic period (the period of the Mishnah, concluding in approximately 200 C.E.) suggests that matters were not so simple. The Mishnah in Bikurim[33] mentioned at the beginning of this chapter reflects some of the ethnic-national elements of Jewish identity that had been so central to biblical Israelite religion. That Mishnah is a discussion of the first fruits that were to be brought to the Temple,[34] and it addresses whether a convert can recite that portion of the ritualized formula in which the pilgrim says, "which the Lord has sworn to our fathers, to give to us." Without discussion or controversy, the Mishnah says that the convert may not recite this phrase.[35]

The ambiguity of the convert's status in the Bible continues, to a degree, in the worldview of the mishnaic period. In these texts, the rabbis establish conversion as a legitimate and fully operative ritual, but the inferior status of the convert remains. Is the convert really "an Israelite in all respects"? Yevamot, as we saw, seems to claim that he is. But Bikurim suggests otherwise. Given the conflicting sensibilities of these texts that become major precedents for later legal authorities, we should not be surprised that even within Orthodoxy, we will find radically different responses to questions regarding what conversion actually is, what a person must commit to in order to convert, and "how Jewish" a convert really is.

One final Mishnah is critical to our understanding of a number of contemporary responsa. Again in the tractate Yevamot, the Mishnah asserts: "If a man is suspected of intercourse with a slave who was later emancipated, or with a heathen who subsequently converted, he must not marry her. If, however, he did marry her, they need not be separated."[36] The significance of this passage in later responsa is enormous. Between the time of the Mishnah and the modern period, the principle that one may not convert for any ulterior motive became well established. As the number of people who wished to convert for the purpose of marrying a Jewish man or woman increased, the issue raised by the Mishnah became much more commonplace. The Mishnah here distinguishes between "before the fact" and "after the fact" circumstances, stating that such marriages are not ideal and should not be performed; but if they were performed, there is no reason to forcibly separate the couple or to declare the marriage null and void.

The profound, even ironic, differences between the biblical and rabbinic traditions should not go unnoticed. In the biblical period, marriage to an Israelite spouse was the most obvious means of effecting "conversion." In the rabbinic period, conversion was a barrier to subsequent marriage, if the couple had already had intercourse. Interestingly, however, the Mishnah gives no reason for this prohibition.

Tractate Geirim, a minor tractate not formally part of the Mishnah and typically dated somewhat later, is devoted largely to matters of conversion.[37] For our purposes, and in order to be able to follow the Orthodox debates that will unfold centuries later, one particular passage from Geirim is essential: "Anyone who converts [in order to marry] a woman, for love or out of fear, is not a convert. Thus, Rabbi Judah and Rabbi Nehemiah used to say that all those who converted in the days of Mordecai and Esther are not [valid] converts, as it is written, 'and many of the populace were converting to Judaism, for the fear of the Jews had fallen upon them.' And anyone who does not convert *lesheim shamayim* [for the sake of heaven], is not a [legitimate] convert."[38]

Here, for the first time, we find mention of the motivations of the convert and the stipulation that the conversion must be free of any ulterior motive.[39] Geirim goes even further: in addition to listing negative conditions that must be avoided, it specifies that the conversion must be "for the sake of heaven." It does not, however, offer any explanation of what that phrase means. Is it simply the absence of those negative conditions? Does it require complete allegiance to halakhah? On this critical issue, Geirim is silent. But this new requirement would become the object of enormous discussion and controversy in subsequent generations, and would complicate still further the ambiguous status of many converts in Jewish communal and legal life.[40]

Rabbinic Images of Conversion in the Talmudic Period

The stipulation in Geirim that conversions must be performed "for the sake of heaven" does not appear in the *baraita* that we saw in tractate Yevamot. But the Gemara, the later talmudic discussion of this passage, does reflect this consideration:

> Both a man who became a proselyte for the sake of a woman and a woman who became a proselyte for the sake of a man, and, similarly, a man who became a proselyte for the sake of a royal board, or for the sake of joining Solomon's servants, are not proper proselytes. These are the words of R. Nehemiah, for R. Nehemiah used to say: Neither lion-proselytes, nor dream-proselytes nor the proselytes of Mordecai and Esther are proper proselytes unless they become converted at the present time.
>
> . . . R. Isaac b. Samuel b. Martha said in the name of Rav: the halakhah is in accordance with the opinion of him who maintained that they were all proper proselytes.
>
> Our Rabbis learnt: No proselytes will be accepted in the days of the Messiah. In the same manner, no proselytes were accepted in the days of David or in the days of Solomon. Said R. Eleazar: What scriptural [support is there for this view]? "Behold he shall be a proselyte who is converted for my own sake," he who lives with you shall be settled among you, he only who "lives with you" in your poverty shall be settled among you; but no other.[41]

The conflict in Yevamot is instructive. The view quoted in the name of Rabbi Nehemiah states without equivocation that conversions must be free of any ulterior motive or they are null and void. But Rav disagrees. His disagreement with Rabbi Nehemiah is apparently a broad one; he seems to believe that conversions are proper no matter what the *geir*'s motivation.[42]

Geirim is not the only source to address directly the motivations of the convert. A *baraita* in the tractate Kiddushin of the Palestinian Talmud makes a similar claim: "One who converts out of love, and similarly, a man for a woman or a woman for a man, or converts of Kings' Tables [who sought access to royalty] or converts out of fear of lions[43] and the conversions [in the time of] Mordecai and Esther—these, we do not accept. Rav said, the halakhah is that they are converts, and we do not repel them the way that we repel other converts; rather, we accept them and seek to draw them close."

Note the subtle difference between the claims of Yevamot and Palestinian Kiddushin. Rabbi Nehemiah in the Babylonian Talmud says that people in any of these improper categories are not converts, while the anonymous voice of the Palestinian *baraita* simply says that they are not to be accepted as converts. Rav, of course, says that such converts are to be accepted.

The implicit disagreement between Rabbi Nehemiah of the Babylonian Talmud and the anonymous voice of the Palestinian Talmud would become critical in the modern period. What should Jewish communal policy be? Does, or should, the halakhah hold that, ab initio, such converts ought not be accepted, but if they are accepted, their conversion is valid? Or does, or should, the halakhah follow Rabbi Nehemiah, who holds that, a posteriori, people converting for inappropriate motivations are not valid converts? There is, of course, a third possibility: that the motivations of the convert should not matter at all. The talmudic period saw the development of a variety of texts, and there is support among them for each of these various positions. The rabbis provided no definitive ruling on this issue, and, as we will see, the issue became quite divisive in the period of the post-talmudic codifiers.

Elsewhere, in tractate Bekhorot, the anonymous voice of the Talmud quotes an apparently tannaitic source in a view that receives much attention in later Orthodox discussions: "If a heathen is prepared to accept the Torah except one religious law, we must not receive him [as an Israelite]. Rabbi Jose son of Rabbi Judah says: Even [if the exception be] one point of the special minutiae of the Scribes' enactments."[44]

While many Orthodox authorities have interpreted this passage to mean that each convert is required to observe every iota of Jewish law, others, as we shall see, have thought that the language was not so specific. Many of them have questioned what the prospective convert must actually agree to observe. Must he perform all the demands of Jewish law, or did the rabbis mean that any convert who denies the authority of even one portion of the system of Jewish law should not be accepted? If so, they may not have meant that the convert must actually perform all these commandments; instead, it might have been enough for the prospective Jew to acknowledge the authority of commandments and to recognize his or her current inability to meet those requirements.

The distinction will have extraordinary importance in the modern period, when many nonobservant prospective converts seek to convert to Judaism but want their conversions recognized by halakhic communities. The distinction that we are drawing here is not only a modern one; the idea that what the convert must accept is the authority of the system in principle is a notion reflected in a well-known and oft-cited tale about Hillel the sage:

> Our Rabbis taught: A certain heathen once came before Shammai and asked him, "How many Torahs do you have?" "Two," he replied. "The Written Torah and the Oral Torah." "I believe you with respect to the Written, but not with respect to the Oral Torah; make me a proselyte on condition that you teach me the Written Torah [only]. [But] he scolded and repulsed him in anger. When he went before Hillel, he accepted him as a proselyte. On the first day, he taught him, *alef, bet, gimel, dalet*; the following day, he reversed [them] to him. "But yesterday you did not teach them to me thus," he protested. "Must you then not rely upon me? Then rely upon me with respect to the Oral [Torah], too."[45]

Modern authorities who insist that no conversions can be considered legitimate unless the prospective convert agrees to observe all of Jewish law obviously struggle with this passage. Many take comfort in Rashi's comment that this was not a case of accepting all of the Torah "except for one detail," but rather, a pedagogical "trick" that Hillel used to convince the convert that ultimately, he must simply trust his teacher. Just as the prospective convert can have no view as to what the order of the letters of the alphabet really is without confidence in his teacher, so, too, he should be open to his teacher's lessons about the authority of the Oral Torah. The convert began the process of conversion by denying the authority of the Oral Torah; he simply did not believe that it was from the mouth of God. Hillel was convinced that he would be able to show the prospect otherwise.[46]

A simple reading of the text, however, does not comfortably support Rashi's claim. A more compelling reading holds that what is at stake is the convert's willingness to accept the authority of the Oral Torah. And the narrative is clear; Hillel converts him despite the convert's unwillingness to do so.

A very different narrative in Menaḥot raises similar questions about the degree to which a convert's motivations must be "for the sake of heaven" in order for the conversion to be valid. The story, abbreviated here, relates:

> Once, a man who was very scrupulous about the precept of fringes, heard of a certain harlot in one of the towns by the sea who accepted four hundred gold [denars] for her hire. He sent her four hundred gold [denars] and appointed a day with her. . . . When he came in, she prepared for him seven beds. . . . She then went up to the top bed and lay down upon it naked. He, too, went up after her in his desire to sit naked with her, when all of a sudden the four fringes [of his garment] struck him across the face; whereupon he slipped off and sat upon the ground.
>
> She also slipped off and sat upon the ground and said, "By the Roman Capitol, I will not leave you alone until you tell me what blemish you saw in me." "By the Temple," he replied, "never have I seen a woman as beautiful as you are; but there is one precept that the Lord our God has commanded us; it is called tzitzit, and with regard to it, the expression "I am the Lord your God" is twice written, signifying, I am He who will exact punishment in the future, and I am He who will give reward in the future. Now [the tzitzit] appeared to me as four witnesses [testifying against me]."
>
> She said, "I will not leave you until you tell me your name, the name of your town, the name of your teacher, the name of your school in which you study the Torah." He wrote all this down and handed it to her. . . . She then came to the *beit hamidrash* of R. Ḥiyya, and said to him, "Master, give instructions about me that they make me a proselyte." "My daughter," he replied, "perhaps you have set your eyes on one of the disciples?" She thereupon took out the script and handed it to him. "Go," said he, "and enjoy your acquisition." Those very bedclothes that she had spread for him for an illicit purpose she now spread out for him lawfully. This is the reward [of the precept] in this world; and as for its reward in the future world, I know not how great it is.[47]

The story, which is told as part of a discussion of the reward of scrupulous observance of commandments, makes essentially the same point that emerged from the story about Hillel. In this case, it is Rabbi Ḥiyya who allows a proselyte to convert in violation of Rabbi Nehemiah's ruling that one may not convert out of love or for marriage. This story, in conjunction with other amoraic sources, demonstrates that the amoraim (the rabbis of the talmudic period) are wrestling with the same issues with which their predecessors in the period of the Mishnah, the tannaim, had contended.

One additional aggadic (narrative rather than legal) source is also commonly cited by later authorities. The aggadah in question comes from the tractate Sanhedrin: "What is the purpose of [writing in the Torah], 'And Lotan's sister was Timna'?—Timna was a royal princess, as it is written, *aluf Lotan, aluf Timna*; and by *aluf*, an uncrowned ruler is meant. Desiring to become a proselyte, Timna went to Abraham, Isaac, and Jacob, but they did not accept her. So she went and became a concubine to Eliphaz the son of Esau, saying, 'I had rather be a servant to this people than a mistress of another nation.' From her, Amalek was descended who afflicted Israel. Why so?—Because they should not have repulsed her."[48]

The talmudic passage gives no indication of why Timna should have been accepted. But it does suggest that when people are turned away, the implications for Jewish security in the future can be very problematic.

The importance of these aggadic texts in later Orthodox responsa notwithstanding, the key material of the talmudic period to which later sources refer is the legal material. During this period, Jewish law on conversion, as in virtually all other areas of halakhah, was developed and honed. At the same time, the talmudic sages seem to have perpetuated, intentionally or not, the ambivalence that began with the Torah's use of the term *geir* and that was codified in the tannaitic period. "Let the left hand repel and the right hand draw close"[49] (the rabbis' advice for those dealing with aspiring converts) seems to have been more than a mere aphorism. Its contradictory advice was a primary basis for the competing sentiments expressed in later rabbinic decision-making.

As far as the most controversial element of contemporary halakhah—the motivations of the convert—is concerned, talmudic literature bequeaths to us three positions:

The first holds that the effectiveness of the conversion is dependent upon the motivation of the convert. The second position says that the conversion is valid no matter what the convert's motivations might have been but that those motivations should affect a court's decision as to whether to convert the person. The third position holds that the convert's motivations are irrelevant to the process. This last position may be the one with the most support. It is the view of the Mishnah in Yevamot[50] and the *baraita* in Yevamot's major discussion of conversion;[51] it is also described by Rav as the halakhah.[52] That support notwithstanding, the third position becomes much more embattled as Jewish law moves into its next major phase.

The Post-Talmudic Codes and Medieval Legal Developments

In the writings of Maimonides (1138–1204), the prospective convert's motivation continues to play a central role. In his legal magnum opus, the *Mishneh Torah*, Maimonides introduces the subject: "When a Gentile wishes to enter the covenant and to be gathered under the wings of the Divine Presence, and he accepts the yoke of Torah, he needs circumcision and immersion."[53] Later in the same chapter, Maimonides' interest in intention is expressed much more directly:

> The appropriate way to perform the commandment [of conversion] is that when the convert comes to convert, we investigate him lest [he be converting] for money that he will receive, or for some position of authority that will come his way, or whether it is because of fear that he wishes to enter the religion. If he is a man, we investigate whether he has cast his eye on a Jewish woman; and if she is a woman, we investigate whether she has cast her eye on a Jewish man. If no inappropriate motivation is discovered, we inform him of the magnitude of the weight of the yoke of Torah and of the tremendous efforts required from Gentiles to perform [its commandments]. If they accepted, and

did not change their minds and we see that they have returned out of love, we accept them.[54]

What is new in this selection is Maimonides' notion that the court has an obligation to investigate the prospective convert. Though the *baraita* in Yevamot does not raise this issue, it seems in retrospect that Rabbi Nehemiah thought that only converts with suspect motivations ought to be refused. None of the talmudic sources we examined say anything about the courts investigating. This element seems to be new with Maimonides and raises the significance of motivation to a level that we have not seen before.

As we will see in our analysis of contemporary responsa in future chapters, the intent of these premodern sources, whether mishnaic, tal-mudic, or later, is sometimes not at all clear. Their inherent ambiguity lends them at times to polemic uses. The contemporary student of modern responsa must be sensitive to the diverse positions that these sources contain that allow for a host of different readings. Maimonides' writing on this subject is a case in point.

Because of his inestimable significance in Jewish legal history, virtually all contemporary authorities seek to demonstrate that Maimonides supports their own position. But Maimonides' corpus is sufficiently complex that it is not always clear how compelling these arguments are. Consider one example: Rabbi Shlomo Riskin writes, "Maimonides never mentioned the acceptance of the commandments as a necessary prerequisite for conversion. It is rather the very definition of conversion, the statement of purpose, the matrix from which circumcision and ritual immersion must follow."[55] Riskin bases his view on the fact that Maimonides says, "When a Gentile wishes to enter into the covenant, to be gathered under the wings of the Divine Presence, and he accepts the yoke of Torah," he requires circumcision and immersion. For Riskin, the phrase "he accepts the yoke of Torah" is critical. It is the very definition of conversion.

Given the fact that being "gathered under the wings of the Divine Presence" is highly metaphoric, the reading that Riskin offers is not at all self-evident or obvious. It may be that Maimonides is saying only that "when a person wishes to convert, he requires circumcision and immersion."

Other portions of Maimonides' corpus support this reading more than Riskin's. In the following source, the convert's motivation apparently mattered to Maimonides ab initio, but not at all a posteriori: "A convert whom they did not investigate or to whom they did not make known the commandments and the punishments [for not fulfilling them] but who was circumcised and immersed in front of three judges is a convert. Even if it subsequently becomes known that he converted for some ulterior motive, once he has been circumcised and immersed, he has been removed from the status of Gentile, and he remains suspect until his righteousness can be verified. Even if he returns to Gentile worship, he remains in the category of a Jewish apostate whose marriage is a valid marriage."[56]

Here, Maimonides echoes the view that conversion, once performed, was permanent. However, the previous paragraph of the *Mishneh Torah* might seem contradictory. For while this passage, *Isurei Bi'ah* 13:17, suggests that the conversion is valid regardless of subsequent behavior, paragraph 13:16 suggests otherwise: "And since Solomon converted many women and married them, and similarly, Samson converted [women] and then married, and it is commonly known that they converted for some ulterior motive and that they were not converted by a *beit din*, they were still considered Gentiles and remained in their status of being forbidden. Moreover, their ultimate behavior proves the nature of their original [intentions], for they continued to worship idols and built altars for them, which is why the Writ considered it as if Solomon had built [those altars] himself."

The apparent contradiction stems from the fact that Maimonides' first paragraph states that these converted women "remained in their status of being forbidden" because the motivations for their conversion were improper; but his next statement asserts that "even if he returns to Gentile worship, he remains in the category of a Jewish apostate whose marriage is a valid marriage."

Maimonides was obviously aware that these two paragraphs make very different claims. How, then, would he have explained this tension? One possibility is that the former passage deals with motivations, while the latter addresses issues of behavior. Another is that the former was meant to be exclusively historical, without any prescriptive implications, while the latter is the passage with normative intent. Still, as we will see, some of the modern responsa will make much of this ambiguity in Maimonides' corpus.

Interestingly, Maimonides focuses only on the religious dimension of conversion in this chapter. It is only in the next chapter of the *Mishneh Torah's Hilkhot Isurei Bi'ah* that he addresses some of the ethnic-national elements that we first saw in the *baraita* in Yevamot. At the start of that chapter, Maimonides instructs the court to ask the prospective convert: "What have you seen that you wish to convert? Do you not know that at this time, Israel is oppressed, shoved, swept away and victimized, and suffering comes to them?"[57] Immediately thereafter, Maimonides quotes the well-known elements of the ceremony as described in Yevamot, including the details of some commandments, their rewards and punishments, the same four agricultural laws, and so on.

From the *Mishneh Torah*, it would appear that Maimonides follows the second of the three positions outlined above. The intentions of the convert are not irrelevant (except in the case of Solomon cited above, where the conversions were apparently sham), but neither are they sufficiently critical to invalidate the conversion retroactively. His language in the *Mishneh Torah* requires the court to investigate the convert and his or her motivations, and to act accordingly. Once the conversion has been performed, however, Maimonides indicates that no aspersions may be cast on its validity.

In another critical composition, Maimonides indicates that sociological realia can sometimes trump the theory that he outlines in the *Mishneh Torah*. In a well-known responsum, Maimonides is confronted with a fascinating case.[58] A Jewish man has purchased a Christian servant and has brought her to live with him. The matter was made public by his brother, and the woman was questioned by the local magistrate.[59] Even after intense questioning, she insisted that she was Jewish, and the judge returned her to the Jewish man in question. Now that they are living together, the author of the question to Maimonides asks, must the community take steps to remove her from his domicile?

Maimonides agrees with the assumption of the questioner that the current living arrangement is unacceptable. He responds that the community must either force him to dismiss her from his household or, alternatively, he must emancipate her and then marry her. Maimonides is aware, of course, that this second suggestion is an apparent violation of the Mishnah in Yevamot[60] but notes that he had already issued several rulings in other similar cases that the man should emancipate the slave and then marry her. He justifies this advice on the basis of an edict known as *takanat hashavim*, a rabbinic ruling designed to make matters easier for the repentant.[61] He concludes by insisting that the "couple" choose a date by which she will either leave the household or they will be married, and adds a theological flourish: "Almighty God will repair the damage we have done."

It is instructive that Maimonides does not raise the issue of the woman's motivation for conversion. Nowhere does he suggest that a court ought to investigate the degree of her commitment to commandments or any other theological structures. This case is precisely of the sort that Rabbi Nehemiah had sought to prevent, and it is a category that the court is expected to deny once it has done its investigation. How are we to explain Maimonides' ruling? Is this simply a case in which the law could not be enforced? Why, then, would Maimonides not have said that explicitly? He does seem to believe that the community has the option of forcing her out of the house, so why raise the second alternative?

And how are we to explain his willingness to blatantly disregard the Mishnah in Yevamot? What conclusions might we draw from this responsum about his conception of what it means to be a Jew? Does this apparent inconsistency in Maimonides' corpus allude to a deeper ambivalence of the sort that we saw in his biblical and rabbinic antecedents?

This responsum is not the only one in which Maimonides takes a position in opposition to a Mishnah. In another, Maimonides addresses the query of Ovadiah the Convert[62] as to whether he should emend the liturgy and avoid phrases such as "God and God of our fathers," given his status as a convert. This is precisely the issue addressed by the Mishnah in Bikurim[63] and the Palestinian Talmud's discussion of it.[64] Maimonides' instruction is unequivocal:

You should recite everything as it is, and do not change anything. Rather, you should pray as every Jewish citizen does, whether alone or in public. The critical point is that it was Abraham our Father who taught the entire nation, who gave them wisdom and who made known to them the truth and unity of God. He battled against idolatry . . . and brought many under the wings of the Divine Presence. . . . Thus, anyone who converts until the end of time . . . is a disciple of Abraham our Father and a member of his household. . . . Thus, you should say "our God and God of our ancestors" . . . —there is no difference here between us and you.

A few sentences later, Maimonides refers to the Mishnah in Bikurim, which would seem to forbid this: "This is an anonymous Mishnah and is thus the view of Rabbi Meir, and it is not the halakhah in this case." He cites the Palestinian Talmud's rejection of the Mishnah and concludes his responsum.

Although much of the rabbinic tradition seems conflicted about the desirability and status of converts, Maimonides does not seem to share that ambivalence. His endorsement of Ovadiah is wholehearted and passionate. His language could not be more welcoming or reassuring. The highly theological language of this responsum, along with Maimonides' clear respect for Ovadiah's commitment to Jewish tradition, might have led someone else to be equally intolerant of the woman whom he discussed in the previous responsum, since she did not share Ovadiah's commitments.

But that was not the case. In both instances, Maimonides ruled generously, finding cause for endorsement of the conversion (in the first instance) and the complete Jewishness of the convert (in the second instance). These two responsa—particularly considering his view that converts whose motivations are suspect but who have been converted, anyway, are fully Jewish—indicate an openness to conversion and a tolerance of different paths to Jewish life that will become critical to our discussion of attitudes in the modern world of Jewish Orthodoxy.

The final authority we need to examine in this chapter in order to follow the disputes and debates that will follow centuries later is Rabbi Joseph Ben-Ephraim Karo[65] (1488–1575), author of the *Beit Yosef* and the *Shulḥan Arukh*, which, along with the annotations of Rabbi Moses

Isserles, is the most universally accepted code of Jewish law in the Jewish world. Like Maimonides' work, Karo's is not always internally consistent regarding the issues that we have been examining. There are significant differences between the approaches of the *Beit Yosef*, a commentary on an earlier legal code known as the Tur, and his *Shulḥan Arukh*, which ultimately became the Jewish community's most important halakhic code.

In the *Beit Yosef*, Karo follows Maimonides' claim that the court is obligated to investigate the motivations of the prospective convert.[66] He rules that, a posteriori, all conversions are valid, regardless of whether the courts have investigated, and that it is "obvious" that failure to accept the commandments does not render the conversion invalid after the fact. A phrase that he introduced has since become central to many modern responsa on conversion: Seeking to explain how Hillel could have accepted proselytes who did not meet the criterion of pure motives,[67] particularly because courts are obligated to investigate the prospect, Karo writes that *hakol lefi re'ut beit hadin*, "everything [must be judged] according to the [unique] perspective of the court [in question]." Thus, Karo continues the tradition of Maimonides that apparently requires the court to investigate the convert's motivations but gives the court great latitude to make its own judgment; furthermore, he notes that, a posteriori, these considerations do not invalidate the conversion.

By contrast, the entire discussion of the conversion process is contained in *Yoreh De'ah* 268, a relatively brief section. Nowhere in this section does Karo clearly indicate what is intended by "acceptance of the commandments," nor does he express concern that the notion is ambiguous. Does that suggest that for Karo, as for his predecessors, simply hearing the warnings of the court about some major commandments, some minor commandments, the plight of Israel, and the like, along with a willingness to convert, was sufficient? Karo does not address this question. But this ambiguity, coming on the heels of a tradition that appears at times moderately conflicted about the entire institution of conversion, makes the profound disagreements that we will see in the modern period almost inevitable.

Concluding Thoughts

In our review of contemporary responsa on conversion, we will see that the notion of *kabalat ol mitzvot* (the acceptance of the yoke of the commandments) plays a pivotal role in the rulings that emerge from the Orthodox community. Those authorities who want to force converts to subscribe to the entirety of Jewish tradition argue that *kabalat ol mitzvot* is a nonnegotiable element of conversion. Are they right? That depends on how we read the texts and sources that we have just seen. Does *kabalat ol mitzvot* find mention in the early sources? Clearly, it does. Does it seem to be a sine qua non? Not really. The urgency for this concept appears to have emerged later.

Alternatively, the authorities who wish to make it easier to convert rely on notions such as the discretion of the court, which first appeared in the *Beit Yosef*. Even these authorities do not dispute the claim that conversions need to be "for the sake of heaven." They simply do not agree as to how to define what constitutes "for the sake of heaven." As we will see, precision in defining that term will become increasingly important as time goes on. Why is that? Perhaps the explanation lies in the radically changed social realities that modern legal authorities had to face. Those early giants of Jewish law could never have anticipated the circumstances that their positions on conversion would eventually have to address. What were those changes, and how did they alter the landscape of Jewish communal and halakhic life? We will suggest that the later authorities whom we will examine not only saw themselves engaged in legal disputations but rather viewed their roles as including the creation of social policies that would enable the Jewish community to confront the challenges wrought by profound sociological changes. Their conflicting conceptions of the social policy that they believed would best protect the interests of the Jewish community ultimately led various authorities, all dealing with the same precedential material that we have seen here, to arrive at radically different halakhic conclusions centuries later. It is to examples of these rulings that we now turn.

Two Trends in Nineteenth- and Early-Twentieth-Century German Orthodox Responses to Conversion and Intermarriage

The 1840s witnessed the emergence of a nascent Orthodox attitude toward intermarriage and conversion. By this point in Western European Jewish history, the question of intermarriage and subsequent problem of the religious identity of intermarried couples and their offspring had been transformed from a theoretical issue into a social reality. In Europe, the problem of intermarriage had erupted. Legislation was enacted by various states in Germany in the late 1840s that facilitated intermarriage between Jews and Gentiles. Ḥakham Isaac Bernays (1792–1849), rabbi of Hamburg and teacher of Rabbi Samson Raphael Hirsch and Rabbi Esriel Hildesheimer, was sufficiently disturbed by the rise of intermarriage in Germany to issue an 1843 responsum in German condemning marriage between Jew and Gentile as unthinkable from the standpoint of Jewish law. In addition, Bernays stated that the children of a marriage between a Jewish man and a non-Jewish woman were unequivocally Gentiles. Finally, he acknowledged that while the community had to recognize that intermarriages enjoyed a civil status, the Jewish community could never accept the religious character of such a union.[1]

Bernays's harsh tone in his responsum gives support to Moshe Davis's observation that "the basic cause" of the stringent position that the Orthodox initially adopted concerning intermarriage "was the increase of mixed marriage to the point where it alarmed the rabbinical . . . leaders."[2] Undoubtedly, it was hoped that such a stringent position would discourage and thus impede the rate of Jewish exogamy in the now more open society of Germany.

38

The second factor that contributed to this Orthodox attitude was the growing strength of the Reform movement in Germany. While Reform Judaism may not yet have completely dominated the communal religious life of German Jewry by the end of the 1840s, its ever-escalating influence was apparent. As Steven Lowenstein has observed, the German Jewish community, in spite of many Reform gains, "remained overwhelmingly Orthodox" until the 1840s. These years "were the crucial decade for the creation of a religious Reform movement in Germany."[3]

Reform rabbis now officiated at conversions to Judaism, and two Reform rabbis even advocated rabbinic performance of intermarriages. Moreover, the Braunschweig Rabbinical Conference of 1844 passed a resolution rescinding the traditional Jewish prohibition against intermarriage, declaring that Judaism sanctioned marital unions between persons of monotheistic faiths where the state allowed the children of such unions to be raised as Jews. While the state did not, in fact, yet permit this, the Orthodox were infuriated by this Reform "betrayal" of classical Jewish positions regarding the necessity of endogamy, and they refused to accept with equanimity this Reform challenge to their hegemony over these matters. The German Orthodox rabbinate swiftly and ferociously responded to this Reform rendering of Jewish tradition. According to Adam Ferziger, "Some of the most venomous attacks against all those connected with Reform were voiced. On the other hand, new foci that would characterize the development of Orthodox identity and its relationship to other Jews in later decades began to emerge."[4]

Zvi Hirsch Chajes (1805–55) of Zolkiev, a leading rabbinic scholar of the day, issued a blistering polemic, *Minhat Kena'ot*, in 1845 against Reform Jews and their activities. He attacked Reform Judaism on multiple grounds, expressing outrage at Reform transgressions of the tradition, including changes in the Jewish prayer book, abandonment of the rite of circumcision by the Frankfurt Reformverein, and rejection of the traditional Jewish belief that the Torah was eternal and unchanging.[5]

In 1849, Chajes turned his attention to conversion and intermarriage and added an excursus to *Minhat Kena'ot*, in which he indicates that conversion and intermarriage had taken on a larger valence in the intervening four years and now loomed ever larger. Chajes took particular note of the resolution concerning intermarriage passed by the Braunschweig Conference and contended that such unions were unconditionally prohibited by the Torah and later Jewish tradition. Furthermore, he stated that Gentiles who desired to convert to Judaism for purposes of marriage were to be rejected. He cited approvingly the unyielding stance against intermarriage that the Bible reports Ezra and Nehemiah had taken when they sent away the non-Jewish spouses of their community members more than two millennia earlier, and he stated that it was no less the obligation of the rabbis of contemporary Germany to follow their example and "distance these [intermarried] persons" from the Jewish faith and the Jewish people today.[6] The tone of Chajes's essay was no less stringent and unmoving regarding would-be converts, their Jewish partners, and the children of such unions than was the attitude that Bernays had expressed in his responsum. In an atmosphere in which intermarriage was now possible and in which an emerging Reform rabbinate was challenging Orthodox authority on these issues, Bernays and Chajes thought that the tide of assimilation could be stemmed only by adopting a severe position on these questions.

These same concerns prompted Rabbi Jacob Ettlinger (1798–1871) of Altona to issue a statement on intermarriage and conversion. Ettlinger, a talmudic scholar of prodigious proportions, was a leading halakhic authority in mid-nineteenth-century Germany. In his statement, Ettlinger repeated the declaration that Jewish law did not recognize the validity of a marriage between a Jew and a Gentile. In addition, he declared that children born of unions between non-Jewish mothers and Jewish fathers were non-Jews unless they underwent a formal ceremony of conversion conducted by a qualified *beit din* (Jewish court). Ettlinger thought that no special efforts should be made to bring these persons into the Jewish fold.[7]

This understanding of Ettlinger's position is supported by a responsum that he issued in 1854 in the case of a Gentile woman who had been married to a Jewish man in a civil wedding ceremony and now wanted to convert to Judaism. Ettlinger contended that the rabbis should not allow the woman to convert. Times had changed, and nonobservance and intermarriage now threatened the stability of the community. He observed that if the Orthodox rabbinate was lenient in this matter and accepted the woman as a proselyte, "we will be lenient in other matters as well." He concluded his responsum by observing that there were precedents in Jewish law for the acceptance of such women into the community of Israel but stated that he was uncomfortable with applying these "lenient rulings" in the contemporary era.[8]

An article that Ettlinger published in 1847 in *Shomer Tziyon Hane'eman* sheds light on this ruling and reveals how troubled he was by these issues during that period.[9] In that article, Ettlinger wrote that ritual immersion of a child born to a Jewish mother and a Gentile father should perhaps be required in order to confirm the child as a Jew. This was "due to doubts that were raised in the Tosafot [medieval commentators on the Talmud]."[10] Of course, normative Jewish law—this single source notwithstanding—did not demand such a ritual. As Adam Ferziger has observed, Ettlinger himself conceded that "ritual immersion is not necessary from a legal perspective," and he "saw no halakhic imperative that these boys be immersed in a ritual bath as is required by converts." Nevertheless, Ferziger comments that the citation of this lone medieval passage indicates that Ettlinger was sufficiently concerned over rising Jewish-Christian social interaction in 1840s Germany that he wanted "to maintain some distinction between 'definite Israelites' [born of two Jewish parents] and those whose halakhic status as Jews was unquestionable but whose familial associations might lead them astray."[11] Given that Ettlinger was willing to take such an extreme and unusual stance on the Jewishness of a child born to a Jewish mother and non-Jewish father, it is no surprise that he adopted the position that he did in his 1854 responsum on conversion and intermarriage. He thought that if the rabbinate adopted a relaxed posture on this matter, the strength of the Orthodox and those Jews in the community who were faithful in their observance of the law would only be further weakened. If one considers the writings of Ettlinger in concert with those of men such as Bernays and Chajes, it is clear that by the 1850s, the German Orthodox rabbinate had transformed conversion in cases of intermarriage into a boundary issue in their attempts to rescue Judaism from the threat of dissolution created by the events of Emancipation and Enlightenment.[12]

Seligman Baer Bamberger (1807–78) of Würzburg, a leader of Orthodox Judaism and the preeminent talmudist in southern Germany during this period, issued two responsa that reflect the stringency of these Orthodox authorities. In his *Yad Halevi, Orah Hayim* 145, Bamberger was asked whether a Gentile woman who had been married in a civil ceremony to a Jewish man could now be converted to Judaism. This woman and the Gentile man had even had a son together.

Bamberger responded to this question by immediately citing *Hilkhot Isurei Bi'ah* 13:14, where Maimonides stipulates that candidates for conversion must be examined to determine whether an ulterior motive is behind their conversion. Should they seek entry into the household of Israel for any such reason, they were not to be accepted as candidates for conversion. Having said this, Bamberger noted—as had Ettlinger—that there were precedents in the tradition that would permit such persons entry into the Jewish people, and he cited the well-known case described in Shabbat 31a in which Hillel accepted an individual into the Jewish fold who had ulterior motives when he first sought admission into the covenant of Israel.

Nevertheless, Bamberger—again, like Ettlinger—refused to employ this lenient precedent as a guide in this instance. He stated that unless the rabbi who had posed the question was convinced that the couple would be observant subsequent to the conversion and their Jewish remarriage, the rabbi should be stringent and reject the would-be convert. He observed that the genuine intent of such a couple to lead a traditional Jewish life could hardly be assumed. Indeed, there was no reason to believe that the couple would be any more pious after the conversion than they had been prior to such entry into the Jewish people. After all, they had elected to be married by an officer of the state even before an Orthodox rabbinic court had granted the woman permission to convert. Bamberger concluded that neither the woman nor her husband had any sincere intention to observe Jewish law. Therefore, he stated that he would not offer a lenient ruling in this case and would not approve the conversion. He believed that such a conversion would be illegitimate and that a stringent decision was called for both by Jewish law and the needs of present-day Judaism.

A second decision that Bamberger issued in *Yad Halevi, Oraḥ Ḥayim* 3:46, regarding the case of an infant boy born to a non-Jewish mother and a Jewish father who had been married in a civil ceremony, underscores the consistency of the policy he adopted on these matters. In the brief responsum, Bamberger reported that the Jewish father desired to have his son circumcised so that the boy could be brought into the Jewish community. The rabbi who posed the question to Bamberger reported, however, that the father was nonobservant. Bamberger replied that the father, despite his desire to have his son circumcised, was now no more observant than he had been when "he stood dressed in his frock" before the civil magistrate who had married the couple in a nonreligious ritual. Bamberger stated: "The act of ritual circumcision in this instance should not be performed."

The two decisions that Bamberger issued asserting that children born of Gentile mothers and Jewish fathers ought not to be circumcised are echoed in the writings of other contemporaneous German authorities. On October 31, 1864, Rabbi Bernard Illowy of New Orleans wrote a letter to *Der Israelit*, a leading Orthodox journal in Germany, to solicit opinions from the European Orthodox rabbinate as to whether boys born to non-Jewish mothers and Jewish fathers should be circumcised and converted to Judaism. Illowy addressed himself to Rabbi Marcus Lehmann of Frankfurt (1831–90), editor of the journal, and explained that questions surrounding this issue had been raised in the New Orleans community and that he had forbidden such circumcisions. He stated that the mothers had no intention of raising these boys as observant Jews and that the fathers were flagrant violators of Jewish law. Illowy concluded his letter by asking Lehmann and the readers of *Der Israelit* whether his decision had been correct.[13]

Lehmann published the letter under the title "Die Beschneidung der in Mischehen von nichtjüdischen Muttern gebornen Kinder" (The Circumcision of Children Born to Non-Jewish Mothers in Mixed Marriages), and replied that when a similar situation had occurred in Hamburg, the rabbi there had likewise not permitted such children to be circumcised. Lehmann was of the opinion that this decision was proper and contended that if a blessing had been recited at the ceremony of such a boy, God's Name would have been taken in vain.

However, Lehmann stated that the real issue in these cases centered on the question of the child's status—that is, was the child a Jew or a non-Jew? The answer clearly was that the child was a non-Jew, so Lehmann thought that such a child should not be circumcised in a Jewish religious ceremony, as he had no desire for the "enabling act" of circumcision to facilitate the entry of these children as converts into Judaism. The children of such unions—in which the mothers were Christians and the fathers nonobservant Jews—would never grow up to be loyal Jews. Lehmann stated that it was vital to remember that "Judaism has never sought to make proselytes," and that the fact that their fathers were Jewish was of no consequence in rendering a decision on this matter. Indeed, he predicted that such children, if they were to be converted, would only fulfill the talmudic dictum "Proselytes are as troublesome to Israel as a sore."

Lehmann's article was followed several months later by opinions on the subject issued by Rabbi Dr. Wolf Feilchenfeld of Düsseldorf and Rabbi Dr. Esriel Hildesheimer, then of Eisenstadt in Hungary.[14] While we will deal with the writings of Hildesheimer on the topic of conversion and intermarriage at great length below, it is sufficient for now to note that both these rabbis agreed with Lehmann and Illowy, thus testifying to the stringent trend that marked the policy position of the German rabbinate on these questions.

It was left to Rabbi Samson Raphael Hirsch (1808–88) of Frankfurt to make explicit the logic that stood behind these rulings. The identical question had already come before Rabbi Hirsch, and his response is found in his *Shemesh Marpe*, *Yoreh De'ah* 58. Hirsch acknowledged that the exact stricture of Jewish law—as attributed to Rav Huna in Ketubot 11a—permitted the circumcision of this baby boy for the sake of conversion. However, he thought that there were decisive considerations that required the nonexercise of this permission at this time and place.

Hirsch stated that the status of the son was determined by the status of his mother (Kiddushin 3:12); therefore, from the moment of birth, the boy was unquestionably a Gentile. He could become a Jew only by undergoing the rituals of circumcision and immersion that were performed for the sake of conversion. While conversion was an option, Hirsch argued on the basis of traditional Jewish theological doctrine that it should not be performed. As he explained, the boy, as a Gentile, was obligated only to observe the seven Noahide commandments. According to the Talmud (Sanhedrin 56), when God established His covenant with Noah in Genesis 9, He required that the non-Jew Noah and his progeny observe just seven basic moral commandments. Hirsch reasoned that if the baby remained in the religion of his mother, the possibility of his conducting a moral life pleasing in the sight of God was quite likely, as he would surely—as a German Gentile—observe these basic moral laws incumbent upon all humanity.

Hirsch observed that should this boy be brought into Judaism at the request of his parents, all 613 commandments of the Torah would be thrust upon him. Given the reality of an era in which few born Jews engaged in such observance, Hirsch believed that it would be virtually impossible for this boy—should he be converted—to meet his obligations as a Jew. After all, his mother was a Gentile and his father nonobservant. Even if the mother were to convert, there was virtually no possibility that such people would give their son a proper Jewish education and establish a household where the boy would be brought up to observe the commandments. Hirsch stated that if the baby were to be circumcised ritually and immersed for the sake of conversion, the baby would be burdened with obligations that he would have no need to fulfill as long as he was a Gentile. To convert him and impose these commandments upon him when there was almost no possibility that he would observe them would constitute an unconscionable act on the part of the rabbinic court. Hirsch concluded: "In our age, the responsibility these considerations entail has several times greater significance in regard to a baby who has not yet matured. No one who regards his fellow human being's peace of mind and conscience as holy and inviolable should act so as to endanger that peace of mind and conscience in this way."

Hirsch acknowledged precedents in Jewish law that might allow the acceptance of such women as the boy's mother into the community of Israel despite his own discomfort with applying such "lenient rulings" in the contemporary era. Other Orthodox authorities, as we shall see, were not so hesitant, and these rabbis, anxious to respond from the viewpoint of Jewish law, seized on these precedents to justify their own lenient responses to the challenge posed to Judaism by conversions stemming from intermarriage.

At this point in modern Jewish history, the Orthodox leadership not only believed that a rigorous attitude toward Jewish-Gentile intermarriage and the issues of conversion arising from it could save the Jewish community from its ultimate undoing. Orthodox authorities also aspired to maintain Orthodox hegemony over personal status throughout the community. These two priorities are mirrored in the writings of Esriel Hildesheimer (1820–99), founder and head of the Orthodox Rabbinerseminar in Berlin and the outstanding student of Rabbi Ettlinger. In 1867–68, while Hildesheimer was rabbi of Eisenstadt, Dr. Moritz Benedikt, a prominent neurologist in Vienna, wanted to marry a proselyte who had been converted to Judaism by a Reform *beit din* headed by Abraham Geiger. However, because Benedikt hailed from Eisenstadt, civil law required that he be issued a certificate in his home community permitting him to be married in Vienna, where Benedikt wanted the marriage to take place.

Benedikt wrote Hildesheimer requesting such a certificate, which Hildesheimer refused to issue; the reasons for his refusal are of particular import. First, Hildesheimer stated that as there was an ulterior motive for this woman's converting to Judaism (she wanted to marry a Jewish man), "her acceptance is to be rejected." Second, even if the conversion had included an immersion (*tevilah*), as required by Jewish ritual law (which apparently it did not), Hildesheimer contended that he still could not have accepted Benedikt's fiancée's conversion as valid because the *beit din* that had accepted her into Judaism was Reform. Hildesheimer, in his response to Benedikt, made clear the twin pillars upon which this Orthodox attitude toward conversion and intermarriage has been established to the present day: the belief that the rejection of such persons into the Jewish fold was the wisest policy for the community to adopt in the modern context, and the refusal to recognize the validity of conversions performed by non-Orthodox rabbis.[15] The former point is underscored by Hildesheimer's ruling in the New Orleans case mentioned above. He had also been approached by Rabbi

Illowy on that matter; like Rabbi Lehmann, Hildesheimer stated that the children in question were simply Gentiles and should be regarded as such, and that no conversion should be performed in such cases.[16]

Hildesheimer also dealt with conversion and intermarriage in other places in his responsa. One case is particularly revealing for his attitudes on these matters. In 1879, Rabbi Jacob Hollander of Trier told Hildesheimer that a Gentile man had impregnated a nineteen-year-old Jewish girl and that their child had died. The girl subsequently refused to leave this man and wanted her father's permission to marry him, as she was underage and state law maintained that she could not marry without her father's legal consent. The father stated that he would allow them to marry in a civil ceremony, though he would prefer that the Gentile groom converted to Judaism and that the couple be married in a Jewish wedding ceremony. The groom agreed to convert to Judaism. However, Rabbi Hollander informed Rabbi Hildesheimer that he believed there was no possibility that this couple would be observant subsequent to their marriage. Furthermore, Rabbi Hollander reported that if he refused to convert this young man, the father planned to bring him to a mohel who had already agreed to circumcise the future groom, regardless of the rabbi's decision. The father had stated that he would then bring the couple to a non-Orthodox rabbi to perform the wedding ceremony. Rabbi Hollander asked Rabbi Hildesheimer what he should do in light of all these considerations.

Rabbi Hildesheimer observed that the problem posed by this inquiry was one of the most difficult questions of the modern age, and he stated that it was impossible to deliver a definitive decision in such a case—*shikul da'at* (rational judgment) had to prevail. Obviously, there were legal precedents that could allow the rabbi to rule leniently and accept the non-Jewish husband into Judaism. Nevertheless, Rabbi Hildesheimer maintained that the overwhelming preponderance of the sources frowned on converting a Gentile who, in all likelihood, would be non-observant after the conversion. While Hildesheimer acknowledged that the Orthodox rabbinate could not control what the non-Orthodox rabbinate would do regarding this issue, he told Rabbi Hollander that he should not allow the threat of this man's going to a Liberal rabbi to coerce him into performing the conversion. Consequently, Rabbi

Hildesheimer stated—in light of all these concerns—that he would not sanction such a conversion and urged Rabbi Hollander to maintain the integrity of Jewish legal norms on matters of conversion. In so doing, he asserted, *anu et nafsheinu hitzalnu*—"We will have saved our own souls."[17] Hildesheimer believed that the Orthodox should not accept the spouses and offspring of nonobservant Jews into the community and rejected the notion that conversions to Judaism performed under non-Orthodox auspices had legal validity.

This attitude toward conversion and intermarriage, articulated by Bernays, Chajes, Ettlinger, Bamberger, Hirsch, and Hildesheimer, is summarized and displayed in an *Erklärung*, or declaration, signed by 133 of Europe's most important Orthodox rabbis in 1871. This declaration, which appeared in *Der Israelit*, included the signatures of Bamberger, Hirsch, and Hildesheimer. Disturbed by "attacks in our time against the Jewish law of marriage, attacks likely to destroy the purity [*Reinheit*] of the Jewish family," the signatories prohibited "rabbis, preachers, or other Israelites" from performing marriages that were forbidden by biblical or rabbinic law. The Orthodox stated that these Liberal officiates were "incompetent" to fulfill any rabbinic functions and urged the Orthodox laity to remove these persons from their posts. If the removal of these persons was not possible, the Orthodox rabbinate stated that Jews "faithful to the Law" were obligated to seek out Orthodox rabbis for the performance of rituals relating to personal status, even if this meant going beyond the bounds of the organized and legally sanctioned *Gemeinde* (community) in each city and town.[18]

The issues of conversion and intermarriage had split the Jewish community, with Orthodox and Liberal sectors of the community adopting different postures toward these questions. The period 1840–70 marks the emergence of a stringent Orthodox attitude regarding intermarriage and conversion. Appalled by intermarriage in the Jewish community and angered and disturbed over the rise of a non-Orthodox rabbinate, the initial Orthodox attitude toward this issue was unyielding, designed to protect Jewry and Judaism from the threat of disintegration.

The late nineteenth century signaled the emergence of another Orthodox attitude toward these issues of conversion and intermarriage in the open society of nineteenth-century Germany. A different group of Orthodox rabbis—equally concerned with these phenomena and just as anxious to arrive at a decision in accordance with Jewish law—adopted a lenient posture on these questions. They believed that their position reflected halakhic integrity and that by promoting a policy of inclusion and acceptance, they would thereby promote the future of the Jewish community.

An early sign of this attitude can be found in a responsum of Zvi Hirsch Kalischer (1795–1874), rabbi of Thorn. Kalischer was an Orthodox *mevaseir Tziyon* (forerunner of Zionism), the famed author of *Derishat Tziyon* (1862). He was also a leading halakhic authority in nineteenth-century Europe. When he read Rabbi Illowy's letter and the other rabbis' responses to it in *Der Israelit*, he expressed his own views on the case by responding to Hildesheimer, whom he labeled the "greatest among them." He dissented from their opinion, claiming that "a Jewish sentiment struck root in the hearts of these fathers and they wanted their sons circumcised." Kalischer applauded this desire, saying that it was a "mitzvah to circumcise such children."

Kalischer offered a general excursus on the Jewish attitude toward conversion in general before turning to the status of the children in New Orleans. He stated that all humanity was "the work of God's hands" and that God desired all humankind to receive Torah. However, only Israel, at the time of the theophany at Sinai, was prepared to accept it. Yet God's purpose in granting Israel this precious gift was to enable Israel to conduct itself "as a nation of priests and a holy people" who would bring the truth of God's Torah to the entire world. In this way, any individual who desired "to convert and take refuge in the inheritance of the Lord like Onkelos, Shemaya, and Abtalyon" could enter into the community and partake of this gift of God. Kalischer took an expansive attitude regarding converts and claimed that it was the hope of the rabbis that all persons would come to see the light of Jewish faith.

Having expressed this embracing attitude toward converts to Judaism, Kalischer turned to the case at hand and stated that these youngsters in New Orleans should be circumcised in their infancy, as they would be reluctant to endure the pain of circumcision in adolescence

and young adulthood. These particular children, born of a Jewish father and a Gentile mother, were *zera kodesh*, holy offspring, and he
advised the community to do everything in its power to facilitate their
entry into the Jewish people. Conversely, if these children were not
circumcised by a mohel in a *berit* ceremony when they were infants,
it would be more difficult for them to convert to Judaism as adults.
Thus, Kalischer wrote, "If we do not circumcise [them], we are pushing
[them] away with both hands from the community of Israel." Kalischer
remarked on the possibility that "great leaders of Israel would sprout
from among them. . . . How goodly and pleasant our portion will be"
if such a child were to become Jewish.

Kalischer expressed concern over the fathers of these infants as well.
He interpreted their decision to have their sons circumcised by a mohel
as an act of *teshuvah* (repentance) on their part and thought that the
community was obligated to support them in this deed. Cognizant of
the fact that these children and their fathers would likely be nonobservant, Kalischer nevertheless noted: "At a time like this, there are many
who do not conduct themselves according to Jewish law. . . . We should
circumcise the son with joy. . . . We should not, God forbid, push him
away. In regard to this, it is fitting to say that even sinners in Israel
sometimes perform mitzvot."[19]

Marcus Horovitz (1844–1910), born in Liska, Hungary, at-
tended Esriel Hildesheimer's yeshiva in Eisenstadt as a young man.
Hildesheimer's yeshiva was unique among the Hungarian yeshivot
of its day, as it included secular subjects in its curriculum. This in-
novation, reflecting the open cultural outlook and worldview of the
school's founder, earned Hildesheimer the enmity of many tradition-
alists in the Hungarian Orthodox camp.[20] Horovitz, however, came
to share Hildesheimer's perspective on Judaism and the world. He ad-
mired Hildesheimer greatly and dedicated his volume of rabbinic responsa, *Mattei Levi*, to him. In its introduction, Horovitz described
Hildesheimer as a "prince of Torah and pillar of piety, a man as strong
as iron in his righteousness and like the very essence of heaven for the
purity of his heart.[21]

Horovitz eventually migrated to Germany, where he was educated, as was his teacher Hildesheimer, in *Wissenschaft des Judentums*.

Horovitz's four-volume *Frankfurter Rabbinen*, a history of Frankfurt's rabbis, is a model of nineteenth-century academic scholarship.[22] Horovitz achieved great distinction in Germany and was one of the most prominent members of that country's Orthodox rabbinate. And, like many of his colleagues, he was sensitive to the delicate choices that Orthodoxy had to make if it was to cope successfully with the challenges of the modern era. Horovitz's attitude toward Judaism and the problems created by modernity is perhaps best illustrated by his views regarding Jewish religious pluralism.

Unlike Rabbi Samson Raphael Hirsch, Horovitz did not refuse to cooperate with Jewish religious groups that advocated viewpoints different from his own. On principle, Horovitz opposed the efforts of Hirsch, and others in the German Orthodox world, to separate from the general Jewish community. After 1876, when such separation from the established Jewish community became legal in Prussia, Horovitz registered his protest against *Trennungsorthodoxie* (separatist Orthodoxy) by accepting the post of *orthodoxer Gemeinderabbiner* (Orthodox community rabbi) when it was offered to him in 1878 by the Frankfurt community. Hirsch, who had established a separatist Orthodox community in Frankfurt immediately after the passage of the Law of Secession in 1876, viewed Horovitz's entry into Frankfurt, which had until then been Hirsch's domain, as a personal insult and challenge to his authority. Consequently, he attempted through intermediaries to dissuade Horovitz from assuming the position of community rabbi. Even his teacher Hildesheimer initially tried to discourage him from accepting the appointment. However, Horovitz spurned the advice of his teacher and ignored Hirsch's objections because he felt it essential, if Orthodoxy was to be influential among considerable numbers of German Jews, to participate in the life of the larger community. Horovitz was unwilling to assume a sectarian stance toward nonobservant Jews and, as we shall see, his responsa on the policy to be adopted toward the children of non-Jewish mothers and Jewish fathers reflect this stance.

Horovitz, in his first responsum on the subject, addressed himself to the greatest living Jewish legal authority of the time, Rabbi Isaac Elchanan Spektor (1817–96) of Russia. He wanted to explain his views on the issue and asked for Spektor's reactions to his review of the halakhic

literature related to conversion. Horovitz began by explaining precisely what had motivated him to investigate this matter. A Jew married to a Gentile woman had come to him to say that he and his wife
wanted their child converted to Judaism. The mohel whom they had
approached about circumcising their son had said he would do so only
if Horovitz ruled that it was a commandment to perform the circumcision. Horovitz had responded that he would have to think the entire
situation over for two days.

In the meantime, the couple went to another mohel, who indiscrim-
inately circumcised such children. While Horovitz did not question the
piety of this man, he explained to Rabbi Spektor that he considered
the policy of that mohel unwise. Horovitz feared that although the circumcision might be performed according to the standards of halakhah,
there was reason to fear that the child would not be immersed in a
mikveh under the auspices of a *beit din*. In that event, the child would
not have been converted, but these children, who would be identified
as Jews because of the circumcision ceremony, might well marry other
Jews, in violation of Jewish law. Horovitz, at this point, did not draw
any final conclusions from this consideration; but this anxiety was a
reason given by Rabbis Hildesheimer, Illowy, Lehmann, and Feilchenfeld for prohibiting such a ceremony.[23]

Horovitz told Spektor that three other such cases had come before
him. Once, Horovitz reported, he forbade the mohel to perform the
circumcision because the father told Horovitz that he did not plan to
raise the child "according to the ways of the Torah." Moreover, the father threatened to leave Judaism if Horovitz did not permit the circumcision. Therefore, wrote Horovitz, "If the father wanted to change his
religion, why should I bring his son into the community of Israel?" The
father's threats in this instance were counterproductive and aroused
Horovitz's ire.

In the second case, the father said that he wanted to raise his son "according to the religion of Moses and Israel" and that his wife wanted
to convert. Horovitz reported, "I heard that there were heretics in the
man's family who wanted to persuade him to convert to his wife's faith.
However, the man was determined to reject their advice. I feared that
if I forbade [such a circumcision], he would perform the will of his

family." As Horovitz did not think that there was a clear prohibition against the mohel performing the circumcision, and since he did not want to be the cause of a Jew's "denying the God of Israel publicly," he permitted the circumcision.

In the third episode, Horovitz told the father that he would permit the circumcision of such a child on the following conditions. One, the boy would have to be raised as an observant Jew. Two, the son, at age thirteen, would have to agree to this. Three, either the mother would have to convert and become an observant Jewess or the father would have to hire an observant woman as a housekeeper to ensure that the father and son would have a kosher home.

Horovitz decided that these cases were too many and too complex to be handled on an ad hoc basis, so he consulted the sources for a thorough halakhic investigation. According to Horovitz, the two major questions were: (1) Is it forbidden to circumcise such a child for the sake of conversion? (2) If it is permissible, should the rabbinic court do so? Horovitz was now prepared to deliver his view on the subject for Spektor's critical assessment.

Horovitz wrote that it might initially be supposed forbidden to accept such a child as a convert; normative Jewish tradition, in Horovitz's view, held that a convert should come to the Jewish people and their religion only "from love." As a baby could not possibly come "from love," how would it be possible to conduct a circumcision ceremony, which would facilitate his entry into the Jewish people? Horovitz dismissed this objection by stating that a child had no need to prove "love." That consideration was important only for an adult, because of the possibility of an ulterior motive prompting the individual to seek conversion, a possibility that would not apply to a child. Moreover, citing a ruling attributed to Rav Huna in Ketubot 11a and codified by later Jewish legal authorities, Horovitz noted that it was explicitly stated that a minor could be converted to Judaism by the authority of a *beit din*. Thus, there was no question that a child born to a Gentile mother and Jewish father could be converted; but was it desirable?

Horovitz answered this question by expressing his own views on the proper Jewish attitude toward conversion, for he reasoned that only after determining this general perspective could he decide the proper stance relative to converting these particular boys. Horovitz, noting the talmudic warning "Proselytes are as troublesome to Israel as leprosy," observed that, despite this injunction, the rabbis "never ceased to consider the acceptance of proselytes as a commandment." Indeed, the rabbis "feared locking the door before proselytes." It was for this reason, Horovitz said, that the rabbis held that a proselyte, after he had been accepted as a candidate for conversion, was to be circumcised immediately. Thus, if "it is a commandment [to circumcise] an adult, certainly it is a commandment to circumcise a baby," for there need be no doubt as to the baby's sincerity. In putting forth this reason, Horovitz indicated that the acceptance of such children into the Jewish community provided an opportunity to perform a commandment. Consequently, he implied that it was desirable to do so. The rest of his ruling simply reinforces this interpretation of Horovitz's views, for he went on to raise other possible objections to the acceptance of these children into the community and, as we shall see, to dismiss them.

First, Horovitz quoted Rabbi Haim Heinemann, a German colleague who forbade the conversion of such children on the grounds of the rabbinic principle "Thou shalt not place a stumbling block before the blind." Heinemann, echoing the reasons advanced by Rabbi Hirsch above, reasoned that the baby, if he was not converted, was not obligated to observe the commandments. However, such a child—raised in what likely would be a nonobservant home—if circumcised and later converted to Judaism, would probably transgress the commandments and thus be culpable before God. While it was permissible to accept an adult who, in full responsibility, could make such a decision, Heinemann thought it unfair to accept a child.

Horovitz countered by stating that circumcision was an enabling act. The child, when he was thirteen, could exercise his option to accept or reject entry into the Jewish people. By circumcising him as a baby, the *beit din* simply made his choice, if it were to be an affirmative one, easier. He also produced an additional reason for asserting that the principle "Thou shalt not place a stumbling block before the blind" was not applicable here: "If we compare our Holy Torah and exalted faith . . . to, God forbid, a 'stumbling block,' " one could hold that "it would be a sin to teach Torah to the people Israel." Even to imply this,

Horovitz contended, was an insult "to God and His Torah." Indeed, Horovitz noted that the talmudic dictum "And we grant merit to a person even not in his presence" had been applied by the rabbis in Ketubot 11a as an act of "granting merit" to a child brought before a *beit din* for conversion. Thus, bringing this child into the community was not only permitted but was an act of beneficence.

Having answered the first question, Horovitz addressed the second: "Does the *beit din* actually have the power to circumcise this child?" Horovitz stated that the commandment to circumcise such a child was clearly operative in talmudic times. But was it operative today? In the rabbinic era, the entire people had observed the Law. In the contemporary era, no such assumption could be made. Horovitz painfully observed that most Jews of his time and place were nonobservant and that there was little reason to assume that the children, in most cases, would be observant. In making these observations, Horovitz was simply acknowledging the reality of contemporary German Jewish life. His teacher Hildesheimer had made the same observations and, as a result, had forbidden the circumcision of these children.

Horovitz, for precisely these reasons, thought that the traditional talmudic judgment granting the *beit din* this right should be exercised in the contemporary situation. He said that if the *beit din* refused to permit the circumcision of the child, "the father will find more than enough mohalim who will circumcise the baby, as we well know." Picking up a concern voiced earlier in the responsum, he continued: "And then this circumcised boy will grow up without *tevilah* and without conversion. . . . He will thereby cause the public to stumble, as both in his eyes and the eyes of the world he will be a Jew. Moreover, if by some chance he does observe the commandments, he will be thought a kosher (proper) Jew and will serve as a witness for marriage, etc., and will likely marry a Jewess." It would therefore be better, Horovitz reasoned, for the *beit din* to ensure that the circumcision was performed for the "sake of conversion" than to leave it to chance. Here the environment had a decisive impact upon Horovitz, causing him to interpret Jewish law in a lenient way.

In concluding this responsum, Horovitz expressed the fear that if the father in this situation refused this request, his entire process of repentance might be hindered, "although his end might have been to serve the Creator properly. Thus, if we put him off and do not accept his repentance, he will continue to sin." Horovitz thus chose to interpret this action of the father's—the bringing of his son for circumcision—as an act of repentance on the father's part. Consequently, it was not forbidden. Horovitz stated: "Perhaps, on the contrary, it is a commandment" to circumcise the son immediately. With this word, Horovitz's first responsum came to an end.

However, Horovitz soon wrote another responsum on the matter.[24] Though he had not yet received a reply from Spektor, Horovitz wrote that he had read a responsum of Spektor's on the issue, which he wanted to address. In Spektor's responsum, he had ruled, on the basis of a statement in the *Shulḥan Arukh, Yoreh De'ah* 266:3 ("If a Jew cohabits with a Gentile woman and they have a son, the son should not be circumcised on the Sabbath"), that it was forbidden for sons born to Gentile mothers and Jewish fathers to be circumcised by a mohel in a Jewish religious ceremony. Instead, Spektor had decided that only the son of an observant Jew could be circumcised by a mohel.

Horovitz dissented from Spektor's position, actually citing the same *Yoreh De'ah* 266:3 passage to support his position. Horovitz claimed that the source in question, by declaring that such circumcisions could not be performed on the Sabbath, implied that the mohel had the right to perform such circumcisions on weekdays. He thus reaffirmed his previous conclusion that there was nothing in Jewish law that forbids the mohel to perform the ceremony. The two men were at loggerheads over the issue.

Horovitz also questioned the wisdom of Spektor's proposed solution to the problem. He reported that Spektor had suggested that the rabbinic court should exercise the power that Jewish law (*Even Ha'ezer* 154:21) bestowed upon it to compel a man to leave his wife. This prerogative could be used as leverage to compel "appropriate behavior" in these cases. Thus, the *beit din* should order the man to leave his Gentile wife and, should he refuse, the *beit din* should not allow his son to be circumcised by a mohel.

Horovitz demurred. While he acknowledged that the *beit din* had the right to exercise this authority, there was no obligation to do so.

Indeed, living as he did in the relatively open society of post-Emancipation Germany, Horovitz held that such attempted coercion would only be counterproductive. In language reminiscent of Maimonides' responsum from centuries earlier, Horovitz argued that not only would such a decree be ineffectual; because there was no real power to enforce it, it would hold the Orthodox rabbinate up to ridicule. Spektor, living in the more traditional environment of Russia, still wished to employ the old weapons of coercion to check deviance from norms of halakhic Judaism. Horovitz, on the other hand, understood the impotence of such a threat in the context of nineteenth-century Germany.

For this reason, Horovitz concluded his responsum by suggesting that within the German Jewish environment of the day, the birth of children such as these might bring the fathers back into the Jewish fold: "Their sons may cause them to cast away their evil thoughts." Thus, it would be better, he stated, if a decree compelling the husband to leave his wife not be issued, for it not only would be ineffective but also would discourage these families from embracing Judaism. Horovitz, in his conclusion, held that it was halakhically permissible and sociologically sound for the community not to forbid the circumcision of these children by a mohel, and even to encourage such circumcision. Of course, each case had to be decided on its own merits. However, the *beit din*, in each instance, had to exercise its judgment so as to "speak to the heart of the man and return him to the way of the permissible and the Holy Torah."

Spektor replied to Horovitz, praising his erudition and sensitivity on this issue. However, he apologized that he was, because of his age and illness, unable to comment on the substance of Horovitz's remarks. Thus, what might have been a significant halakhic exchange between a traditional and a Modern Orthodox rabbi on a matter of prime import to contemporary Jewry never took place.

The lenient attitude expressed by Horovitz is reflected in a number of responsa issued by David Hoffmann (1843–1921), a close friend and colleague of Horovitz's. Hoffmann, like Horovitz, immigrated to Germany from Hungary and was a student of Esriel Hildesheimer. Hoffmann was appointed to the faculty of the Rabbinerseminar at its founding in 1873 and succeeded Hildesheimer as rector upon the older rabbi's death in

1899. His collection of responsa, the *Melamed Leho'il*, is a modern Jewish legal literature classic. Hoffmann was undoubtedly the *posek elyon* (leading halakhic authority) of Orthodox Jewry in Germany at the time.[25]

Hoffmann, in a number of cases, dealt with whether a person who desired to convert to Judaism for an ulterior motive—for example, marriage to a Jew—could be accepted. In an initial responsum, Hoffmann noted that the *Shulḥan Arukh*, *Yoreh De'ah* 268:12, states explicitly that conversion for any ulterior motive—including marriage—is forbidden. It might therefore be supposed that such a person could not be admitted into the Jewish fold. However, Hoffmann quickly noted that the Tosafot on Yevamot 24b cited the case of Hillel—who accepted a proselyte who stated that he would convert only on the condition that he be appointed high priest—from BT Shabbat 31; and the case of Rabbi Ḥiyya—who accepted a female proselyte who stated that she wanted to marry one of Ḥiyya's students—from BT Menaḥot 44 as sources that countered the rule as stated in *Yoreh De'ah*. The Tosafot resolved this seeming contradiction by stating that although these persons initially had ulterior motives, Hillel and Ḥiyya "knew that in the end these persons, despite their apparently ulterior motives, were in fact coming selflessly for the sake of heaven." Hoffmann then cited the rabbinic principle *hakol lefi re'ut einei habeit din* (everything depends upon the judgment of the *beit din*) to justify his position. As we pointed out in the previous chapter, this principle grants great discretion to the rabbinic court in deciding cases involving conversion despite the rule found in *Yoreh De'ah* 268:12. As a result of this warrant, Hoffmann stated that Jewish law permitted the *beit din*, if it had reason to believe that such an individual would ultimately become a faithful Jew, to accept the candidate as a member of the Jewish people even if the initial motive prompting that conversion was the desire to marry a Jewish mate.[26] In this particular case, Hoffmann noted that a Gentile man who was already civilly married to a Jewish woman wanted to convert to Judaism prior to the birth of their child. Here, Hoffmann reasoned, there was no reason to suspect the man's motives, as he already lived with the woman. Hoffmann ruled that this man was coming "for the sake of heaven," not for an ulterior motive, so the man should be accepted as a proselyte.

Hoffmann advanced several other reasons supporting his position. First, he noted that the couple would stay together with or without the conversion. By converting the man to Judaism, the *beit din* could prevent the woman from violating the biblical prohibition against having intercourse with a Gentile. Of course, Hoffmann acknowledged that an objection to performing this conversion could be raised on the grounds of the rabbinic legal principle "Do not say to a person, 'Sin,' in order that your friend will gain merit." After all, the woman, by choosing to live with a Gentile man, was, from the standpoint of the Law, a sinner. Therefore, the *beit din* was surely under no obligation to commit a "sin" by allowing the man to convert to Judaism so that the Jewish woman would no longer be in violation of Jewish law. Nevertheless, Hoffmann did not allow this consideration to prevail. He further noted that the woman was now pregnant. Thus, if the *beit din* refused to convert her husband, she would be humiliated and possibly forced to dwell alone should the husband leave her because of the *beit din*'s refusal to convert him.

Hoffmann also expressed concern for the children who would be born from this union should their father not be converted. These children, who were halakhic Jews, might be drawn after their father and his religion should he not be converted. "And these sheep," Hoffmann said, "how did they sin?" Hoffmann clearly desired that Jewish law be applied in a way that would make it likely that these children would identify as Jews when they became adults, and he feared that a stringent decision that would have these children grow up with a non-Jewish father would serve neither the cause of family unity nor the interests of a Jewish community that confronted the challenge of constituency retention in an open society.

Hoffmann did not appear to be completely comfortable—despite the discretion granted him by the principle "everything depends upon the judgment of the *beit din*"—with his holding in this case. He even concluded his responsum by stating that the conversion of such a Gentile to Judaism by the *beit din* was not the halakhic ideal. In fact, it was an *isura zuta* (minor prohibition). Nevertheless, he allowed considerations of family unity and constituency retention to trump this concern and stated: "It is beneficial that the *beit din* commit this minor infraction in receiving the convert and training him in the religion so that legitimate offspring [*zera ma'alyah*] will issue from him." This decision indicates that Hoffmann thought the optimal stance for the Jewish community to adopt regarding conversion and intermarriage in the modern situation was a lenient one of inclusion and acceptance, justified by the flexibility granted the rabbi by the halakhic tradition. Other decisions that he issued confirm this view of his position.

In a similar case, Hoffmann was asked if it was permissible to accept a woman as a convert who wanted to marry a Jewish man. As in the previous responsum, he cited the halakhic principle *hakol lefi re'ut einei habeit din*, "everything depends upon the judgment of the rabbinic court," at the outset to indicate that it was permissible to accept this woman as a candidate for conversion despite her seemingly ulterior motive.[27]

Hoffman gave several other reasons as to why she should be accepted into the community. First, Hoffmann claimed that the couple would simply be married in a civil ceremony should the rabbi refuse to receive the woman as a proselyte. Thus, the man would violate the biblical prohibition against cohabiting with a Gentile, a development that Hoffmann wanted to avoid. Second, Hoffmann stated that if an Orthodox rabbi rejected the woman, she might go to a Liberal rabbi (*ehad meihahadashim*) who would accept such converts. Hoffmann ruled that it would be better for an Orthodox rabbi to convert the woman than leave it to the Liberals. In this way, he believed, "the evil would be kept to a minimum." Ironically, the rise of a Liberal rabbinate, which led to a stringent position on conversion and intermarriage in the writings of Orthodox rabbis from 1840 to 1870, appears to have been a factor in the acceptance of proselytes by Hoffmann writing in this later period.

Hoffmann concluded this responsum by expressing some of the same discomfort that he had conveyed in the previous one. He stated that the woman should be received if she assured the court that she was converting "for the sake of heaven" and that she intended to observe laws of Shabbat, kashrut, and *niddah* (family purity). While he seems to have believed that the woman would never be truly observant, his last sentence indicates that conversion "for the sake of heaven," which included practice of the commandments, remained his ideal standard. Nevertheless, he appears to have considered the goals of constituency retention and inclusion paramount in this case and thus allowed the conversion.

In another case, Hoffmann addressed whether it was permissible to perform a wedding ceremony for a man who was born of a Gentile mother and a Jewish father, who had been raised as a Jew, and who now desired to marry a Jewish woman. As a baby, the man had been circumcised by a mohel, but it was unclear whether he had been ritually immersed for purposes of conversion. The case was further complicated by two other factors: the man considered himself Jewish and, indeed, paid a tax to the Jewish community; and the rabbi who posed the question, in light of this last fact, doubted that the man would agree to "acceptance of the yoke of the commandments," as he had identified himself as a nonobservant Jew throughout his life.[28]

Hoffmann stated that, in the event that the rabbi insisted upon a conversion for this man, he would not need *hatafat dam berit* (the drawing of a drop of the "blood of the covenant" from the penis), as he had been circumcised as a baby by a mohel in a religious ceremony.[29] In addition, Hoffmann stated that there was a legal presumption that this man was a Jew, for he may well have been ritually immersed when he was young and had considered himself—and had been considered by others—a Jew. Yet, there remained the possibility that he was a non-Jew, in which case his marrying a Jewish woman would involve a serious violation of Torah law. Hoffmann ruled that it would be best if the man received *tevilah* prior to marrying the woman, but added that it was permissible to receive him without insisting upon a strict fulfillment of the demand of *kabalat ol mitzvot* (acceptance of the yoke of the commandments).[30]

If the rabbi felt uncomfortable with this last point, Hoffmann advised that *kabalat ol mitzvot* should include acceptance of commandments such as honoring one's parents and loving one's neighbor. Ceremonial commandments, which the man would undoubtedly reject, were conspicuously missing from Hoffmann's list. As a final consideration, Hoffmann stated that if the man refused *tevilah*, it was still permissible to marry him to a Jewish woman because he was a *safeik yehudi,* a Jew of possible status. Nonetheless, Hoffmann urged the rabbi to find someone other than a rabbi to perform the ceremony and ruled that the traditional formula for Jewish blessings, which includes God's Name and mention of His Sovereignty, not be recited at the wedding. Instead, he stated that it was permissible to recite, in place of the traditional formula, the phrase "We bless the Creator of man."

Hoffmann's commitment to a policy of constituency retention and inclusion led him to advocate an extraordinarily flexible and even idiosyncratic approach to issues of personal status and intermarriage. Jews had to be kept within the "congregation of the faithful," even if that meant creating novel ceremonies that were far from halakhically conventional. Hoffmann, in another responsum, dealt specifically with *kabalat ol mitzvot* in a highly complicated case:

> A *kohein* [a Jew of priestly status who is not permitted to marry a convert, according to Jewish law] married a non-Jewish woman in a civil marriage, and she gave birth to a son who was circumcised and who subsequently died. Now the non-Jewish woman is [understandably] in distress [on account of the death of her infant son]. She also believes that her infant son was a Jew, and since she thinks—as a result of that mistaken supposition—that she is not of the same religion as her child,[31] she wishes to convert and marry the *kohein* according to the laws of Moses and Israel. Moreover, there is reason to fear that if the [Jewish] court does not agree to convert the non-Jewish woman, she will go mad. What should the court do?[32]

Hoffmann was clearly aware that Bekhorot 30b states that a proselyte who rejects even a single item of rabbinic law is to be rejected. Inasmuch as Jewish law explicitly forbids a *kohein* to marry a convert, it would thus seem that the rule in Bekhorot would make it impossible for an Orthodox rabbi to accept such a woman—one who fully intended to marry a *kohein*—as a convert. However, Hoffmann stated that there was no halakhic requirement to ask this woman if she intended to observe each of the commandments. In this way, the ruling in Bekhorot could be circumvented.

Hoffmann permitted the conversion of this woman despite her intention to marry a *kohein* because he believed that the woman should be accepted for the sake of her husband and their children. Repeating concerns voiced in earlier responsa, Hoffmann reasoned: "Certainly, it is better that she should convert so that her offspring will not be lost from Israel and so that a Jewish man will not receive *kareit* from heaven on her account."[33] However, Hoffmann stated that *kiddushin* should not be performed, for "it is preferable for her to live together with him in a civil marriage than to be [halakhically] married to him." In short, the prohibition of a *kohein* marrying a convert was more severe than the prohibition that forbids a *kohein* from living with a convert without the rites of Jewish marriage. Thus, he urged the rabbi to have the couple live together after her conversion without a religiously sanctioned union![34]

The multiple contexts and audiences that Hoffman had to address were demanding and tested his ingenuity as a *posek*. Because of his commitment to traditional Jewish legal injunctions, he upheld the classical halakhic prohibition that forbids a *kohein* to marry a convert; and because of his overriding commitment to a policy of constituency retention and inclusion, he allowed the conversion and allowed a couple not married according to Jewish law to live together.

This responsum highlights Hoffmann's deep concern for the way that Judaism was perceived by the German public as well as the compassion that he found inherent in Jewish tradition. A woman's mental health was of paramount concern to him: "In [this] case, we should also fear that if the woman does become insane because we do not accept her, this would constitute, heaven forbid, a desecration of God's Name, for [non-Jews] would say that the Jews do not care about non-Jewish women and do not worry whether they become ill and insane." This factor notwithstanding, it remains clear that Hoffmann's views, in relation to the offspring of intermarriage, are consistent with those of Kalischer and Horovitz and are opposed to the rulings issued by the Orthodox authorities cited in the first part of this chapter.

Several issues that we have been examining coalesce in a startling responsum that displays the delicate lines that Hoffmann had to follow in these matters of conversion and intermarriage even as he once again promoted a policy of constituency retention and inclusion. In *Melamed Leho'il, Even Ha'ezer*, number 10, Hoffmann addressed "the matter of whether or not we should accept for conversion a non-Jewish woman who already married a Jew in the secular courts while she was non-Jewish." The problem once again was that conversion for an ulterior motive was halakhically unacceptable. In order to make the claim that this conversion was permissible, Hoffmann again felt constrained to "prove" that no ulterior motive existed. In this instance, Hoffmann did so by arguing that the civil marriage was effectively "marriage." Consequently, the couple had no vested interest in Jewish *kiddushin*. After all, they already lived together; it could not be said that the prospect of their ritual marriage after conversion constituted an ulterior motive for conversion. His argument to support this conclusion is fascinating.

Hoffmann opened his responsum with a justification of this stance, citing a position from the responsa of the *Beit Yitzḥak* claiming that it was forbidden to convert such a woman to Judaism. He contrasted this position with one quoted by another rabbinic figure, Shalom Kutnah, in his *KaTorah Ya'aseh*. Kutnah had argued that since secular law also makes divorce difficult, and since formal dissolution of the relationship cannot take place without those same courts, civil marriage in these circumstances should be considered, a posteriori, tantamount to "marriage."

Hoffmann supported this latter position and even extended it by quoting from the famous Mishnah from Yevamot 24b: "If a man is suspected of intercourse with a slave who was later emancipated, or with a heathen who subsequently became a proselyte, he should surely not marry her. If, however, he did marry her, they need not be parted." To prove that no ulterior motive for conversion existed in this case, Hoffmann wished to demonstrate that a "marriage" was already in place. Hoffmann cited with approval the view that, while the Mishnah frowned upon such a marriage between a Jew and "an emancipated non-Jewish woman who subsequently converted," the rabbis nonetheless considered it marriage, that is, *kiddushin*. Hoffmann stated that the same could be said for the relationship between this Jewish man and non-Jewish woman who desired to convert as a result of the civil ceremony that had already been performed.

Hoffmann's desire to permit the conversion was so powerful that he referred approvingly to this argument, knowing that it represented what can, at best, be termed a creative misinterpretation of Yevamot 24b.[35] After all, when the Mishnah says, "If . . . he did marry her," it unquestionably refers to some halakhically valid form of *kiddushin*. The Mishnah's marriage involves a man who was Jewish by birth and a woman who was Jewish as a result of conversion. In contrast, the case before Hoffmann involved a man who was Jewish by birth and a non-Jewish woman civilly married to that man who now wanted to convert. In drawing an analogy between the case in the Mishnah and the one before him, Hoffmann took tremendous liberties with the legal precedent. However, as we have demonstrated repeatedly, Hoffmann was so completely committed to an agenda of inclusion in a modern social situation where his laity had unprecedented legal and denominational options that he was willing to adopt this stance. Hoffmann was concerned as well with the maintenance of the Orthodox community for which he was responsible, leading him to read the Mishnah eisegetically to make his case for leniency and inclusion.

Hoffmann again revealed his ambivalence about his own decision by acknowledging that his "open-arms" policy had its dangers as well. He warned the Orthodox community to be vigilant, noting that his holding had its limits. In cases where women who wished to convert had been refused, they should not then be allowed to marry Jews in a civil ceremony and subsequently invoke this ruling to "compel" Orthodox rabbis to convert them. Hoffmann stated: "If, before she was married [civilly], she had already asked the rabbi to convert her and he refused because he saw that she was converting for the sake of marriage, then, [even though she was married civilly], the rabbi should not accept her [as a proselyte]. Without this [restraint], all non-Jewish women whom the rabbis do not wish to accept will go and become married in a civil ceremony. Then, they will afterward say, 'The rabbis had no choice but to answer, "Amen." ' "

Whether anyone would have attempted to invoke Hoffmann's precedent in this manner is difficult to say. However, this section of the responsum demonstrates that Hoffmann was well aware of the perils implicit in his position. One can only conclude that Hoffmann pushed the elasticity inherent in Jewish law to its limits in order to adopt a lenient and inclusive stance on matters related to conversion and intermarriage.

In concluding this survey of German Orthodox rabbinical attitudes toward conversion and intermarriage, it will be instructive to turn to a responsum issued in 1928 by Rabbi Menachem Mendel Kirschenbaum (1894–1942) of Frankfurt. Rabbi Jakob Hoffmann (1881–1956), the Frankfurt *orthodoxer Gemeinderabbiner* from 1922 to 1937, had invited the Polish-born Kirschenbaum to leave his native Kraków to come to Frankfurt in 1927 to serve as *av beit din* (head of the communal rabbinical court). Such an invitation from a German Orthodox rabbi to an Eastern European one was not unusual during this period, as the era's German Orthodox rabbis often recognized that their Eastern European colleagues had greater halakhic expertise than they did. Rabbi Kirschenbaum himself was the product of a traditional yeshiva education, and his responsa are collected under the title *Menaḥem Meishiv*.[36]

In the responsum under consideration, Rabbi Kirschenbaum was asked if the existence of a Liberal rabbinate should be a factor in determining whether Orthodox rabbis should receive Gentiles who desired to marry Jews as proselytes. The rabbi who addressed his question to Kirschenbaum observed that there were "proselytes who have not been converted by Orthodox rabbis, but who have been converted by rabbis who are not scrupulous in requiring ritual immersion."[37] The questioner, noting that these persons "now live together [with Jews] despite the fact that such unions are forbidden," asked, "Is it better that we accept converts such as these [under Orthodox auspices], for, after all, a posteriori, such persons are converts?"

Kirschenbaum responded by citing Yevamot 47b: "If a man comes to become a proselyte at this time . . . he is taught some of the major and some of the minor commandments. What is the reason for this instruction? So that if he desires to withdraw, let him withdraw." Kirschenbaum noted that Rashi stated that the phrase, "If he desires to withdraw," meant that "he will not convert." Rashi continued: "Let him withdraw," as, *vela ichpat lan* —"and it does not trouble us." Kirschenbaum turned the plain meaning of this Rashi on its head and utilized this passage of Rashi as a textual warrant to advise his questioner and other Orthodox rabbis to perform conversions in instances where a non-Orthodox rabbinate would usher these Gentiles into the Jewish community if Orthodox rabbis would not. He wrote:

> In the event that it does trouble us that the Gentile will dwell with a Jewish woman—*aval al kol panim ichpat lan* ["and here it does trouble us"], [we should conduct such conversions]. For in our case, [Jews and Gentiles] will certainly continue to dwell together, and if those non-Orthodox rabbis mentioned above accept them as Jews, then, according to the Holy Torah, they are not genuine converts. Yet they will be registered as proselytes in the community registry, and after many years they will eventually marry other Jews. And *shuv ichpat ve'ichpat lan* ["troubles us over and over again"]. Therefore, it is better to receive them and not ask whether they are converting for an ulterior motive.

Kirschenbaum feared that if the Orthodox rabbinate did not conduct such conversions, these people would mistakenly be considered part of the Jewish community by Jew and non-Jew alike. Moreover, the error would be compounded because these persons, converted by Liberal rabbis, would have offspring who would be identified as Jews and who might subsequently marry Jews of incontrovertible halakhic status. Kirschenbaum found the matter to be of grave concern to the community and reasoned that an Orthodox rabbi not only was permitted to receive such persons as proselytes but, because these people would be accepted by a Liberal rabbi if the Orthodox rabbi should refuse them, was urged to accept them.

The acknowledgment of a social reality in which Jews and non-Jews mixed freely as equals in an open society, and in which the presence of a non-Orthodox rabbinate meant that Liberal Jewish clergy were prepared to sanction the entry of these non-Jews into the community as proselytes, led Kirschenbaum to formulate a "creative halakhic posture" that allowed for the entry of Gentiles who had married Jews into the community as Orthodox proselytes.

This chapter has shown that two major attitudes toward conversion and intermarriage developed in the Orthodox camp in Germany during the nineteenth and early twentieth centuries. The first attitude, so strict as to be described as *lehumra* (stringent) by one of its own proponents,

Jacob Ettlinger, marked the initial Orthodox response to intermarriage and conversion as well as infant circumcision of children born to a Jewish father and a non-Jewish mother in the modern world. Advocates of this view were unyielding in their resolve not to admit into the Jewish world Gentiles civilly married to Jews or their progeny when the non-Jewish parent was a woman. Furthermore, they neither recognized the right of non-Orthodox rabbis to admit such persons into the Jewish fold nor allowed the existence of such a rabbinate to influence their own stance on the matter. This may well have been because at this earlier period of modern Jewish history, they still had hopes of retaining hegemony over the entire Jewish community. They may also have felt that the only way to save Judaism from the dissolution that such marriages and conversions promised was to adopt a stringent stance. They clearly represent one response of the Orthodox Jewish community to the social reality of the modern world.

A second Orthodox attitude toward these issues developed in the late 1800s and early 1900s. This stance, marked by leniency and informed by the same commitment to Jewish law as the first, indicates that this other group of Orthodox leaders thought that the halakhah contained other resources and precedents that were better suited to the realities confronting the Jewish people during this period. These responsa illustrate how Orthodox authorities tried to walk a careful path between capitulation to the laissez-faire inclinations of many German Jews, on the one hand, and, on the other, an adherence to stringent Orthodox standards that might ultimately have pushed their community into the arms of Reform and beyond their reach altogether. These authorities increasingly came to rely on the variegated nature of Jewish law to expand the courses of action available to them. They recognized that modernity was radically limiting the nature and extent of their authority and that the Jews of Germany were no longer tied to them by compulsion or inclination. These Orthodox authorities capitalized on some of the tensions and even contradictions in the halakhah regarding conversion in order to issue lenient opinions on these matters. As a result, they interpreted the halakhah so as to admit into the Jewish fold people who were attempting to intermarry, and they encouraged the acceptance of children born to Gentile mothers and Jewish fathers into Judaism. These rabbis did not recognize the legitimacy of conversions to Judaism by non-Orthodox rabbis, but the existence of a Liberal rabbinate was a major factor influencing their decisions to admit these people into Judaism.

Three Hungarian and Central European Writings on Conversion and Intermarriage

At the end of the eighteenth century and during the first years of the nineteenth, the impact of Emancipation and Enlightenment on Jewish religion and society, which would eventually be considerable, was felt barely, if at all, in Hungary. The Hungarian Jewish community was still overwhelmingly religiously observant. The Reform Movement had not yet appeared as a major force on the Central European Jewish scene. Endogamy was still the rule, as significant interaction between Jews and Christians as social equals continued to be extremely rare. This apparent quiescence is reflected in the sermons and legal opinions of Orthodox rabbis of the period, captured perfectly in a homily delivered by Rabbi Moses Schreiber (1768–1839) of Pressburg (Bratislava) on Purim in 1795.

Better known as the Ḥatam Sofer, Rabbi Schreiber was considered the architect of ultraorthodox Judaism. It was he who took the mishnaic statement *ḥadash asur min haTorah* ("All that is new is forbidden by the Torah"—Orla 3:9) out of context, employing it to condemn even the slightest deviation from received Jewish custom and practice as a major violation of Jewish law. While the Ḥatam Sofer regularly employed his legal writings and sermons to inveigh against religious and social trends that he found disturbing,[1] he did not do so in this Purim homily. Apparently, he felt no need to express alarm over conversion or intermarriage at the time. His Purim sermon attests to the calm still surrounding these issues in the Central European Jewish world of the time.

70

At the outset of his homily, Rabbi Schreiber commented on Yevamot 109b, where the Talmud states that proselytes cause *ra* (evil) to befall Israel. Schreiber interpreted this statement as embodying rabbinic "complaint" against the tendency of some converts to observe the commandments in an overly scrupulous manner. Such superstrict adherence to Jewish practices established a standard of conduct that few born Jews could attain. Here the Ḥatam Sofer was clearly drawing on select classical Jewish teachings that articulate a positive attitude toward proselytes and their exemplary patterns of conduct.

Schreiber then addressed the traditional rabbinic opposition to conversion *lesheim davar* (for any ulterior motive).[2] According to Jewish tradition, the motives of one who would enter "under the wings of the Divine Presence" should be as selfless as the motives that prompted the archetypal convert Ruth. However, that same tradition spoke of the many proselytes welcomed by Mordecai after the evil Haman and enemies of the Jews had been routed. These converts were seen as coming to Judaism because they feared the power of the Jews, as described in the final chapter of the Book of Esther. The Ḥatam Sofer—who viewed all laws of Judaism as eternal—thus felt constrained to explain how Mordecai could ignore the proscription on the acceptance of proselytes who were motivated to convert for intentions other than the purely spiritual.

The Ḥatam Sofer resolved this problem by recourse to the famous talmudic story found in Shabbat 31a in which a prospective convert says to the great tannaitic sage Hillel, "Convert me on the condition that you teach me all the Torah while I stand on one foot," to which Hillel responded, "That which is hateful to you, do not do to your friend." According to medieval rabbinic commentary, Hillel brought this man into the Jewish fold despite his demand because he regarded the Gentile as having begun a process of instruction in Torah that would ultimately transform him into a selfless adherent of Judaism (*mitokh shelo lishmah, ba lishmah,* "even when appropriate deeds are performed for the wrong motives, eventually they will be performed for the right ones").

Mordecai, Schreiber argued, had done nothing more than follow Hillel's model. While he received into the fold proselytes whose motives could initially be regarded as suspect, Mordecai knew "in his soul that he would study Torah with them so that even though they did not initially come for selfless motives, they ultimately would do so for the appropriate reasons" (*shelo lishmah, yihyeh lishmah*). These persons were destined to become righteous proselytes, for they stood "in awe of the Torah and its commandments as well as the One Who commanded it." Rabbi Schreiber proclaimed: "The rivers clap in great joy" because even the descendants of the evil Haman became "righteous proselytes." The entrance of these individuals into the Jewish fold therefore immeasurably enriched *teveil yisra'eili* (the Jewish world).[3]

Schreiber's positive attitude regarding conversion is also reflected in his legal writings. In an 1810 responsum, he referred to a case that a seventeenth-century rabbi had confronted. A man had come to the rabbi with suspicions that his Gentile maidservant had replaced his own newborn son, whom he feared had died at birth, with her own baby boy. The man wanted to know whether this child, who he suspected was not his son, should be circumcised by a mohel and raised as a Jew. The rabbi, the Ḥatam Sofer reported, stated that the child should be circumcised for two reasons. First, the man was not certain that the child was not actually his. If the child was his, the son should certainly be entered into the covenant of Abraham.

Second, even if the child was a Gentile, "What do we lose if we enter the son of a Gentile under the wings of the *Shekhinah*? Circumcise him!" Commenting upon the ruling of this earlier rabbi, the Ḥatam Sofer stated that the rabbi's instruction was incomplete. The child's uncertain halakhic status as a *safeik yisra'eil, safeik goy* (possible Jew, possible Gentile) could have been completely remedied by having the child immersed in a *mikveh* through the agency of a *beit din* "for the sake of conversion."[4]

In another responsum, the Ḥatam Sofer was asked whether one ought to recite the blessing for conversion over a minor who is brought by his mother for conversion by a *beit din*. While Ketubot 11a provides a warrant for this practice, the *Shulḥan Arukh, Yoreh De'ah* 268:7 asserts that such a child has the right to protest and annul his conversion when he matures. The blessing said at the time of his conversion might therefore become, in retrospect, a "blessing in vain," and the rabbi, in the case at hand, held that perhaps it ought not to be recited in the ceremony involving such a minor. The Ḥatam Sofer acknowledged that a strict reading of the law might well lead to such a conclusion. While an a posteriori act of renunciation of Judaism was theoretically possible, the Ḥatam Sofer stated, "We have not heard of such a thing when the mother brings him." Hence, the blessing should be recited.[5]

In analyzing the attitudes and evolution of Hungarian Orthodox rabbinical attitudes toward conversion, these texts are significant. First and foremost is the fact that Schreiber offered no objection to conversion on religious or social grounds. Second, he adopted legalistically lenient positions, which testify to his assumption that the converted children would be raised in a traditional Jewish community. Indeed, in the second responsum, he not only presumed that the child would be raised as an observant Jew but also found it very unlikely that a child raised in such an environment would ever wish to repudiate his Jewishness. Schreiber's positions in these responsa indicate that while Jewish-Gentile contacts did occur, leading to issues related to conversion, neither assimilation nor intermarriage was a problem for his community at the time.

By 1817, signs of a Reform movement in European Judaism had emerged. The Ḥatam Sofer inveighed against Reform in the 1819 *Eileh divrei haberit*, and in an oft-quoted responsum several years later, he stated that if secular law permitted it, "it would be advisable to push [the Reformers] beyond our borders. Our daughters would not be given to their sons, nor our sons to their daughters—they to theirs and ours to ours."[6]

The Ḥatam Sofer recognized that his position in this responsum was completely theoretical, as the governmental authorities would not grant the power of excommunication to the Orthodox rabbinate. Nevertheless, this opinion points to a Jewish world on the cusp of momentous changes and indicates that the Orthodox rabbinate could no longer take the religious traditionalism of the community for granted.

A responsum written by Rabbi Akiva Eger (1761–1837) makes plain how this realization shaped rabbinic rulings on conversion. Though he served for most of his career in Prussian Posen, Eger was born in Eisenstadt, then a Hungarian city, and was educated in Hungarian yeshivot. He was a cherished colleague of the Ḥatam Sofer; indeed, Eger's daughter became the Ḥatam Sofer's second wife after his first wife died. Eger was thus an intimate of the foremost circles of the

Hungarian Orthodox rabbinate. His responsum addresses the issue of "an uncircumcised Gentile" who had approached a rabbi to ask to be circumcised and converted to Judaism.[7]

At the outset of his responsum, Rabbi Eger noted that the rabbi who sent him this query was concerned, first of all, about the illegality of conversion to Judaism, as such acts were forbidden "by the law of the kingdom." Governmental prohibition of conversion to Judaism was common in many parts of Central Europe during much of the nineteenth century. Indeed, while the Hungarian government granted equality to Judaism as a state-recognized religion in 1867, the Hungarian government would not acknowledge the right of a Christian to convert to Judaism until 1895.[8] Eger was sensitive to this reality and stated that all Jews—especially a rabbi—must obey the dictates of the king. Consequently, in those regions where conversion to Judaism was prohibited, the rabbi should not officiate at a conversion.

Having addressed this significant practical concern, Eger dealt with the conversion itself. The prospective convert had told the rabbi of his intention to travel to a locale where conversion to Judaism was legally permitted; so he did not ask this rabbi to convert him but only to teach him *Mikra* (Bible) and the daily prayers. While this was not, strictly speaking, against the law of the land, the rabbi was still wary of giving religious instruction to this would-be Jew. He therefore asked Eger whether he was permitted to teach the prospective convert, bearing in mind the talmudic rule that forbids the instruction of a Gentile in the study of Torah. The rabbi asked Eger whether this rule applied to a Gentile intending to convert.[9] Eger responded by first citing the dictum of the Maharsha (Rabbi Samuel Eliezer ben Judah Halevi Edels, 1555–1631), who, commenting on the well-known story of Hillel in Shabbat 31a mentioned above, concluded that one need not be concerned about the admonition found in Sanhedrin 59a, "One who instructs a Gentile in Torah deserves death," as the deed of Hillel indicated that "it is permitted to teach Torah to a Gentile who comes for purposes of conversion."

Then, however, Eger sought to dismiss the application of the ruling advanced by the Maharsha. On the basis of a comment in the Tosafot on Yevamot 24b, Eger stated that Hillel knew that this man desired to convert for the sake of heaven and therefore converted him immediately—prior to offering him instruction. As no contemporary rabbi possessed the wisdom of Hillel, no present-day authority could follow his example; so the ruling of the Maharsha was irrelevant for modern-day rabbis. Eger refused to grant his questioner permission to instruct this potential convert and, in so doing, effectively banned conversion in almost all cases. The logic of his position meant that a rabbi could no longer instruct a Gentile who desired to become a Jew, nor could any rabbi claim sufficient insight to know a priori—as Hillel had—the motives of a would-be proselyte.

The Eger responsum's strict interpretation stands in sharp contrast to the sort of leniency previously allowed by the Ḥatam Sofer in matters related to conversion and illustrates how the attitudes of at least one segment of the traditional Hungarian rabbinate had begun to shift. This rigid ruling reflects a socioreligious context in which Reform was on the rise. Jewish-Gentile social interaction was now beginning to occur with greater frequency, and the religious behavior of converts after conversion could no longer be taken for granted. As Adam Ferziger has noted, Eger had come to a personal "recognition that a transformation had taken place" and that "nonobservance" was now "a permanent characteristic of modern Jewish life. What the Ḥatam Sofer may have seen as a ferocious but passing danger, Rabbi Akiva Eger considered as an irreversible trend."[10] These factors clearly influenced the position that Eger put forth in his responsum.

Eger's was not the only Orthodox rabbinic response to this changed situation. His pupil Rabbi Eliyahu Guttmacher of Posen reacted two decades later in a radically different manner to the transformed reality. An analysis of his writings will reveal this other response.

Eliyahu Guttmacher: An Inclusive Approach

Eliyahu Guttmacher (1795–1874) was a well-known mid-nineteenth-century Central European rabbi born in Borek, in the district of Posen. As a youth, he studied with Akiva Eger, and for the rest of his life regarded Eger as his most outstanding teacher. Guttmacher's writings grant us another insight into the evolving approaches regarding conversion among the Hungarian Orthodox rabbinate and those who fell within its orbit.

Writing in 1838–39, Rabbi Guttmacher responded to a rabbi who asked whether it was appropriate to accept an individual for conversion who intended to marry a *kohein*. Guttmacher noted that Jewish law brooked no compromise on this matter: the rule prohibiting a priest from marrying a convert was clear. Guttmacher wrote a brief, straightforward responsum in this instance and did not use the case to issue a policy statement regarding intermarriage and conversion. He simply stated that the rabbi should not perform the conversion.[11]

Two decades later, the social situation concerning intermarriage between Jews and Gentiles had begun to change,[12] and Guttmacher was compelled to formulate a stance on these matters. In 1858, he dealt with a case in which a Gentile man in Meizeritsch desired to convert in order to marry a young orphaned Jewish woman. The rabbi who posed the question to Guttmacher believed that the young man would probably become observant. The prospective *geir* had studied and apparently accepted the Thirteen Principles of Maimonides as the authoritative beliefs of Jewish faith and had familiarized himself with the siddur and the traditional order of Jewish prayer. The rabbi was inclined to carry out the conversion but wanted Guttmacher's approval.[13]

Guttmacher noted that Judaism permitted the rabbi to accept this young man as a proselyte but said that the applicant should produce a secular legal document stating that it was legally permissible for him to convert before the rabbi could conduct the conversion. Guttmacher, like Eger, wanted to observe the regulations of the secular authorities. Although Guttmacher shared the concern of his teacher over legality, he was apparently untroubled by the matter of teaching Torah to Gentiles, despite Eger's opposition to it.

Guttmacher then turned his attention to the substantive matter of Jewish law in the matter before him and focused the first part of his discussion on the passage in Yevamot 109b concerning the "evil" that will befall those who convert Gentiles to Judaism. Basing himself on the commentary of the medieval Tosafot on this passage, Guttmacher limited the scope of this dictum by claiming that it applied only to those who converted Gentiles to Judaism hastily or to those who sought out Gentiles in order to seek their conversion. In his opinion, only active proselytizing on the part of Jews was forbidden.

In the case of individual Gentiles who of their own accord sought admission into the Jewish people, Guttmacher adopted a different attitude—even when this request derived from a yearning for a Jewish mate. He claimed that there was greater *aḥrayut* (accountability) for those rabbis who rebuffed such would-be converts than for those rabbis who accepted these persons into the Jewish faith despite their nonspiritual motives, even if legitimate doubts remained about the sincerity of their intent to become completely observant following conversion. Guttmacher stated that the *din* (law) supported this stance because even if the potential convert misled the rabbinic court about his intent to observe the commandments, the conversion was still upheld as valid once the appropriate rites of entry were performed under the supervision of a qualified *beit din*.

Furthermore, if the candidate for conversion was worthy and the rabbinic court rejected him, the damage to the Jewish people could potentially be catastrophic. Guttmacher thus opposed the stance of his teacher Rabbi Eger and justified his own position on the basis of the talmudic legend found in Sanhedrin 99b concerning Timna and the Jewish Patriarchs—Abraham, Isaac, and Jacob. According to this legend, Timna beseeched the Patriarchs to convert her to Judaism. They refused her request to convert, believing her desire to be impure; they thought that she was motivated to enter Judaism by her love for the Patriarchs alone. Guttmacher noted that, because of their rejection, Timna was prevented from building a *bayit ne'eman* (faithful household) in Israel. Instead, she married a non-Jew, and the Jewish people were ultimately severely punished, for, according to Jewish legend, Timna bore Amalek, the eternal archetype of all enemies and persecutors of the Jewish people.

Guttmacher suggested that the Patriarchs would have better served the Jewish people had they adopted the more generous model later employed by Hillel. By referencing this story in a discussion of what should be done in the case of the young man whose motives for conversion were impure, Guttmacher was indicating that he differed with his teacher Eger—Eger having refused to grant present-day legitimacy to conversion based on Hillel's precedent. Guttmacher held that those rabbis who would be stringent regarding conversion should bear in mind their own burden of culpability. Rejecting a *nefesh tov* (good soul) constituted a graver threat and danger to the Jewish people than the responsibility involved in accepting an individual who was *eino ra'ui* (not worthy).

As a result of these considerations, Guttmacher ruled that the rabbi should be lenient in this case and accept this Gentile man as a convert to Judaism. He stated that it was of little import that he had an orphaned Jewish girl in mind as a future marriage partner. Despite the stricture in *Yoreh De'ah* that disallowed conversion prompted by an "ulterior motive," Guttmacher did not regard this "ulterior motive" as a decisive ground for rejecting this man. Rather, he averred that the man's conversion and his subsequent marriage would constitute the fulfillment of a "great mitzvah" for the Jewish people.

Nothing in this responsum indicates that Guttmacher expected anything less than complete Jewish observance from this potential convert. Guttmacher concluded by stating that he rendered an explicit judgment on this matter precisely because his rabbinic colleagues, and the Jewish people as well, needed to be aware of the dire consequences that might result from a refusal to accept a potential proselyte. In the contemporary period, there was no reason to fear that converts would cause Israel to stray "from the correct path." Israel does that without them! "On account of our many sins, *peritzim* [lawless violators]" now lead our people, he explained. Hence, all negative statements about converts no longer apply. Indeed, given the piety of many converts, "Would that we could learn from them."

Seven years later, Guttmacher expressed a similar position in another case. Writing in 1865–66, he observed that the civil governments by then commonly permitted civil marriage between Jews and non-Jews.[14] These couples had no intention of dissolving their bonds, and many of these unions had already produced children. The question that Guttmacher addressed in this responsum was whether civilly married women could be converted, as non-Jewish women now "desired to enter into the religion of the Jews," and the Jewish "husbands also awaited this act of *ḥesed* [kindness] that would allow them to be united with their wives in Jewish marriage."[15]

By framing the question in this way, Guttmacher showed that he was inclined to rule leniently in the case before him and accept these women into the Jewish fold. Guttmacher and his rabbinic interrogator knew that there were halakhic obstacles to the conversion of such women. Indeed, Guttmacher cited these problems at great length. At the same time, he recognized in this responsum—as he had in the earlier one—that other precedents could be employed that would permit the conversion and subsequent entry of these women into the Jewish community. These couples had already fulfilled "their desire," that is, consummated their unions, so there could no longer be grounds for claiming that their aspiration for conversion was prompted by an ulterior motive. Guttmacher concluded that the conversions should be performed for these women. It could even be said that the desire of these women to convert to Judaism was *devar hashem* (an act done for the sake of God).

Advancing an argument that would later be adopted by other Orthodox rabbis,[16] Guttmacher contended that such women should be converted to Judaism "to save the husband" from violating the legal prohibition against a Jew from having intercourse with a Gentile. According to Jewish law, the punishment for a Jewish man who disobeys this law is *kareit*, excision from heaven. Guttmacher thought that the rabbis were duty-bound to prevent such transgressions inasmuch as they had the legal options to do so in these instances. Clearly, the task of the rabbi—insofar as he was able—was *lezakot* (to grant merit) to Jews.

Guttmacher observed that if each Gentile woman married to a Jew converted, all future children who might issue from their unions would also be Jews. Any older children, born prior to the conversion of their mothers, should be converted as well. Undoubtedly, Guttmacher was concerned with the unity of the family as well as the status of the non-Jewish wives and the religious state of their children. His halakhic stance was diametrically opposed to that of Rabbi Eger.

In an additional responsum regarding a potential convert and his family, Guttmacher reconfirmed his stance. In this instance, a man who wished to convert had a Jewish wife who had previously apostatized from Judaism and embraced Christianity. This woman had given birth to a son and daughter fathered by this Gentile man and was currently pregnant for the third time. She had stated that she and her children now wanted to return to Judaism, and her husband had approached a rabbi, desiring to convert. This rabbi submitted the question to Guttmacher, noting that there seemed to be an ulterior motive involved, for the wife's Jewish mother and siblings had stated that they would share the family's apparently considerable wealth with her and with her husband and children only on the condition that the entire family embraced Judaism. Thus, Guttmacher was being asked not only whether to convert this Gentile man to Judaism but also whether it was legitimate to deal with an entire family seemingly prompted by the base motive of financial gain.[17]

Guttmacher began by pointing out that the wife and children were already halakhically Jewish. After all, Judaism technically does not recognize the possibility of "apostasy," that is, conversion to another religion. The classical reasoning for this is based on the rabbinic dictum in Sanhedrin 44a: "A Jew, even when he sins, remains a Jew." While the woman in this case had committed a sin by "marrying" her husband and "converting" to Christianity, her act of intermarriage could not remove her status as a Jew. Her children were Jewish.

Guttmacher defined the children as *anusim* (compelled ones), a term reserved in halakhic literature for forced converts away from Judaism and others who are not allowed to express their Jewishness publicly, through no fault of their own. If the rabbinic court did not accept their father as a Jew, the children could not be rescued from their "Gentile state," even though they were—strictly speaking—Jews. If the father were not accepted as a convert, the rabbis would have "pushed the children away with two hands from the community of Israel."[18] Guttmacher contended that the rabbinic court was therefore obligated to rescue the children from that fate by accepting the father as a convert, even if this act was *ketzat neged hadin* (a bit contrary to the law).[19] The rabbinic dictum (Shabbat 4b) "Do not say to a man, 'Sin so that your friend will gain merit' " should be ignored in this instance. While the *beit din* might be faulted for committing a "minor sin" in accepting such a candidate as a proselyte, the subsequent mitzvah that would flow from this act of acceptance would offset this "minor transgression," for should the father convert, he would actually fulfill the biblical commandment "Be fruitful and multiply."

Guttmacher then returned to the oft-quoted passage in Yevamot 109b condemning those who accept Gentiles as converts to Judaism, and he again dismissed it as legally irrelevant because its terms were limited by special conditions. He claimed that the passage only meant to condemn active efforts at outreach, that is, "to mix *zarim* [strangers] among the Jewish people." The rule was applicable only if there was no compelling reason to accept the Gentile candidate into Judaism. In this case, there had been no outreach efforts to convert the father. He had approached the rabbi concerning conversion on his own accord. Moreover, "in this instance, there is *ta'am usevara* [good cause and reason]" to perform the conversion. Consequently, Guttmacher reasoned, "It is a commandment to do so."

Finally, the rabbinic principle "Everything depends upon the judgment of the rabbinic court" provided an additional warrant for performing the conversion. If the rabbinic court decided that such a conversion constituted a *tovah* (benefit) for the Jewish people, it was imperative—there was *tzorekh* (a need)—that the conversion be conducted so that this man and his family could be ushered into the Jewish community.

Guttmacher maintained that the court in question had an obligation to "rescue" the woman and her children—as they were Jews—from the "sin" and "negative influence" of living with a non-Jewish husband and father. Therefore, it was "permissible to accept him" as a convert. While the rabbi and the rabbinical court had good cause to doubt that the man would be an observant Jew subsequent to his conversion, it could not be known with certainty that he would return to his former ways. Indeed, he might even become an observant Jew. Therefore, for the sake of his family and in light of the precedent concerning Timna in Sanhedrin 99 that he had also referenced in a previous responsum, Rabbi Guttmacher concluded that the conversion of this man would constitute a *tovah* for the Jewish community. The man should be accepted as a proselyte, and the family should be welcomed back into the Jewish people. By converting the father, a *pisul* (blemish) would be removed from the family.

Rabbi Guttmacher was no less aware than was his teacher Eger that Jewish life in mid-nineteenth-century Hungary and Central Europe was marked by changed socioreligious circumstances. His responsa reflect his judgment that the optimal policy for the Orthodox rabbinate to adopt regarding conversion in light of these conditions was one of leniency and accommodation. His colleagues in Hungary disagreed. In their view, only a stringent stance on conversion could save the Jewish community from dissolution in an era of religious reform and nonobservance. We now turn to an analysis of their position.

Later Developments in Hungary

When, on July 28, 1849, the government of Lajos Kossuth proclaimed Jewish civic emancipation, it was conditioned on the reform of Judaism and a rabbinical assembly that would call for the modernization of the community. Jews were required to abandon their particularity as a prerequisite for full emancipation. Many members of the "enlightened-progressive" sectors of the rabbinate applauded this trend toward "Hungarian nationalism." However, the ultraorthodox were bitter opponents of all attempts at modernization. A rabbinical assembly in Mihalowitz in 1866 formally forbade all changes in synagogue ritual and architecture and went so far as to prohibit secular education and the study of foreign languages.[20]

The government continued to push for Jewish integration into Hungarian life, and in December 1867, a bill sponsored by Minister of Education and Religious Affairs József Eötvös removed whatever barriers remained for individual Jews by elevating them to a position of civil and political equality enjoyed by individual Christians, even though Judaism itself was still not accorded full status as an "accepted religion" by the government. Eötvös intended to promote further Jewish acculturation by calling a Jewish Congress in 1868–69 that would centralize the institutions of the Hungarian Jewish community and enable the influence of progressive Jewish elements to grow. The Orthodox leadership of Hungary actively resisted all such attempts at consolidation. They were successful in promoting their own cause, and the legal unity of the Hungarian Jewish community was soon broken. The government permitted the Orthodox to create their own educational and administrative institutions apart from those of the liberal elements in the community. While intermarriage remained, at most, a marginal phenomenon by contemporary standards, the rabbinic leadership of the Orthodox community remained keenly aware that "secular tendencies" had caused the erosion of traditional Judaism even among observant Jews in France and Germany, and the leadership fought tenaciously to resist such an outcome in Hungary. All this provides the backdrop for the responsa that the Orthodox rabbinate would display toward conversion.[21]

In one responsum, Rabbi Judah Aszod (1794–1866), head of the rabbinic court as well as *rosh yeshiva* (head of the yeshiva) of Dunaszerdahely, addressed the question of an abandoned, partially circumcised four-year-old *asufi* (boy of unknown lineage) whom a Jewish couple now wished to adopt as their own. Since the boy had been found in a city where a majority of the citizens were not Jewish, the prospective parents wanted to know if a conversion was required.

Aszod stated that there was no reason to assume that this boy was Jewish. The boy was partially circumcised, so there was a possibility that he was Jewish, but there were stronger grounds to assume that he was not—for example, the boy spoke no Yiddish. Aszod further surmised that if the mother had been Jewish, she would have left him in a Jewish neighborhood, as Jews are known as *raḥmanim benei raḥmanim* (compassionate people who are the children of compassionate people); but the boy had been left in a lodging of Gentiles. Finally, because he had been found in a city where the majority of residents were not Jewish, Rabbi Aszod ruled that the boy should be considered a non-Jew. He surely required *hatafat dam berit* (the drawing of the blood of circumcision) in order to be converted. Even if he were a Jew with an improper circumcision, a number of authorities (including Rashi, the Ran, Turei Zahav, and the Tur) held that he would need to be recircumcised. Aszod ruled that this boy needed to be circumcised and immersed no less than any other Gentile who sought entry into Judaism and the Jewish people.

Though Aszod acknowledged that it was halakhically permissible to convert this boy, he ruled that such a conversion should not be performed. First, there was no obligation to bring a minor child like this one into the Jewish community. Aszod advised the prospective parents to wait until the boy was old enough to seek conversion on his own. Aszod feared that in the world of contemporary Hungarian Jewry, the boy might well be nonobservant. It was better for him to remain an unconverted Gentile living among Jews than to be formally admitted into the community. The era when the Ḥatam Sofer could approvingly cite a rabbi who wrote, "What do we lose if we enter the son of a Gentile under the wings of the *Shekhinah*? Circumcise him," had long since passed. Aszod believed that the optimal policy for the Jewish parents would be to send the boy out into the world—to a judge or magistrate—and have the secular authorities assign custody so that neither the individual Jew involved nor the community could be accused of any perfidious act. His perception that Jews occupied a precarious position in the world despite Emancipation, combined with his defense of the tradition against changing socioreligious norms, led him to issue an opinion completely at odds with the position Guttmacher had put forth in the response discussed above.[22]

Rabbi Akiva Yosef Schlesinger (1837–1922), born in Pressburg (Bratislava), became one of the most fanatical spokesmen for ultraorthodox Judaism in the modern world.[23] Schlesinger's vehemence against conversion in the modern era cannot be viewed apart from the vitriolic judgments he passed against religious Reform in particular or from his opposition to acculturation in general. His view on conversion was just one dimension of a larger ideological struggle and was decided on the basis of his uncompromising determination to protect traditional Judaism from all threats, internal and external. His "Note on the Acceptance of Converts Who Have Increased in Our Time," appended to the second edition of his *Lev Ha'ivri* (1865), reflects the attitude toward conversion that had come to dominate the most extreme elements in the Hungarian Orthodox community.[24] Schlesinger complained that his was a lawless era in which every Jew "does what is right in his eyes" and follows the ways of the Gentiles. He criticized as well the majority of Jews in present-day Hungary, who had internalized a modern notion of *ḥeirut ḥadat* (freedom of religion). He claimed that the "number of persons who attach themselves to the House of Jacob has increased." Schlesinger admonished his fellow Jews to follow the strictures of Judaism: "Know, my brothers, the will of God as contained in His Torah and observe His Law."

Schlesinger noted that the Talmud in Pesaḥim 87b proposed that "God exiled Israel only so that they should add proselytes to the community." However, he countered, the sages also said, "Proselytes are as troublesome to Israel as a sore" (Yevamot 109b). To explain this statement, he referenced Rashi, who, in opposition to other commentators on this passage, stated: "This is because they are not scrupulous in their observance of the commandments, and Israel learns from them." Citing Yevamot 24b, Schlesinger observed that converts were not to be accepted in "the days of the Messiah, or in the days of David and Solomon," for then one could not be certain whether their motives were selfless.

Schlesinger acknowledged that Israel might be redeemed on account of those Gentiles whose motives for conversion were pure and contended that the Pesaḥim passage applied to them. However, the Yevamot 109b passage referred to those who converted for ulterior motives—either out of fear of Jewish power or on account of their "lust" for Jewish partners. These people were like the *eirev rav* (mixed multitude)[25] in Exod. 12:38, which attached itself to Israel during the time of the exodus from Egypt and from whom have descended those Jews who have oppressed the Jewish people "in our generation," "those Sadducees and heretics, who are not descended [genuinely] from the Children of Israel." It would have been better had they remained in their Gentile state, for these apostates are "worse than idolaters." These are the people of whom the Talmud states in Niddah 13b, "These converts delay the coming of the Messiah." Why should one be surprised that the "heretics" among the Jewish people—that is, the Reform—have accepted them? After all, "One species of heretic has found another of his kind." Israel would rejoice if those Jews who follow the ways of the Gentile would leave the Jewish fold altogether.

Schlesinger continued his polemic by contending, as had Eger, that the seemingly expansive and inclusive precedent involving Hillel in

Shabbat 31a was more restrictive than commonly interpreted. Citing the writings of Isaac Luria, Schlesinger argued that Hillel converted persons during the tannaitic period whose motives were seemingly not selfless because he recognized "the root of their souls," that is, he knew that their intentions were ultimately pure. However, he asserted, "we" today are not the equals of Hillel and are unable to rely upon "such esoteric teachings" and insights. Instead, the community must rely solely upon "the words of this Torah that are written in our pure *Shulḥan Arukh*, which states that prospective converts should be discouraged from entering the Jewish people." Schlesinger observed that prominent rabbinic authorities, commenting upon the halakhah in *Yoreh De'ah* 268:2, state: "We need to threaten the would-be proselyte. Perhaps in this way, we will separate him from Israel."

Schlesinger concurred, "It seems to me that in our day, everyone needs to do his utmost to discourage them." As the Jews are not as oppressed as in previous generations, "we need to do our utmost to be stringent with them. Righteous proselytes alone" are to be accepted, not those who "innovate the religion or perform the commandments according to their [own personal] viewpoints." Converts must accept all the Torah, neither adding to nor subtracting from it. Should they deny even a single law, they are to be rejected, he ruled, drawing on the talmudic opinion expressed in Bekhorot 30b.

The Talmud (Yevamot 109b) therefore says, "Evil after evil befalls those . . . who jump to increase converts and *meshumadim* [apostates]." Schlesinger concluded his excursus with, "Guard your spirit, and after careful examination," be certain that prospective converts will be *sha-leim* (complete) Jews, "distinguished [from non-Jews] by name, language, and dress, and by the wearing of ritual fringes, earlocks, and a beard." Only then should converts be accepted into the Jewish people.

The responsa of his older colleague Maharam Schick (1807–79) display exactly the same, if not more radical, sentiments. Educated in Pressburg under the tutelage of the Ḥatam Sofer, Schick served in Hungary throughout his career and was rabbi in Hust from 1861 until his death. In a responsum written in the early 1870s concerning a baby boy born to a Jewish mother and Gentile father, Rabbi Schick acknowledged that Jewish law imposed an obligation upon a *beit din* to circumcise such a child.[26] After all, the boy was halakhically Jewish. Nevertheless, Schick argued that the court was not required to fulfill its mandate in this instance. The rabbinical court had the same right to refuse services to this boy born of an intermarried Jewish mother as it would have in the instance of a "Jewish sectarian" such as a Karaite. The mother, as evidenced by her union with a non-Jewish man, was no better than such "heretics" and privileges that would normally be accorded a Jew under halakhic prescriptions could be denied her offspring. Schick believed that the Jewish community should, as a matter of urgent policy, "be distant from them. We have no obligation to attach them in any way [to our people and our religion]."

Schick recognized that his ruling represented a stringent departure from normative Jewish practice. After all, the child's mother was Jewish, and he conceded that many rabbinic colleagues would disagree with his ruling, given the clarity of Jewish law on this issue. Nevertheless, he insisted that his decision against circumcising the child was proper policy for the Orthodox community to adopt, as the erection of "such a fence and border might well establish a boundary that would prevent licentiousness and put a stop to Jewish women marrying Gentile men." Citing the stipulation in *Yoreh De'ah* 334:1, "Excommunication is imposed upon one who deserves it, even if there is reason to assume that this will cause his defection from the fold," to warrant his position, Rabbi Schick maintained that "we are authorized to create a *seyag leTorah* [fence around the Torah] here" and not perform the circumcision.

Rabbi Schick concluded his responsum by urging other rabbis to agree to this ruling but cautioned that in *dor parutz hazeh* (this licentious generation), it may well be that "sinners" who marry Gentile men and women will not consider the commandment of circumcision to be of import. Such a "fence" might well prove ineffectual. Such persons might even rejoice in such a prohibition. Therefore, each rabbi must exercise *shikul da'at* (discretion) before erecting such a "fence."

In an 1875 responsum,[27] Schick dealt with the same issue and expressed an identical viewpoint to the one he had articulated in the first responsum. This case involved a widow who had married a non-Jewish man in a civil ceremony, despite having received several warnings not to do so. She was now pregnant by her non-Jewish husband and already had one son from her first husband (presumably Jewish). The rabbi who posed the question to Schick wanted to know whether he should refuse to circumcise a new son should one be born to *haperitzah hahi* ("that shameless woman") as a result of her union with this *areil* ("uncircumcised man").

Schick, noting that, according to the law, such children should be circumcised, nevertheless repeated the position reported above and argued that there was reason—perhaps even an obligation—to go against convention "in order to stand in the breach against this evil woman in this licentious generation." Otherwise, others might follow her example and commit this *to'evah* (abomination). Schick added, "We should not fear being stringent here, even if this causes her to apostatize." Indeed, she should be expelled from the synagogue and not allowed to purchase kosher meat. "Anything that can possibly be done to distance her from Judaism" should be done, for she has "no portion or inheritance in our midst. The truth is that such a great act of abomination should arouse the children of Israel to stand in the breach."

Schick went so far as to cite the *Shulḥan Arukh, Even Ha'ezer* 260:16, which states that a woman who intermarries should be flogged for having violated an injunction of the Torah. He urged all Jews to heed the teachings of the biblical Ezra, who had instructed that Jews who intermarry sin against God and disobey His commandments. Schick employed the same phrase that the Ḥatam Sofer had, regarding religious reformers: "Your daughters should not be given to their sons, nor your sons to their daughters."

Despite all this vitriol, Schick acknowledged that the law required the *beit din* to circumcise the boy on a weekday. But he again stated that the need to establish a *seyag leTorah* trumped the law in this instance. Any community that has the ability to "erect a fence" that would strengthen Judaism is required to do so. Schick contended that previous generations had not hesitated to refuse circumcision in such instances and that their basis for this decision was the warrant provided by *Yoreh De'ah* 334:1 that granted them the authority to excommunicate nonobservant Jews for the benefit of the community even if that caused them to leave the Jewish people. He thought that the rabbis in his generation should follow their example and do no less. And, he concluded, should his generation of pious Jews fail to distance itself "from the dwellings of these evil people, . . . we might well begin to follow their ways." The need for erecting and upholding a boundary against the forces and individuals who threatened to undermine traditional Judaism mandated strong measures.

The stringency and harsh tone in the writings of Rabbi Schick as well as Rabbis Schlesinger and Aszod on issues of conversion and intermarriage testify to the impact that social reality had on these rabbis' religious consciousness and on their doctrinal rulings. Their writings bespeak the transformations that marked Hungarian, and overall Central European, Jewish life in the nineteenth century. During the first decades of the 1800s, when traditional rabbinic leadership could take the religious observance of the community for granted, the Ḥatam Sofer could take a relaxed attitude toward conversion. His successors did not have this luxury. During the course of the century, when large sectors of the community were nonobservant and attracted to religious Reform, they no longer deemed this attitude appropriate. Though a rabbi of the status of Guttmacher advocated a policy of inclusion that would retain as many Jews as possible within the ambit of the community, the consensus that ultimately dominated the Hungarian Orthodox rabbinate on matters of conversion and intermarriage was diametrically opposed to the Guttmacher position. The posture of the majority was a reasoned, sectarian approach designed to protect "authentic Judaism" from the forces of dissolution that had already undermined, and threatened to erode even further, a traditional Jewish way of life and belief. Interestingly, the stringent trajectory that evolved in the approach most of the Hungarian Orthodox rabbinate adopted regarding conversion by the latter part of the century ran counter to the lenient direction that marked the evolution of German Orthodox rabbinical attitudes toward conversion during this same period.

Four Europe and the United States in the Modern Period

After the Holocaust, leaders of world Orthodoxy were faced with doing everything in their power to enhance Jewish unity and increase the number of Jews in the world. Jewish life had been on the precipice of utter destruction. One-third of the world's Jews had been murdered by the Third Reich. European Jewry—the heart of Jewish learning, tradition, and vibrancy—had lost more than 90 percent of its ranks. Traditional Jewish life had been virtually eradicated. Since even the defeat of Nazism could not guarantee Jewish recovery from such a trauma, one might have expected halakhic authorities to employ conversion law in the process of healing and recovery.

Some halakhic authorities (as had been the case with some of the German and Hungarian authorities we examined in previous chapters) did seek to lower the bar of admission sufficiently to allow other sorts of Jews into the Jewish people. But some other authorities proved no less rigid after the Holocaust than before. The trauma of the Holocaust led some of these leaders to reach out to Jews everywhere (and to non-Jews who wished to join their ranks); for others, it spurred a "circling of the wagons," a determination to protect the integrity and standards of what little was left of the traditional Jewish world.

Both responses, as we will see, were in evidence in post-Holocaust European and American Orthodox circles. Given the demographic damage that the Jewish people had suffered during the Shoah, some rabbis adopted a more embracing approach toward conversion standards. Others, despite the ravages of the mid-twentieth century, were not so inclined, and these men affirmed the most unbending standards regarding conversion.

One theory about the rise of a new, more stringent, Orthodox rabbinate in the mid- to late twentieth century has been offered by sociologist Charles Liebman, one of the twentieth century's most important students of Orthodox Judaism. Liebman contends that there has been an "apparent growth in what has been called 'religious extremism' in Jewish Orthodoxy in the contemporary period."[1] He points to a tendency on the part of "extremist authorities" to "emphasize the objective, the ordained," while implicitly denying or minimizing the authority "of the subjective, the optional and personal interpretation."[2]

Liebman's characterization of Orthodoxy does not always conform to what we have seen, particularly in the work of Rabbi Esriel Hildesheimer and Rabbi David Hoffmann, who emphasized the subjective and the personal over the "objective and ordained." But another element of Liebman's thesis, one that will become critical as we glance at the work of Eastern European authorities and American halakhic decisors, explains why Hildesheimer and Hoffmann did not conform to the larger picture of "religious extremism" that he describes. To explain why some Orthodox authorities represent an exception to the tendency toward "extremism," Liebman introduces another category: "social isolation" from other segments of the Jewish world. The greater the sense of Jewish communal and political unity that informs an Orthodox authority, argues Liebman, the less likely such an authority is to issue stringent rulings that would ignore or alienate substantial portions of the (less observant) Jewish community: "In the pre-emancipation period, extremist tendencies were probably present among many, if not most, Jews—rabbinical leaders in particular. But these tendencies were in tension with and held in check by a sense of responsibility for the material and physical welfare of the entire community, and by the network of interrelationships between more and less religious Jews."[3]

Liebman's thesis suggests that what held Hildesheimer and Hoffmann in check, even if they did have "extremist tendencies," was an abiding sense of responsibility for the larger Jewish community, a sense that was a vestige of the pre-Emancipation period. Paradoxically, the same forces unleashed by Emancipation that dissolved the political parameters of the premodern Jewish community, thereby causing an attenuation in Jewish commitment and observance on the part of many

Jews, also afforded Orthodox rabbinical authorities the social latitude to render even stricter interpretations of Jewish law in matters such as conversion and intermarriage than had many of their predecessors. That would explain the gradual progression that we will see in this chapter from authorities such as Hoffmann, whom we discussed above in chapter 2, to a lesser degree of flexibility with Rabbi Yehiel Yaakov Weinberg, and to what might be called "extremism" with Rabbi Mordecai Yaakov Breisch. The extremist tendency will become even more apparent as we move to the American scene later in the chapter. With Liebman's thesis in mind, we begin our discussion of post-Holocaust Europe and America.

The Impact of the Shoah on Attitudes toward Conversion: Rabbi Yehiel Yaakov Weinberg and the *Seridei Eish*

Our survey of postwar Europe begins with Rabbi Yehiel Yaakov Weinberg, a survivor of the Nazi destruction of European Jewry, and his responsa, titled the *Seridei Eish*. Rabbi Weinberg, the last head of the Orthodox Rabbinerseminar in Berlin prior to its destruction by the Nazis and one of the greatest rabbinic scholars of his era, survived his internment in a concentration camp during the Holocaust and lived in Switzerland until his death some two decades after the war.[4]

When intermarriage and conversion are considered, Rabbi Weinberg's responsa evince many of the moderate characteristics of authorities who had preceded him, such as Hoffmann. In an undated responsum,[5] Weinberg addressed a question from a German rabbi concerning the permissibility of converting a woman to Judaism who had already been civilly married to a Jewish man. The woman was now pregnant by this man and was apparently willing, if the rabbi agreed to convert her, to observe the Sabbath, kashrut, and laws of family purity. "Is it *mutar* [permissible]," the rabbi wanted to know, "to receive her?"

Weinberg began his responsum by asserting that most rabbis would forbid such a conversion on several halakhic grounds, the primary one being that conversion *lesheim ishut*, for purposes of marrying a born Jew, is not allowed. However, in a manner reminiscent of some of

Hoffmann's remarks, Weinberg observed that a number of other Jewish legal authorities did permit such conversions, on the grounds that if the couple continued to live together without the benefit of conversion, they might come to commit *aveirot ḥamurot* (weightier sins). In such an event, *yeish lehatir isur kal* ("it is permissible to permit a lesser infraction") and convert the person to Judaism. Thus, relying upon the rabbinic dictum cited earlier, that "everything depends upon the judgment of the rabbinic court," Weinberg ruled that it was possible to receive this woman if, in the judgment of the rabbinical court, she came to convert *lesheim shamayim* (for the sake of heaven). In fact, Weinberg held that the court should be inclined "to be lenient if there is a fear that if she is not accepted as a convert, she will remain with [the Jewish man] in her Gentile state."[6] In this case, Weinberg reasoned, the man would certainly not divorce her if the rabbi rejected this Gentile woman as a proselyte. Thus, she would continue to live with this Jewish man even while she was not a Jew—a serious violation of biblical law.

Moreover, Weinberg stated that the woman could be viewed as coming to Judaism "for the sake of heaven" and not for the ulterior purpose of marrying a Jewish man. After all, she already lived with this man and was pregnant with his child. If she would agree to observe the laws of Judaism outlined above, she should be accepted by the rabbi as a convert.[7]

The responsum reflects Weinberg's belief that Jewish law allowed a degree of latitude to the individual rabbinic court in adjudicating such cases. In this sense, it reveals that Weinberg was not eager to establish an unbending standard that would cover each and every case of conversion and intermarriage. Rather, it shows that Weinberg, like some of his aforementioned predecessors, believed that Jewish law countenanced a role for independent decision-making in such cases. He thus stood among those rabbinic authorities who ruled leniently—in that he allowed such conversions at all—and not strictly on this matter.

Weinberg addresses virtually the same case in yet another responsum.[8] He cites a number of precedents, concluding that "what emerges from all this is that it is permissible to convert her." Yet despite the apparent ease with which Weinberg reaches this conclusion, careful reading shows that he must have been more ambivalent than his language initially indicates. Several paragraphs after concluding that it is permissible to convert the pregnant woman, he asserts that "it is incumbent on everyone to warn the woman that she must accept [the authority of the commandments] completely in her heart, to observe the laws of the Torah in all their details." This is a natural demand for an Orthodox authority to make; but one wonders how seriously Weinberg thought it would be taken. After all, how likely was it that this woman and her husband, who had flagrantly violated Jewish law and social mores by marrying a woman in a civil ceremony, would now live a life committed to the details of Jewish observance? Though Weinberg says nothing explicit about what must have been a powerful internal conflict for him, this language mandating that the woman be warned about how she must live suggests that the decision to allow the conversion was far more painful for him and fraught with difficulty than the plain language and bottom-line ruling of the responsum might indicate.

In another responsum on conversion,[9] Weinberg's position was more stringent. He was asked whether individuals converted to Judaism by Liberal rabbis should be permitted burial in a Jewish cemetery. Weinberg acknowledged that sometimes these rabbis performed the conversions *kedin ukhedat* (according to Jewish law). Nevertheless, he ruled, basing himself primarily upon Rabbi Moshe Feinstein, his contemporary and the foremost American halakhic decisor of his day (who, in turn, also periodically quoted Weinberg himself),[10] such conversions were not legally viable. Therefore, if possible, the Orthodox rabbi in a given community should publicly protest the burial of such "Jews" in a Jewish communal cemetery. However, if the Orthodox rabbi, because of public pressure, could not prevent such a burial, he was not obligated to initiate a public controversy over the matter. Rather, the rabbi should simply warn the Orthodox members of the community to be buried at least "eight *amot* [cubits] from the graves of such false converts," which was double the distance usually considered by halakhah to be an individual's personal space.[11]

Most significant for our purposes are Weinberg's closing comments, in which he went beyond the specific question posed to him to a consideration of the entire issue of conversion and intermarriage. Weinberg was alarmed that so many Gentiles were converting to Judaism for purposes of marriage, particularly under the auspices of non-Orthodox rabbis. Significantly, this did not lead him to urge Orthodox rabbis to perform these conversions. Instead, taking a more stringent and less accommodationist position, Weinberg stated that "in our generation, it is impossible to maintain Judaism except through war and strength of spirit. There are boundaries one cannot cross with indifference." Such conversions, performed by Liberal rabbis for the purpose of marriage, were "meaningless exercises and appear ridiculous to the best of Christians as well. A Jew who marries a convert of this type knows that he is throwing dirt in the face of his fellow creatures." Weinberg thought that the most prudential strategy that the Orthodox could adopt in response to the problem was a strict one designed to save the Orthodox Jewish community from potentially destructive forces. In this way, Weinberg eventually came to urge the same course of action that Orthodox rabbis such as Ettlinger and Hildesheimer had put forth a century earlier.

This was not the only responsum in which Weinberg articulated disdain for Reform. He adopted a similar position in a later responsum[12] on whether it was permissible to perform a circumcision for the son of a Jewish man and a non-Jewish woman. In the course of his legal argument, Weinberg made revealing comments about his assessment of how Orthodoxy should address destructive forces emanating from outside the community. He worried that performing a circumcision for such a child would lead to a situation in which "people will assume that he is a Jew and will permit him to marry a Jewish woman." Weinberg also feared that permitting the circumcision would "strengthen the hands of the transgressors, who marry Gentile women and are not ashamed, when their child is born, to bring him into the covenant of Abraham our Patriarch as if the child were a complete Jew." Weinberg decided that standards must be kept high: "It is a commandment to erect a fence to protect our holy Torah and not to circumcise him."[13]

The child in question, of course, was non-Jewish, since his mother made no claim of being a Jew. But at the conclusion of his responsum, in what sounds almost like an aside, Weinberg extended the restriction further: "And even the son of a Gentile woman who was converted by the rabbis of Reform should not be circumcised. . . . Rabbinic councils must issue decrees that no mohel should perform a circumcision for one who was not converted according to Torah law." Here, Weinberg did not raise even the theoretical possibility that some Reform conversions might be acceptable; indeed, his comment about the child of a female Reform convert was appended to a responsum about a completely non-Jewish child, with no apparent effort on his part to distinguish between the two cases.[14]

In another discussion of the same issue,[15] Weinberg's language is even clearer: "If they circumcise him, people will assume that he is Jewish, and [the fact of his non-Jewishness] will be forgotten. . . . Woe to us if we allow this to happen. We should do nothing to cast in a positive light those who marry non-Jewish women. On the contrary, we must distance ourselves from them and separate ourselves from them, declaring that their sons and daughters are absolute Gentiles and that it is forbidden to marry them."

Though Weinberg differed in significant ways from the Orthodox authorities who had preceded him in Germany, the positions he took were by no means his alone. That his stance was representative of other Orthodox rabbinic opinion on the subject can be seen in a lengthy responsum by Rabbi Mordecai Yaakov Breisch of Switzerland, author of the _Ḥelkat Ya'akov_, as well as in a shorter one by Isaac Halevi Herzog, first Ashkenazic chief rabbi of the State of Israel. (We will see other responsa by Rabbi Herzog in the next chapter, when we examine conversion in Israel. The particular responsum discussed in this section, though by an Israeli authority, addresses the Diaspora.)

Rabbi Mordecai Yaakov Breisch and the _Ḥelkat Ya'akov_

Rabbi Breisch's writing on our subject was occasioned by his reading the responsum discussed previously by Rabbi Menachem Mendel Kirschenbaum of Frankfurt that urged Orthodox rabbis to convert persons who desired to enter Judaism for purposes of marriage.[16] Rabbi Kirschenbaum, writing in 1928, feared that if Orthodox rabbis refused such persons, they would simply go to Liberal rabbis who would then convert them, but obviously not in what Kirschenbaum considered a halakhically legitimate manner. Consequently, they and their progeny would be considered Jews by some members of the Jewish community and would quite likely intermarry with other Jews. Kirschenbaum, fearing this development, thought that the Orthodox had a genuine stake in ensuring that these persons were properly converted by legitimate Orthodox authorities. Upon the publication of Kirschenbaum's responsum in 1937, Breisch responded.[17] Reflecting the prevailing perspective within Orthodoxy, which already saw itself as standing apart from the non-Orthodox Jewish community (thus reflecting the "social isolation" described by Charles Liebman in the theory discussed at the beginning of this chapter), Rabbi Breisch expressed astonishment that Western European rabbis such as Kirschenbaum were not able to reject converts of this type. Almost all of them, Breisch claimed, came for purposes of marriage, not for more "pure" religious or theological purposes. Furthermore, it was their intention to marry "unobservant sinners" who were only *yehudim le'umiyim* (ethnic Jews).

Elaborating upon this category, Breisch maintained that such a Jew made a mockery of Judaism. Because he was simply an "ethnic Jew," it was virtually impossible that his prospective spouse would observe the commandments of the Jewish religion. At most, there could be a commitment to Judaism only in a cultural and nationalistic sense, but not a religious one. Breisch ruled—drawing upon a host of Jewish legal precedents—that these applicants should not be converted to Judaism. Even if the proper initiatory rites of circumcision and ritual immersion were followed, these persons were not to be accepted despite halakhic precedent that could be interpreted as holding that these persons were to be received as converts—that is, as Jews. For, Breisch ruled, failure to accept the "yoke of the commandments"—a halakhic requirement for conversion that, by definition, could not be fulfilled in these cases— "was one of the things that annuls a conversion even a posteriori [after the conversion ritual has already been performed]."

In opposition to other more lenient authorities such as Rabbi Eliyahu Guttmacher and Rabbi David Hoffmann, Breisch opined that there was no justification for the view that the rabbinic court should commit the "minor infraction" of admitting an insincere proselyte into Judaism so that the person's Jewish partner could be saved from the "grave sin" of cohabiting with a Gentile. (Here Breisch clearly had in mind a responsum by Hoffmann[18] on the matter that had advanced this as a major consideration in permitting the rabbinic court to perform such a conversion.) In Breisch's view, these people and their progeny would undoubtedly be nonobservant. If a conversion were to take place, even more sins would be committed, as all would be unobservant Jews. Breisch ruled that it would be preferable not to convert the Gentile so as to avoid "condemning" the children—assuming that the Gentile seeking conversion was a woman—by obligating them to observe the commandments. Here again, Breisch stood in opposition to his more lenient colleagues earlier in the century, though his argument echoed the stances of Rabbis Seligman Baer Bamberger and Samson Raphael Hirsch in the previous century on the same matter.[19]

In concluding this responsum, Breisch stated that it should be irrelevant to the Orthodox whether such persons would go to non-Orthodox rabbis for conversion if refused by the Orthodox. Observant Orthodox Jews would certainly investigate a prospective spouse's lineage, so there was no need to worry that the children produced by a union not sanctioned by halakhah would ever be considered legitimate Jews by the observant community, and thus there was no danger of accidental intermarriage. Even if an investigation should uncover the fact that an Orthodox, as opposed to a Liberal, rabbi had presided at such a conversion, the conversion would still be invalid and the individual and her descendants would be "non-Jews." Jewish law had an absolute standard on this issue that could not be compromised, and "reliance upon leniencies [in this matter] would constitute a defacement of the borders of the truth."

As suggested above, Breisch's responsum bespeaks an Orthodoxy that saw itself as socially apart from the non-Orthodox Jewish world and that attempted to establish objective and strict standards of Jewish law in the areas of conversion and intermarriage. It displays the characteristics of religious extremism that Charles Liebman considers a hallmark of Jewish Orthodoxy in the contemporary world.

Liebman's thesis is further supported by a fascinating responsum in which Breisch reprints a responsum issued by Chief Rabbi Isaac Halevi Herzog of Israel (whom we will discuss at greater length in the next chapter, when we address conversion in post-Independence Israel). Rabbi Herzog's earlier responsum, published in Breisch's corpus *Ḥelkat Ya'akov*, was issued in reply to a decision rendered by the Agudath Harabanim (Rabbinical Union) in Switzerland regarding a teacher whose wife's father was a non-Jew and whose mother, though born a Jew, had apparently converted to Christianity prior to her marriage. The Agudah, because it was engaged in a *milḥama keveidah* (intensive war) against conversion in Switzerland (presumably because most were done for the sake of intermarriage), decreed that this Jewish man could not be accepted as a teacher in the Jewish community's school. The rabbis of the union then wrote to Herzog, informing him of the decision and requesting his reaction.[20]

Herzog approved of the decision: "You have done according to the Torah and the commandments. . . . For [the type of conversion now taking place], not done for the sake of heaven, is like a rot in the household of Israel." The question posed to Herzog, of course, was not technically about conversion but about a specific case of employment. Nonetheless, Herzog used it as an opportunity to discuss the phenomenon. As we shall see, Herzog appears to have viewed conversions not done "for the sake of heaven" as causing intermarriage rather than as a logical outcome of social conditions where Jews and Gentiles socially interacted with each other.

What is particularly fascinating about this responsum (and what lends further support to Liebman's thesis) is that Herzog, who (as we will see in the next chapter) could be quite lenient regarding questions posed to him within the State of Israel, was very stringent in this case. He was more lenient in Israel because in that country, a society Jewish in both population and culture, the convert would by definition be instilled with a profoundly Jewish identity and would be part of an observable Jewish community. (We will see a similar phenomenon in the next chapter with another Israeli authority, Rabbi Shlomo Goren, in the case of Paula Cohen.)

The same disagreements over conversion and marriage in discussions of halakhic decisors in Western Europe at this time also occurred in those to the east. One issue that the Eastern European authorities had to address was how to handle a prospective convert who was already living with a Jewish partner. As we discussed in chapter 1, the Mishnah in Yevamot 2:8 had ruled centuries earlier that a man who had had intercourse with a slave could not free her and then marry her. Despite this explicit ruling, Maimonides stated that a man could marry such a woman, apparently because he recognized that there was little that the court could do to force her to leave his home. Performing the conversion and then allowing the Jewish man to marry his former concubine would save the Jewish man from committing the even graver sin of living with a Gentile woman.[21] As we shall see, some early modern and modern Eastern European authorities took note of this position, and in arguments that reflect the reasoning of both Maimonides and Hoffmann, they decided not to fight social reality. They argued that if a Jew's non-Jewish partner sought to convert, the rabbinate should not refuse him or her on the grounds that the conversion would be for the sake of marriage. Rather, the rabbinate should claim that since the couple was already living together without conversion, the conversion would be "for the sake of heaven."

It is important to note that this orientation, which aptly reflects the phenomenon that Liebman discusses with regard to the twentieth century, extended back to the mid-nineteenth century. According to one of these authorities, Rabbi Solomon Tabak of Hungary (1832–1908), roughly a contemporary of Rabbi David Hoffmann, "if he is living with her when she is still a Gentile, and no one can prevent him from doing so, it is clear that she has converted for the sake of heaven."[22] Similarly, the *Imrei David*, Rabbi David Halevi Horowitz of Stanislav, ruled that it was permissible to convert a woman to Judaism who had been civilly married to a Jewish man and had had children with him. As he stated, "We, in our rabbinic court, are able to immerse such a convert without examining motives." The *Imrei David* claimed that rabbinic sources stating that a person is not to be accepted as a proselyte if he or she intended to marry a Jewish spouse applied only to cases where the union could be discouraged. In cases such as this, where there was no doubt as to the union of the two people, the convert was to be accepted.[23] This accommodationist stance is also reflected in a responsum of Rabbi Judah Leib Zirelson (b. 1860), a Russian scholar shot by the Nazis in 1941. He writes that "the Gentile women, by marrying their

Jewish young men [in civil ceremonies] . . . have already achieved their goal entirely. Therefore, they are completely removed from a desire to convert for the sake of marriage."[24]

Even Rabbi Ḥayim Ozer Grodzinsky of Poland (1863–1940), a staunch opponent of Reform Judaism in the West and of secular education in the East (in addition to being a vehement anti-Zionist), seems to have acknowledged the limitations on the court's power. He opines, "It appears that the legal conclusion has to be that even if she does not convert, she will stay with him as a Gentile; then in this case, there is no element of 'for the sake of marriage.' "[25]

As expected, this leniency was not accepted by all authorities. Rabbi Meir Arik of Poland (1855–1926) dismisses the notion that simply because a couple lives together, the non-Jewish partner's desire to convert should be considered "for the sake of heaven." He insists: "The argument . . . that since he is living with her from the very outset completely openly, she senses nothing is wrong with her situation, and that therefore, we should not call such a conversion 'for the sake of marriage,' is totally unconvincing. For it is probable that her partner[26] now wishes to live with her legitimately and not in violation of social norms, and it is because of that that she is coming to convert."[27]

Technically, Rabbi Arik's assessment of the situation is correct and would probably have aptly characterized the situations examined by Hoffmann in the West and by Tabak, Zirelson, and Grodzinsky in the East. The reason for the different ruling, Liebman's thesis would explain, is that Arik's strict rulings were not held in check by a commitment to Jewish peoplehood in the broadest sense, while the other authorities were willing to mischaracterize—perhaps even consciously—the situation in order to extend consideration to a population whose loyalty they had lost but whose destiny they sensed that they still shared.

Arik's orientation is shared by yet another early-twentieth-century figure, Rabbi Ḥayim Eleazar Shapira of Hungary (1872–1939). While arriving at essentially the same conclusion as Arik, Shapira employs language that is more theological and psychological. His acerbic tone reflects his sense of nonobservant Jews as an entirely "other" class: "I am astonished [at the rabbis who rule otherwise], for how is it conceivably possible to say that the conversion will be a genuine one for these participants in an intermarriage, who deny the God of Israel and the Torah of Moses? After all, the Gentile woman is coming with him because of the impure love that has grown between them. And even if they insist that their purpose now is to convert, it is obvious that is because of their desire to live together now unfettered and unbothered by the Jewish parents of one of the partners."[28]

Arik's and Shapira's positions, when compared with those of Tabak, Zirelson, and Grodzinsky, evince the same variegated system of Jewish law that we saw in the West. The radical differences among the positions endorsed by these authorities, despite their access to precisely the same precedents and the fact that they were addressing virtually identical situations, suggest that factors other than the simple application of legal precedent were at play. Halakhic decision-making, as we have observed elsewhere, is as much a matter of social policymaking as it is jurisprudential analysis.

After the Shoah, one might have expected a more inclusive orientation among Orthodox authorities that would have emphasized an ethos of group solidarity among all Jews regardless of religious orientation. Liebman's claim that "[extremist] tendencies were in tension with and held in check by a sense of responsibility for the material and physical welfare of the entire community, and by the network of interrelationships between more and less religious Jews" is very telling. Despite the horrors of the Shoah, Jewish social policy after the war was not as different from that of the prewar period as might have been anticipated. If anything, the forces for moderation, motivated by a sense of responsibility for Jews everywhere, had been destroyed, and a number of Orthodox legal authorities urged the Orthodox community to adopt a rigid policy of exclusion regarding those Jews who had married outside the faith and their families. As we will see in the next chapter, it would be the State of Israel that would force on a number of Orthodox authorities a sense of responsibility for Jews at large.

The American Experience

American Judaism offers another fascinating lens through which to examine halakhic responsa as models of social policymaking. In America, where Judaism developed as a voluntary community on a congregational model devoid of communal legal status from the very outset, one might have expected Orthodox authorities to cast a wide net, reaching out to and speaking for as broad a swath of American Jews as possible. But as we will see, that was not the overall response. Indeed, American Orthodox rabbis have evinced many of the same qualities and proclivities as their European counterparts in the debate on conversion. Among those most committed to preserving a sense of shared peoplehood or, perhaps, seeking to navigate the yet uncharted waters of such an open host community, some of the tendencies toward leniency we observed in Europe are preserved. Yet because Judaism in America has displayed an essentially socially isolated form of denomi-national religious life, many other Orthodox rabbis saw themselves as issuing responsa for their community and their community alone. For these rabbis, the more exclusionary approach described by Liebman became the standard response to conversion candidates of dubious intentions.

Rabbi Moshe Feinstein and *Igerot Moshe*

Nowhere is the Liebman thesis as clearly applicable as it is in the opinions of Rabbi Moshe Feinstein. Rabbi Feinstein, born in Belorus-sia in 1895, immigrated in 1937 to America, where he became head of the Mesivta Tiferes Yerushalayim in New York. A prolific author of responsa, Rabbi Feinstein was the leading Orthodox rabbinic author-ity of his time in the United States, and possibly in the world. His responsa reflect an unyieldingly negative attitude toward the accep-tance of proselytes who come for purposes of intermarriage, even when such conversions are conducted by Orthodox rabbis. In addition, Fein-stein, like all Orthodox authorities before him, rejected the validity of conversions performed by non-Orthodox rabbis. However, he did not adopt the position that the Orthodox ought to conduct conversions of problematic candidates.

A responsum that Feinstein issued in 1950 indicates his views on the subject. A rabbi asked Feinstein whether it was permissible to bury a woman converted to Judaism by a Conservative rabbi in a Jewish cemetery. Apparently, the woman had identified herself and had been identified by others as a Jew in her community of Canton, Ohio. It appeared that she had converted in order to marry her Jewish spouse. As the conversion was performed by a Conservative rabbi, Feinstein stated, "Behold, it is simple that the conversion [was] nothing. . . . This rabbinic court of the Conservatives is *pesulin* [unfit] to be a *beit din* as [Conservative rabbis] are *koferin* [deniers] of many of the principles of Judaism and deny many negative commandments." Their testimony is thus invalid, "for anyone who accepts the shameful title 'Conservative' upon himself is assumed to be *mufkar* [lawless] with regard to many prohibitions in the Torah and to be in *kefirah* [apostasy] against many of the principles of Judaism. . . . Consequently, it is evident that no conversion performed by a Conservative rabbi has legal standing."[29]

Feinstein's views on this matter are reflected in several other responsa—issued in 1960, 1963, and 1971—in which he reiterated his position that conversions performed by non-Orthodox rabbis were unacceptable under any circumstances.[30] Regarding Reform rabbis, he stated: "Even if no one witnesses their transgressions of Torah, the name 'Reform' testifies to the fact that they are heretics"[31] and therefore unfit to conduct conversions. When dealing with the issue of Conservative rabbis utilizing a *mikveh* under Orthodox control, Feinstein ruled: "It was proper not to allow them to use the *mikveh* for purposes of conversion."[32] Feinstein regretfully acknowledged that in certain locales, the *mikveh* was built with funds from the broader Jewish community, which meant that the Orthodox community could not exercise exclusive control over how the *mikveh* was used. In those cases, the Orthodox would have to content themselves with silence; but this was not the halakhic ideal.

Feinstein's refusal to accept the validity of conversions conducted by non-Orthodox rabbis does not, of course, distinguish him in any way from other Orthodox rabbinic authorities. In fact, none, to our knowledge, has issued legal rulings accepting the validity of conversions performed by the Liberal rabbinate.[33] What distinguishes Feinstein and many of his contemporaries on this issue is that they, unlike many others who preceded them, did not see the existence of a non-Orthodox rabbinate as relevant in calling for the admission of these would-be proselytes into Judaism under Orthodox auspices. This is due not only to their interpretation of Jewish law; rather, the virtual unanimity of this stringent interpretation is partly conditioned—in light of the considerations put forth by Liebman—by the distance that these rabbis feel from non-Orthodox communities. They do not feel themselves to be part of a wider community that must accommodate these non-Orthodox elements. As a result of the pluralistic-voluntaristic nature of the contemporary American Jewish community, where no Jewish denomination is legally accountable to another, they are not compelled to do so. On the contrary, the reality of modern Jewish life allows them to view these nonobservant elements as a counterpoint, leading them to feel that they must protect Judaism against the destructive forces that these elements promise to unleash. Ever vigilant against these "uncommitted" Jews, they have no reason to fear, as Breisch stated above, that non-Orthodox converts will somehow mistakenly be identified by the Orthodox as genuine Jews.

Returning to his 1950 responsum, it is now possible to understand why Feinstein—like Weinberg after him—ruled that the woman from Canton, converted by a Conservative rabbi, should not be buried in a Jewish cemetery. However, noting that the Orthodox rabbi might not be able to prevent this, Feinstein stated that the Orthodox rabbi of the community should at least warn the Orthodox Jews there to be buried at a distance of no less than "eight cubits" from such a person, a stipulation that we saw earlier in this chapter, in Rabbi Weinberg's *Seridei Eish*. Furthermore, Feinstein advised that it would be best for other Jews in the community to stay away from those who had been converted in such a manner. The responsum thus suggests that the Orthodox were evolving toward a position of greater sectarianism vis-à-vis the larger Jewish community—or, at least, were being urged to do so by rabbinic leaders such as Feinstein.

This responsum of Feinstein's, as well as others cited here, reflects the same tendency that marks the responsa of other contemporary rabbinic figures described in this chapter. Nowhere in Feinstein's responsa on this matter is there a discussion of how the "convert" or his or her family might feel about these issues. In this sense, Feinstein's responsa stand in opposition to those issued by David Hoffmann, who sometimes considered such concerns in his rulings.[34] For Feinstein, and for other rabbinic figures who agreed with him, such considerations could potentially have tempered the desire to establish a clear legal standard on this matter. Consequently, his responsa can be viewed as an attempt to fix "the objective, the ordained" aspects of Jewish law in this area, as opposed to "the subjective, the optional, and personal interpretation" (in Liebman's formulation).

Feinstein's interpretation of Jewish law as possessing an objective and absolute standard on this matter can be seen in additional views that he put forth in his 1950 opinion, as well as in other responsa. As to whether it was permissible to bury a woman converted to Judaism by a Conservative rabbi in a Jewish cemetery, Feinstein noted that the fitness of the Conservative rabbi to officiate at such a conversion was not the only issue; just as crucial, if not more so, was *kabalat ol mitzvot,* expected of every proselyte.[35]

In a series of responsa, Feinstein made it clear that "acceptance of the yoke of the commandments" was a requirement on which the halakhah could not compromise. In a manner reminiscent of Breisch, Feinstein contended, time and again, that even if a conversion was conducted by an Orthodox rabbi, it was invalid if the candidate did not comply with the requirement of "acceptance of the yoke of the commandments."

In 1950, several months after Feinstein had issued his ruling in the Canton case concerning the burial of the woman converted by the Conservative rabbi, Feinstein dealt with a case involving a Jewish man who was married to a Gentile woman who had been converted to Judaism by an Orthodox rabbi. While discussing this matter—which dealt with whether the couple's child, conceived when the mother was still a Gentile, needed to be redeemed in accordance with Jewish tradition, at thirty days of age—Feinstein observed of the woman, "But if this convert is like most in this country," she was insincere when she orally pledged to observe the commandments. Feinstein, reflecting what he knew about social realities in the United States, assumed that the woman, as well as her husband, was probably still nonobservant despite her conversion. Therefore, he held, "It is more likely that [this woman and other converts like her] are not converts at all, and they remain in their Gentile state."

Of course, Feinstein did not know whether this was the case in this instance. He could only presume that such women were nonobservant. What is critically important is that Rabbi Feinstein did not consider the key issue to be the identity of the rabbi who performed the conversion. Rather, there was need for a sincere "acceptance of the yoke of the commandments" before a qualified rabbinic court, which had to consist of Orthodox rabbis. Even if the rabbis who constituted the *beit din* were Orthodox, acceptance and observance of the commandments on the part of the convert remained the sine qua non for a valid conversion, not the Orthodox denominational composition of the court.

In several other cases, Rabbi Feinstein reiterated his view that conversions conducted even under Orthodox auspices were invalid if there was not a genuine commitment to observe the commandments of Judaism. For example, in a 1952 case involving a Gentile woman already civilly married to a Jewish man of priestly descent, Feinstein ruled—in direct contradistinction to David Hoffmann, whose responsum Feinstein cited as approving such a conversion—that such a conversion was unacceptable because Jewish law forbade the marriage of a proselyte to a *kohein* (priest). As this woman would undoubtedly remain with her husband, she could not possibly fulfill the requirement of *kabalat ol mitzvot* expected of every proselyte because her very marriage would be a sin. Even if she were to be converted by an Orthodox authority, "her conversion would be as nothing." In 1963 and in 1968, Feinstein ruled that this requirement could not be compromised.[36] Even if a prospective convert were circumcised and immersed before a qualified rabbinic court, Feinstein stated that if he "did not accept the commandments, he is not a convert."[37] Feinstein insisted on the same "objective" legal ground that his peers Breisch and Herzog did.

In light of Hoffmann's responsum on precisely the same issue, it is important to ask why Feinstein arrives at such a radically different conclusion. In part, Feinstein's approach is colored by sociology. Un-like Hoffmann, who harbored a hope that the social currents he was witnessing might be temporary,[38] Feinstein knew that he and his core-ligionists were a minority among a firmly entrenched non-Orthodox majority. Feinstein's approach can also be partly explained if we recall that debates about conversion are never simply about conversion, but rather about Jewish identity. In insisting on the primacy of *kabalat ol mitzvot*, Feinstein is doing much more than issuing a ruling on con-version; he is adopting an essentialist posture and establishing a firm definition regarding what is and what is not legitimate Judaism.

Feinstein essentially acknowledges as much. In another responsum, on whether converts who had not been observant were to be considered "true" converts, he was clear: they were not.[39] Unlike Hoffmann, who seemed willing to ignore the likelihood that the prospective convert was not going to be observant,[40] Feinstein is unwilling to gloss over that potentiality.[41] He makes it clear that what is at stake is not simply conversion but a conception of what is genuine Judaism. Speaking of the convert, Feinstein writes: "And even if he says that he accepts the commandments but we know that in truth he does not, [his statement and the conversion are] nothing. . . . And furthermore, I cannot under-stand the reasoning of the rabbis who err in this. For even according to their own reckoning, what value are they bringing to the Jewish people by accepting converts like these? For it is obviously not good for either God or the Jewish people that converts like these should be mixed into the Jewish people. And as for the ruling, it is clear that these are not converts at all."

As far as Feinstein is concerned, it made no sense to do anything that might accord any legitimacy to the varieties of Judaism that had become so popular among the Jews of America. Indeed, whereas Hoff-mann referred to Reform rabbis as *meḥadeshim* ("innovators")[42] and Weinberg referred to them as *rabanei hareforma* (Rabbis of the Re-form),[43] Feinstein avoids calling Reform or Conservative rabbis by a neutral description or by the appellation *rav* or *rabanim*. Instead, he uses an artificial construct, a transliteration of the English word "rabbi" into Hebrew letters,[44] indicating that there is no Hebrew word for what this person is. This "rabbi" is no rabbi, and his Judaism is not Judaism.

Liebman's thesis is most suggestive in explaining the hard-line approach exemplified by Feinstein. America, where Feinstein wrote, had no central communal institution parallel to the German *Gemeinde* to reinforce awareness of the needs and conditions of less observant Jews. Feinstein was not required to issue rulings for the entire community in matters of conversion and intermarriage. In contrast, the *Gemeinde* remained an important reality in Germany for a rabbi like Hoffmann. The ongoing *kehilah* (communal) structure of the German Jewish world meant that strong cultural and familial ties bound Jews of all types together. Hoffmann and his students therefore felt a strong sense of responsibility for the entire Jewish community regardless of their personal standards of what proper Jewish belief and conduct ought to be. Liebman's thesis can thus account for an orientation in which Hoffmann felt responsible for Jews who were not part of his Orthodox community, even as it helps explain why Feinstein did not—at least on the issue of conversion and intermarriage.

Like Breisch and Herzog, Feinstein was keenly aware that most people seeking to convert in the modern period did so *lesheim ishut*, for purposes of marriage to a born Jew. Unlike Weinberg and other authorities, however, Feinstein was not willing to rely upon the rabbinic principle "Everything depends upon the judgment of the rabbinic court" to allow these conversions. Instead, expressing his desire for absolute standards to be established in this area of Jewish law, he held such conversions, except in the rarest of cases, to be unacceptable. Thus, in 1963, Feinstein stated that he was uncomfortable with conversions linked with intermarriage even when all requirements for conversion were fulfilled by the convert and supervised by an Orthodox rabbinic court.[45] While Feinstein did not entirely rule out these conversions—in view of the fact that "there are some cities where sometimes it is impossible for the rabbi to ban them totally"—he believed that the majority of Orthodox rabbis in the present day "did not want to engage in matters concerning conversion at all."

Feinstein's interpretation of Jewish law in this matter fits into Liebman's categories—for it obviously represents Feinstein's efforts to "emphasize the objective, the ordained" while limiting the authority of "the subjective, the optional, the personal." In addition, it reveals a significant Orthodox authority as resistant to the demands of the non-Orthodox community, for which he apparently did not feel personal rabbinic responsibility. His interpretations expose more than just his own view concerning the standards of Jewish law on the subject; they display the tendency toward religious extremism that Liebman sees as the hallmark of Jewish Orthodoxy in the modern era. Feinstein's positions—like many others, lenient and stringent, discussed in these pages—reflect the use of legal decision-making as a tool of Jewish social policy.

Responsa of Rabbi Simcha Levy and Rabbi Jack Simcha Cohen

In order to trace the evolution of Orthodox halakhic attitudes toward conversion and intermarriage in the last sixty years, it is essential to contrast the view expressed by authorities such as Feinstein with the positions advanced by Rabbi Simcha Levy and Rabbi Jack Simcha Cohen. In 1949, Levy, a former president of the Orthodox Rabbinical Council of America (RCA) and chairman of its Halakhah Commission for over two decades, responded to a query submitted by Orthodox rabbi E. Louis Cardon of Salt Lake City. Rabbi Cardon turned to Levy and the Halakhah Commission for guidance in a case where Cardon feared that if he refused to convert a candidate who came for purposes of marriage, the couple might go to a Reform rabbi, who would convert the Gentile partner. In that event, the Gentile would incorrectly be identified as a Jew by the community, even though a conversion conducted by a Reform rabbi would be invalid. Cardon wanted to know whether he ought to convert the Gentile to Judaism.

Levy, a pulpit rabbi in Perth Amboy, New Jersey, who was familiar with social trends in American Jewish life, wrote a responsum in which he "reluctantly" permitted the conversion, "lest the family turn to a Reform rabbi and be lost in its entirety."[46] Levy required a Jewish court of three Orthodox rabbis to oversee the conversion and a period of study in which the prospective convert would have to demonstrate sincerity. Levy also raised the ancillary issue of the Jewish status of children born to an unconverted Gentile mother and Jewish father. He held that if a decision was made to raise the child (presuming it was a boy) as a Jew, the parents were to have the boy circumcised in the presence of a rabbinic court and were to be informed that the child, when he was older, was to be immersed ritually for purposes of conversion. Thus the child's identity as a Jew would be secure. Levy could not have been happy about these compromises, for it is clear that these were thoroughly nonobservant households. But he seems to have believed that the alternative to this halakhic flexibility, given the social realities of American Jewish life, was worse.

Levy's consistency on this matter, as well as his unease with this decision, is evidenced in an address he delivered at the 1952 convention of the RCA. Emphasizing that he was speaking as an individual and not in his capacity as chairman of the Halakhah Commission, Levy stated that he "would not rule out conversion where the purpose was marriage of a non-Jew to a Jew under certain circumstances." While he obviously did not see such a conversion as the halakhic ideal, he claimed that Jewish law contained precedents that "might guide the *beit din* to permit conversion [in cases] . . . where the alternative was something worse—the possibility where the Jewish partner to the marriage might be lost to Judaism."[47]

Clearly, the existence of a non-Orthodox rabbinate was a decisive factor in Levy's holding that Orthodox rabbis were sometimes permitted to perform conversions in cases of intermarriage. Levy had ample legal precedent on his side, as witnessed in the writings of David Hoffmann and others. More significant, and consistent with Liebman's thesis, Levy's rulings reflect that some members of the Orthodox rabbinate and the people attending their synagogues saw themselves as part of the same community as their non-Orthodox Jewish counterparts. While it is not surprising that a nominally Orthodox Jew would seek out a non-Orthodox rabbi to perform a conversion if an Orthodox rabbi refused him, Levy's attention to this consideration reflects the relatively weak position that Orthodoxy occupied in the American Jewish community at this time. Painfully aware that the Orthodox were a small minority in places such as Salt Lake City in the late 1940s and early 1950s, Yeshiva University–trained, Modern Orthodox rabbis like

Levy, and perhaps other Orthodox rabbis in the United States, were compelled to deal with nonobservant elements of the Jewish community. Thus, moderating factors led people such as Levy to find a way of officiating at these conversions. "Social isolation" from those who were nonobservant was not a viable option for the Levys of the Orthodox world. His responsum and speech are indicative, to borrow Liebman's notion, of an Orthodox rabbinate that elected to live with an entire Jewish community, and not just with the Orthodox segment of it.[48]

Lest Levy be misconstrued, it should be emphasized that there were precedents in Jewish law—albeit lenient ones—to admit such persons into Judaism, which makes clear that Levy was as wedded to the Jewish legal system as a more stringent colleague might have been. Indeed, his decision—despite any discomfort he may have felt—to employ these precedents reveals that he considered these lenient rulings better suited to deal with the contemporary realities confronting Judaism and the Jewish people than the more stringent ones.

Most Orthodox authorities did not follow Levy's lead. He came to stand nearly alone in the Orthodox rabbinic world in his decision to make such public declarations on the matter. One of the few other well-known American Orthodox rabbis who similarly decided to engage with the non-Orthodox world on conversion and intermarriage was Rabbi Jack Simcha Cohen, whose responsum almost four decades later on the conversion of children of Gentile mothers and Jewish fathers was considered radical by some.

By the time Cohen addressed this issue in the 1980s, there was a great deal of Orthodox sentiment against allowing such conversions. In chapter 2, we mentioned that Rabbi Dr. Bernard Illowy of New Orleans had ruled in 1864 that the child of a Gentile mother could not be circumcised, and he ordered mohalim not to perform such a ceremony. Indeed, he was generally hostile to the idea of conversion.[49]

Rabbi Jack Simcha Cohen reached the opposite conclusion.[50] In a responsum published in 1987, he suggested that "children born to Jewish fathers and Gentile mothers may be converted during infancy by a proper *beit din*. Thus, Jewish men with Gentile wives who bring their infant children to a *beit din* for conversion purposes should not be rejected."[51] Though Cohen reached a conclusion radically different from the prevailing Orthodox thought of his time, based partly on variant readings of several key talmudic and legal texts, he acknowledged that these readings were rooted in more substantive differences with much of the rest of the Orthodox world on this subject. Though he did not itemize them, it is clear that in Cohen's responsum, at least three factors distinguish his orientation from that of Rabbi Moshe Feinstein.

First, in a move reminiscent of Hoffmann, Cohen takes pains to point out the emotions in the situation that confronts him: "In a recent case, a Jewish family adopted an infant Gentile girl and after a few years came to rabbis to formally convert the child. The parents were informed that a *beit din* could not properly convert their adopted daughter (aged five) because the parents did not observe the laws of Shabbat. Imagine the trauma attendant upon such an episode."[52] While Feinstein, or even Weinberg, might not have denied the emotional difficulty for a family that was denied conversion, it is clear that any such trauma was not a legally relevant factor for them. For Cohen, however, it was.

Second, Cohen acknowledged that he was motivated by a very different set of policy assumptions from those of authorities such as Weinberg and Feinstein. Toward the end of the responsum, he wrote: "The principle of insulating the Orthodox community against the sin of intermarriage may necessitate that all who marry out of the faith should be kept at a distance rather than welcomed to the fold. Though we disagree with this orientation, discussion of its halakhic merits is not within the purview of this presentation."[53]

Finally, Cohen was thoroughly comfortable with a less mechanical, more variegated sense of Jewish law and tradition: "Though the ideas expressed may appear somewhat bold or innovative, they are grounded in traditional principles of Talmud scholarship. . . . Our concern is not to suggest that the analysis herein is the sole interpretation of the talmudic text, nor the only reliable theory of the Codes. Such is certainly not the case. Indeed, Torah may be interpreted in numerous ways dependent upon the wisdom and intellectual acuity of scholars, and their final decisions."[54] The suggestion that there are multiple approaches to this problem, each equally valid, is a significant departure from the rhetoric of Feinstein.

While it would be impossible to demonstrate conclusively why Cohen ultimately adopts such an accommodating stance, so at odds with Illowy, whom he mentions in his responsum, several factors suggest themselves. First, over 125 years elapsed between Illowy and Cohen. Illowy, whose responsum was dated 1864, was writing long before intermarriage became a norm. Thus, he could have allowed himself the luxury of believing that either history or even his halakhic approach might stem the flood of intermarriage. Rabbi David Hoffmann, who wrote that his own leniencies might have to be reconsidered if intermarriage became rampant, seems to have harbored the same hope. But by the time that Cohen was writing, it was clear that a new norm had emerged. No halakhic stringencies were going to stem the tide of massive waves of intermarriage, both in the United States and beyond.

When he wrote his responsum, Cohen was rabbi of Congregation Shaarei Tefila in Los Angeles. While Shaarei Tefila is an Orthodox congregation, the Jewish community in Los Angeles is generally much more liberal than the large Jewish communities elsewhere in the United States, particularly on the East Coast. Cohen knew the social reality facing his community and thought it best to address it directly. Orthodoxy required a more open, not a more exclusive, policy, he felt. Cohen is thus separated from Illowy by time and place, and from Feinstein by place, in terms of geography and in terms of the nature of his community.[55]

It is critical to remember that Levy and Cohen were, in many respects, lone voices, even among Orthodox rabbis of their generation and even on the West Coast. In the vast majority of cases, it is the exclusionary posture of Rabbi Moshe Feinstein that has been adopted by American Orthodoxy.

From Deal to Denver: Communal Efforts to Address the Conversion Issue

Our representative survey of the Orthodox treatment of conversion in America could not be complete without mention of two high-profile, community-wide attempts to address conversion issues. The first example is that of the Syrian Sephardic community and its 1935 ban on conversions (reaffirmed in 1946 and 1972);[56] the second—an attempt to bridge the denominational divide in a halakhically acceptable fashion—took place in Denver in the late 1970s and early 1980s. Both cases, despite obvious differences, support the application of Liebman's thesis that conversion policy can be seen—at least in part—as a reflection of the rabbinate's conception of the boundaries of the community for which it is responsible.

The Syrian Sephardic community is, in many respects, as insular a community as one can find in American Jewish life. As a result of deeply embedded communal mores, more than 90 percent of the community's population is married to a partner from among its own ranks. But America, as we have seen, can be corrosive to such mores. Thus, in 1935, in an attempt to ensure that the openness of life in the United States would not undermine the public culture of observance and communal loyalty among the Syrian Sephardic community, its leadership declared a community-wide ban on marriage to converts. The rabbinical proclamation of February 1935 reads, in part:

> We have observed the conditions prevailing in the general Jewish community, where some youth have left the haven of their faith and have assimilated with non-Jews; in certain cases, they have made efforts to marry Gentiles, sometimes without any effort to convert them, and other times an effort is made for conversion to our faith, an action that is absolutely invalid and worthless in the eyes of the Torah. We have therefore bestirred ourselves to build and establish an iron wall to protect our identity and religious integrity and to bolster the strong foundations of our faith and religious purity that we have maintained for many centuries going back to our country of origin, Syria.[57]

The halakhic implications of this attitude become even more starkly revealed soon after the statement quoted above: "We . . . do hereby decree . . . that no male or female member of our community has the right to intermarry with non-Jews; this law concerns conversion, which we consider to be fictitious and valueless. We further decree that no future rabbinic court of the community should have the right or authority to convert male or female non-Jews who seek to marry into our community."[58]

Two dimensions of the aforementioned proclamation bear note. First, the phrase "general Jewish community" refers not to a group of Jews with whom the authors seek affinity but rather to a group contrasted with those for whom their "country of origin, Syria," is still a defining characteristic. Second, the notion that efforts to convert non-Jews to Jewish life constitute an act that is "fictitious and valueless" is hardly supported by the rabbinic precedents and numerous responsa that we have seen. Even Rabbi Feinstein would not have made this claim, and other Orthodox authorities would have disagreed with this assertion. Nonlegal factors are at work in this instance, and the ban on conversion issued by these rabbis is a powerful reminder that Jewish legal pronouncements in this area reflect rabbinic attempts to formulate social policy and establish social limits for a community.

This attitude was not unique to the Syrian Sephardic community in the United States; a complete ban on conversions had already been instituted in the Syrian community of Argentina prior to the American ban, for similar reasons. In 1927, Rabbi Shaul David Setton of the Syrian Jewish community of Buenos Aires issued an edict that reads, in part: "Because life in this city is exceedingly wanton, and everybody does as he pleases, there is no rabbi serving the Jewish community, whose authority is respected by the government or by any other party. Hence, anyone who wishes takes an unconverted Gentile woman for his wife or chooses laypersons at random (to serve as witnesses) and 'converts' her in their presence. . . . Therefore I dispersed announcements that it is forbidden to accept converts in Argentina until the end of time."[59]

The Israeli rabbinic community took the ban so seriously that it refused to marry the children of people who had been converted in Argentina in violation of this edict. Years later, the Israeli rabbinate found a way to respect the stance of their Argentinean colleagues while nevertheless accepting these South American converts by taking prospective Argentinean converts to Uruguay, not far from Buenos Aires, and converting them there. Officially, the ban remains in effect, even if honored more in the breach than the observance.[60] The overwhelming pressure on even the Israeli rabbinate to find a solution for a problem in Argentina is testimony to the difficulty that any community experiences when trying to insulate itself completely from other communities that have different standards of religious behavior.[61]

In dramatic contradistinction to the isolationist tendency of the Syrian community, we turn now to a case in which building warmer relations with the non-Orthodox world came to be seen as a desideratum. In 1977, two Orthodox rabbis, both known as mavericks, appeared in Denver as speakers in adult education programs.[62] One was Eliezer Berkovits, a professor emeritus of Hebrew Theological College in Chicago. He had been ordained at the Hildesheimer Rabbinical Seminary in Berlin and was the *talmid muvhak* (most stellar student) of Rabbi Yehiel Yaakov Weinberg,[63] who warned the Denver community that the issue "who is a Jew?" was destroying Jewish unity.

The second was Steven Riskin, then rabbi of the Lincoln Square Synagogue in New York (later known as Shlomo Riskin, who eventually served as chief rabbi of Efrat, south of Jerusalem). Riskin stated that passages from the Talmud and Maimonides that deal with conversion allow for a lenient attitude concerning the applicant's commitment to observance of the commandments. Orthodox rabbi Stanley Wagner of Denver thought that "Berkovits and Riskin had offered theological justification for conversion as an ongoing process, not a contract signed as a condition of admission,"[64] and their lectures prompted him to initiate a bold and flexible experiment regarding conversion in Denver. Within a few weeks, seven Denver rabbis of all denominations met, determined to find a way to provide for a single, citywide conversion apparatus.

Ultimately, these rabbis worked out a system whereby prospective converts would for several months take a class on the fundamentals of Judaism, to be taught by rabbis across the denominational spectrum of the Jewish community. After the class, a panel of rabbis representing different movements would examine the candidate; if the panel found the candidate fit for conversion, a *beit din* of Traditional rabbis would perform the conversion. (These "Traditional" rabbis were Orthodox rabbis whose congregations had adopted more liberal practices, such as the use of microphones on Shabbat, mixed seating, and the like; no mainstream Orthodox rabbi was willing to participate.)[65] Needless to say, if a male candidate were not already circumcised, he would undergo circumcision or, in the more likely event that he was already circum-cised, *hatafat dam berit* (symbolic ritual circumcision). Men as well as women would be immersed in a *mikveh*. Participants who converted through this program would agree to basic Jewish observances (such as fasting on Yom Kippur, joining a synagogue, and lighting candles for the Sabbath and holidays). Dietary laws were mentioned, as was "keep-ing a Jewish household," but both practices were left vague. This not only made it possible for Reform applicants to accept the *beit din*'s stipu-lations, but also protected Traditional rabbis from the accusation that they had not required converts to commit to a Jewish life of observance.

Elements of this compromise are reminiscent of Rabbi David Hoff-mann's suggestion that a rabbi, in certain situations, should receive a promise from the prospective convert that he would be observant, but not have the applicant swear that he would be. And just as Hoffmann's "solution" has left him open to critique in the years since he wrote, so, too, everyone involved in the Denver compromise was left somewhat vulnerable; critics from both right and left assailed the compromises their colleagues had made. What both left and right shared, however, was a sense of despair in the highly charged aftermath of the project's failure. As Orthodox rabbi Jerome Lipsitz commented some time after the de-bacle: "Why have two separate types of Jews? . . . We want to create a Jew all of us can recognize as a Jew."[66] The radical difference between his perspective and that of Rabbi Moshe Feinstein cannot be overstated.

By 1982, the Denver arrangement had become tenuous. Traditional rabbis felt that they had compromised too much, pushing too many people through the conversion process simply in order to keep pace with the need (about 750 people were converted through the Denver arrangement). In March 1982, unrelated to the unfolding experiment in Denver, the Reform movement adopted a position affirming patrilineal descent as sufficient for confirming Jewish status upon a child born of a Jewish father and a non-Jewish mother if the child were raised as a Jew. Such a departure from classical Jewish law caused a further rift with Orthodoxy; in retrospect, one can easily imagine the Orthodox participants in the Denver project wondering why they were going to such great lengths to create interdenominational unity when the Re-form movement was so unconcerned with such considerations.

On June 17, 1983, six years after the initial agreement, Orthodox rabbis announced that they were withdrawing. The *Intermountain Jewish News* published an article discussing the withdrawal, shining a spotlight on a program that had hoped to operate in relative secrecy. Harold Jacobs, president of Orthodoxy's American Council of Young Israel, responded: "We have no choice but to draw the line, clearly, as to who is a Jew and who is not, as to what limits and basic standards of elementary Jewish identity and personal conduct we must insist upon. . . . It is time that Orthodoxy put the rest of the Jewish community on notice: no longer will 'Jewish unity' be bought at the expense of Jewish identity. For Klal Yisrael today, that is too high a price."[67] Jacobs was addressing the twin concerns of boundary maintenance and constituency retention. He clearly reflected the stance that Feinstein had adopted on this matter—that the community for which he was responsible was limited to those who observed Jewish law and who could be defined as Jews from a halakhic perspective. He would not construct a definition of Jewish peoplehood and community that would embrace nonobservant persons as Jews, no matter how involved they were in the Jewish world beyond Orthodoxy.

These sentiments were more strongly expressed by the *Jewish Observer*, an American Jewish journal associated with the Agudath Israel: "While compromise for the sake of unity can often make good sense, when dealing with basic principles of faith, 'compromise' is actually a sell-out. . . . It is time that all Orthodox rabbis recognize that Reform and Conservative Judaism are far, far removed from Torah, and Klal Yisroel is betrayed—not served—when Orthodoxy enters in religious association with them."[68] As far as the experiment being tried elsewhere, the *Observer* warned that "other communities contemplating this type of interdenominational cooperation [ought to] take note of the awesome pitfalls involved and step back from the abyss."[69]

Concluding Observations

When the *Observer* issued its warning in terms of the "awesome pitfalls" involved in interdenominational cooperation, it had in mind not only halakhic statutes and standards, but images of what would constitute wise social policy for the American Jewish community. As we have seen, concern with Jewish social policy was also the province of noted halakhic experts. Though they usually wrote in highly technical and legalistic language, their concerns focused not only on the letter of Jewish law but on a vision for Jewish society that they knew their rulings would help to shape.

Rabbi Moshe Feinstein asked those Orthodox rabbis who might "compromise" on what he deemed objective legal standards what good they could be contributing to the Jewish people by reinterpreting those standards and allowing nonobservant converts into the Jewish people. Of course, his is not a purely legal argument but one based on a vision of Jewish life and a conception of what ought to lie at the heart of Jewish identity. What Feinstein and the *Observer* have in common is that their vision of Jewish life does not have room for varieties of practice very different from their own. In their view, rather than strengthening the Jewish people, such accommodation weakens the future of Jewish life. Authorities like Feinstein authored their legal opinions in such a way as to further the vision for Jewish life that they held dear.

As Orthodox rabbis, these were men deeply committed to the sanctity of Jewish law. Halakhah was not merely a tool or a ruse, but an end in itself. Yet while working with the same basic halakhic materials and the same precedents, these *posekim* issued vastly different rulings. Their widely divergent opinions resulted not only from legal considerations but from fundamentally different conceptions of which people constituted their communities, how they hoped the Jewish world would look in the future, their assessments of the likelihood of that world either surviving or coming to be, and their fundamental notions of what principles and commitments lay at the core of Jewish life. This debate about the future of Jewish life took on additional urgency when Jews had to rule not only for their Orthodox compatriots but for all the Jewish citizens of a sovereign Jewish state. It is to the Israeli context that we now turn.

Five Israel
Conversion to Judaism in a Jewish Society

It should come as no surprise that halakhic discussions of conversion in Israel since the advent of the State have been appreciably different from what we have found elsewhere, even as they have built on the same foundational legal sources that underlie any Orthodox halakhic discussion, regardless of time or place. It seems almost inevitable that defining Jewishness in a Jewish state would be a different enterprise from doing so in a context in which Jews were a minority, often a powerless one. The famous language of the Talmud (Yevamot 47a) that instructed the court to say to the prospective convert, "What reason have you for desiring to become a proselyte? Do you not know that Israel at the present time is persecuted and oppressed, despised, harassed, and overcome by afflictions?" certainly resonated with Jews in Europe, and might even have made sense to some in America. However, does it ring true in a country in which Jews are the majority and in which Jews sit in the seats of power?

When examining rulings in this chapter on conversion in Israel, we will look not only at halakhic rulings issued by Orthodox rabbis; we will also examine secular legal opinions from Israel's courts, including the Israeli Supreme Court, inasmuch as awareness of their holdings— in a country where there is secular Jewish sovereignty—has sometimes had direct influence on Orthodox decision-making and has at other times established the contours within which such decision making has been made. We are well aware that Israeli courts have been mindful of the need to steer clear of religious matters, even though the boundary between what can be defined as a religious issue and what can be seen as a legitimate matter of overarching public policy that the secular courts must adjudicate is unavoidably often ambiguous.[1]

In keeping with the focus of this book, we would underscore that our attention in this chapter will be on halakhic authorities and how their decisions regarding questions about conversion have been affected by the twin facts that Israel is a Jewish state with a Jewish majority and that *posekim* in Israel are making not only religious policy but public policy for a national entity. Our interest remains centered on what halakhic authorities have said and how their being situated in a Jewish body politic has affected their worldview and their rulings on conversion.[2]

What sort of shift has the Israeli context created? Has Jewish sovereignty prompted a shift toward greater flexibility in standards for conversion or, conversely, toward the "religious extremism" of which Charles Liebman speaks?[3] One could plausibly expect either. A shift toward greater flexibility, we might imagine, would stem from some authorities' arguing that in an Israeli context, devotion to the Jewish State (as opposed to commitment to the halakhic process, as demanded in BT Bekhorot 30b) might be a legitimate means of satisfying the traditional requirement that conversions be "for the sake of heaven." After all, these rabbis were now responsible for an entire Jewish society with a wide range of behaviors. They could thus not retreat into the denominationally insular subgroups that a voluntaristic diaspora community structure had permitted and encouraged, which might have led them to seek a more inclusive basis for judging would-be converts. Conversely, a shift toward less flexibility might come from the coupling of governmental power with religion, creating a situation in which religious authorities would believe that with the government vesting them with authority under secular laws, no one could pressure them into compromising their ideals of tradition by accommodating prospective Jews who they felt were not genuinely converting "for the sake of heaven."

Both phenomena have found expression in the writings of Israeli authorities. We begin with a survey of the views of five chief rabbis of the state as a means of examining the Israeli Orthodox perspective on conversion. Our chronological analysis begins with Rabbi Abraham Isaac

Kook and continues with Rabbi Ben-Zion Meir Uziel, Rabbi Ovadiah Yosef, Rabbi Isaac Halevi Herzog, and Rabbi Shlomo Goren.

Rabbi Abraham Isaac Kook: First Ashkenazic Chief Rabbi of Israel

Given his reputation for writing responsa that reached out to the broadest swath of the Jewish world, Rabbi Kook might have been expected to follow the approach of Rabbi David Hoffmann and others who had argued that in order to preserve Jewish unity, standards for conversion had to be more flexible than a simple reading that some of the sources dictate—but this was not the case.

Rabbi Kook's generally restrictive attitude toward conversion is perhaps most clear in a responsum that addresses whether a couple already married in a civil ceremony may be converted and subsequently given a traditional Jewish wedding ceremony.[4] Unlike Hoffmann and his ilk, who saw the existence of a civil relationship as reason to argue that the conversion was no longer for the sake of marriage (and therefore could be construed as a proper conversion, "for the sake of heaven"), Kook insisted that once a couple had married in a civil ceremony, they could never be allowed to convert or have *ḥuppah vekiddushin* (a traditional Jewish wedding ceremony). In language that is as uncompromising as is Feinstein's about converts who are not observant, Kook denies even the possibility of seeing the issue in any other way: "With regard to accepting converts, those who have already formed forbidden relationships—a Jewish man with a Gentile woman, or a Gentile with a Jewish woman—I do not understand what the question is, for who is [sufficiently] regarded and who is [sufficiently] distinguished to transgress the famous words of the Tosefta . . . that one who is suspected of having intercourse with a Gentile woman who later converts may not marry her."

Kook's phrase "for who is [sufficiently] regarded and who is [sufficiently] distinguished" is a paraphrase of a talmudic source[5] in which a well-known rabbi denies that he has any real stature or standing. This seems to be Kook's way of suggesting that those rabbis who have found a way around the simple meaning of the Tosefta have exceeded their authority. His unwillingness to consider any of the arguments presented by those who take a permissive stance on this question is even clearer at the beginning of the next paragraph of his responsum: "And it is clear that far be it from any *beit din ḥashuv* [important court] to give them a priori permission to convert, and [it should] not allow them to have a traditional Jewish wedding ceremony even after they convert, as I have written. And I see no reason to dwell on this matter, given its utter simplicity."

Kook's final words in this responsum characterize much of his writing on the subject—he distinguishes between the halakhic dimensions of his argument and the "social policy" foundations of his decision. Having made a careful halakhic case for his view that such conversions and marriages should not be permitted, Kook concludes by explicitly noting that the foundation of his perspective is a sense of the battle that was raging in Jewish society at the time: "[It becomes clear that now that there are] people who are called rabbis who transgress with impudence[6] the words of our sages, [it is incumbent] upon all scholars and rabbis to gird their loins and to stand up against the breaches, and to make every attempt [to ensure] that all the words of our sages be upheld, like a peg that cannot be dislodged,[7] as befits them and their sacred words. Blessed be the One who chose them and their learning. And happy is he who stands in the breach, to protect the purity of Israel, may good blessing be bestowed upon him."

In other instances, Kook mentions what we might call "extra-halakhic" considerations. In a 1918 responsum, he writes that the Jewish father of a non-Jewish child is technically not the halakhic father of such a child;[8] thus, it might be suggested that the father has no relationship to the child at all and may not bring him to a *beit din* to be converted. However, Rav Kook then posits that halakhic factors are not the only issue to consider; since the father does feel a "natural love" (*ahavah tivit*) for the child, the father has the right to submit this child for conversion, so long as the mother does not protest.

Note that this extra-halakhic consideration does not lead to a lenient position in the responsum as a whole. Despite this apparent leniency on the matter of the father's relationship to the child, Kook refuses to approve any conversion in which there will not be *kabalat ol mitzvot*, acceptance of the yoke of the commandments. He insists that acceptance of the yoke of the commandments is *ikar shel hageirut* (the very essence of the conversion) and that without such acceptance, the conversion is meaningless and void.[9]

While Kook's insistence on *kabalat ol mitzvot* was well-grounded in Jewish law, his position was also apparently motivated by the same cultural phenomena that might have led some authorities to acquiesce and to be more lenient in defining the standards required for conversion. In another responsum,[10] Kook insists that one could halakhically defend the policy of allowing a Jewish mohel to circumcise a child born to a Jewish father and a non-Jewish mother, and he offers a detailed halakhic defense of doing just that. He then argues that this would be bad public policy, changing direction completely, explicitly noting that there is a difference between defensible legal positions and good public policy: "Considering all this is only from the point of view of the halakhah. However, considering the quagmire into which you might be pulled, that he and his parents might come to believe that he is Jewish even without conversion, and on account of our many sins . . . [more] intermarriages might result. It is obviously necessary for us to maintain our guard [*la'amod al hamishmar*] and not give them a mohel to perform a circumcision even without a blessing . . . until we know that their intent is to convert, sincerely for the sake of heaven."

Rav Kook's readiness to distinguish between halakhic considerations and public policy concerns is evident in yet another responsum, slightly related to our issue. Kook faces a question that many earlier *posekim* had also confronted: Can one convert a man who, because of medical considerations such as hemophilia, cannot be circumcised? Kook, like most other authorities, says no.[11] But what is particularly interesting in his responsum is the clear distinction that he makes between halakhic and policy considerations. Toward the conclusion of the responsum, he gives the halakhic reason that such a conversion should not be permitted: "[I]f we decide that we shall allow a conversion on the basis of ritual immersion and acceptance of the yoke of the commandments [without circumcision], behold, he immediately becomes obligated for circumcision . . . and each day he is under the threat of *kareit*." That is the simple halakhic objection to such a conversion. But as in the previous responsum we cited, Kook also offers a policy-based justification. At the beginning of his response, he writes, "In my humble opinion, we should not go about creating such ambiguous situations, since there is no predicting the enormity of the failings that will emerge from this, when it becomes known that simply on the basis of a doctor's opinion we are lenient and accept converts like this without circumcision."

Rav Kook's stringent standards for conversion raise a question that has not arisen in our examination of these responsa thus far: Did his being situated in the Land of Israel (he wrote before the State was actually created) affect his view of the societal battles that needed to be fought? Did his distance from Europe contribute to his sense that the only legitimate response to the changing sociological realities was to raise the barriers higher?[12]

Rabbi Ben-Zion Meir Uziel: First Sephardic Chief Rabbi of Israel

Rabbi Ben-Zion Meir Uziel (1880–1953) was the first Sephardic chief rabbi of the State of Israel. Born in Jerusalem, where his father had been a leading halakhic authority in the Sephardic community and headed the rabbinical court, Uziel was appointed ḥakham bashi (Sephardic chief rabbi) of Jaffa in 1911. He left Palestine for two years to serve as rabbi of the Jews in Salonika, but returned and became chief rabbi of Tel Aviv in 1923. In 1939, he was appointed a chief rabbi of the Land of Israel.[13]

Uziel's life's work was devoted to the concept of Jewish peoplehood. In a testament only two days before his death, he wrote: "I have kept in the forefront of my thoughts the following aims: to disseminate Torah among students, to love the Torah and its precepts, Erez Israel [the Land of Israel] and its sanctity; I have emphasized love for every man and woman of Israel—in body, in spirit, in speech, and in deed, in thought and in meditation, in intent and in act, at home and in the street."[14]

Uziel's legal work reflects this orientation as well. For example, in his collected responsa, *Piskei Uziel*, he discusses whether to convert the non-Jewish spouses of Jews who had already intermarried. In contra-distinction to Hildesheimer, who refused to sanction such conversions, and to Weinberg, who accepted them grudgingly and only if the rabbi could elicit a promise that they would become observant Jews, Uziel seems almost eager to convert them out of moral conviction. He asserts that the conversion is necessary not only for the sake of the Jewish partner[15] but for the children of such unions as well. His language is enormously instructive:[16]

> Even were we not concerned [about repairing the situation of the transgressing father who married a non-Jewish woman] and were willing to say "let the rope follow the pail,"[17] nonetheless, for the sake of their children it is obvious that we are obligated to bring them close [to the Jewish people by converting them]. It makes no difference whether they are the children of a Jewish woman [who is living with a Jewish man], in which case they are absolutely Jews, or whether they are the children of a non-Jewish woman [who is married to a Jew]. Either way, they are the seed of a Jew, and they fall into the category of wayward sheep [who need to be protected].[18]
>
> I am afraid that if we reject [the children] altogether by rejecting the parents, we will be brought to Judgment [before the Master of the Universe], who will say to us, "You have not brought back the strayed, or looked for the lost."[19]

By quoting this last verse from the famous chapter 34 of Ezekiel, in which God accuses Israel of not having sought stray sheep with love, Rabbi Uziel makes clear his sense of the rabbis' obligation. Jewish leaders are responsible for bringing Jews back into the fold; this is true, he seems to suggest, even if it means converting people who are not going to live strictly according to the dictates of Jewish law. Uziel's language is reminiscent of Hoffmann's in *Melamed Leho'il* 2:83, when Hoffmann asked of the children of intermarried adults, "and these [innocent] sheep, how have they sinned?" As was often the case with Hoffmann, this responsum is a treatise on morality and social policy as much as it is about how to address a particular case in light of the many legal precedents at his disposal. Because Hoffmann saw this case as about much more than "law" in its narrowest sense, he was able to adopt a position very different from Rav Kook's approach.

Despite his similarity to Hoffmann, Rabbi Uziel's approach is radically different from that of most other Orthodox leaders, especially those of the same general period. Recall the responsum we saw by Rabbi Moshe Feinstein, who refused to accept such converts: "I cannot understand the reasoning of the rabbis who err in this. For even according to their own reckoning, what value are they bringing to the Jewish people by accepting converts like these? For it is obviously not good for either God or the Jewish people that converts like these should be mixed into the Jewish people."[20]

Relative to such views, Uziel seems much less concerned about applying the objective and strict standards of Jewish law in the area of conversion that Charles Liebman considers to be the hallmark and direction of Jewish Orthodoxy in the contemporary world than he does with affirming a posture that allows for greater inclusiveness. Elsewhere, reflecting on the status of a convert who does not observe all the commandments, Uziel writes: "A convert who accepts the commandments and the punishments [for nonperformance], even if he does not perform [the commandments], we accept him after we inform him of the minor and major commandments, their reward and their punishment. Even if he will sin and be punished, it is nonetheless a privilege for him to have the [reward] for those commandments that he will perform."[21] Uziel's language is an obvious paraphrase of Yevamot 47a, which (unlike Bekhorot 30b, for example) makes no mention of the prospective convert's committing to any particular religious observances or standards. In that talmudic passage, the court is obligated to inform the applicant of some of the commandments, but it is not required to elicit a statement from the convert that she or he will actually observe these commandments. Indeed, that passage in Yevamot is noteworthy for its apparent sense that joining the Jewish people is more about throwing one's lot in with the fate of the Jews than it is about any theological or halakhic commitment. In a radical departure from some of his Orthodox predecessors and contemporaries, Uziel seems to take this approach.

In certain respects, Rabbi Uziel is even more liberally inclined than Rabbi Hoffmann. In a responsum on conversion in the aftermath of civil marriage, Hoffmann had ruled leniently but added a caveat that "should the obstacles multiply" (that is, should mixed marriage become commonplace), it would become necessary to erect a high barrier and cease the conversions at once.[22] Uziel takes the opposite approach. Because intermarriage is becoming so common and because it is a dire threat to the future of the Jewish people, conversion must be used as often as possible to limit the number of such cases. He writes: "We have every right to [permit] this conversion in order to save a Jewish man or woman from this serious transgression, which has become a blight on the House of Israel and is likely to bring devastation to our people. For it is written (Mal. 2:11–12): 'For Judah has profaned what is holy to the Lord—what he desires—and espoused daughters of alien gods. May the Lord leave to him who does this no descendants dwelling in the tents of Jacob.' "[23]

Uziel's use of the Malachi verse in this way, while not unheard of in responsa literature, is unusual.[24] Its appearance here is more than a rhetorical flourish. Uziel, in resorting to a genre of literature rarely quoted in responsa, appears to be suggesting that there could be instances in which adherence to the letter of the law can blind Jewish leaders to their ultimate responsibility. Jewish law, he seems to imply, must be located within the larger framework of Jewish life and Jewish purpose. This notion has perhaps best been expressed by Robert M. Cover, in his now-classic "*Nomos* and Narrative":

> We inhabit a nomos—a normative universe. We constantly create and maintain a world of right and wrong, of lawful and unlawful, of valid and void. . . . The rules and principles of justice, the formal institutions of the law, and the conventions of a social order are, indeed, important to that world; they are, however, but a small part of the normative universe that ought to claim our attention. No set of legal institutions or prescriptions exists apart from the narratives that locate it and give it meaning. For every constitution there is an epic, for each decalogue a scripture. Once understood in the context of the narratives that give it meaning, law becomes not merely a system of rules to be observed, but a world in which we live.[25]

Albeit in very different language, Uziel is saying much the same thing. Jewish law, he insists, needs to be located within a framework larger than rules alone. In language that also evokes the work of constitutional theorist Ronald Dworkin's sense of principle,[26] Uziel seems intent on reminding his reader that to lose sight of the ultimate goal of Jewish law—that is, the creation of a Jewish society for the purpose of serving God—is to do Judaism and God a grave disservice.

Although both Hoffmann and Uziel ruled "leniently" when it came to permitting conversion for a couple already civilly married, their views of civil marriage were not identical. Hoffmann, it may be recalled from chapter 2, cited Shalom Kutnah and relied on Kutnah's ruling that because civil marriage bound the couple to each other in a significant way, the conversion to Judaism would not be for the sake of marriage per se, and thus should be allowed.[27] Uziel did not share Kutnah's and Hoffmann's charitable view of civil marriage. In a responsum devoted to civil marriage (which he wrote to critique a responsum in which a Rabbi Avraham Price of Toronto had coined the phrase "*kiddushin* by civil marriage"),[28] Uziel concludes: "Marriages performed in civil courts have no standing whatsoever . . . [and] a woman married in a civil marriage may leave her husband without a get [Jewish divorce], since such marriage has no element of *kiddushin*."[29] They have, he insists, no sanctity or validity, and thus, Rabbi Price's phrase "*kiddushin* by civil marriage" is internally contradictory and nonsensical.[30]

Uziel's passion for "saving" the people in such situations occasionally led him to make contradictory assertions about civil marriage. For example, the responsum just cited was vehement in its denial of any authority to civil marriage; but in another responsum, Uziel seems to view civil marriage very differently.[31] Asked whether a non-Jewish woman who had already borne children within her civil marriage to a Jewish man should be allowed to convert, Uziel does not seem conflicted; the difference between his approach and the position expressed in the responsum of Rav Kook discussed earlier could not be more radical. Like Hoffmann, Rabbi Uziel recognizes the couple's relationship in this case as a marriage of some sort:

> This non-Jewish woman is already married to a Jewish man, and as she has now entered into the covenant of the Jews, she will be drawn ever closer to her husband's family and his Torah. Furthermore, those children she has already given birth to and those she will have in the future will be complete Jews.[32] This is similar to the [talmudic cases

of] Hillel and Rabbi Ḥiyya,[33] who [were] certain that [their students] would ultimately become complete converts. [They were thus] permitted or, even more correctly, obligated, to bring these [converts] close and to draw them into the covenant of the Torah of Israel. Thus, [they were also] ridding [Israel] of the blight of intermarriage, which is a serious blight in the vineyard of the house of Israel.

Uziel does not permit himself some of the justifications that his predecessors had employed. He does not delude himself into believing that this woman will be observant, at least not right away. He does not claim that her desire to convert is selfless. Nor does he suggest that intermarriage is now only a small problem, but that if it were to spread, a different approach would be necessary. On the contrary, fully cognizant of the numerousness of such cases (a situation not unlike the one facing the Jewish people today), he felt secure in asserting that the only legitimate path was one of inclusion.

Uziel was not, of course, advocating a flagrant violation of explicit halakhic precedent; for an Orthodox rabbi, such a position would be unthinkable. But his corpus on conversion seems to consistently take advantage of the multivalent nature of the precedents at his disposal and to formulate an expansive, open-arms policy designed to bring as many persons as possible into the Jewish fold. That this might mean accepting some people who do not fall into the most narrowly and rigidly construed conception of those converting "for the sake of heaven" does not seem to disturb him greatly. A convert is a thoughtful individual, Uziel explains. "If he does not [explicitly refuse to accept the commandments after he has been informed of them], we accept him, and he will bear [responsibility for his own] sin, and [the community of Israel] is not responsible for him."[34] Uziel claims that any other attitude would make it fundamentally impossible to perform conversions: "We should not demand of him that he fulfill all the commandments, and it is not even necessary that the court know that he will fulfill them, for if we do not [adopt this policy], no converts will be accepted into the Jewish people. For who would be willing to guarantee that this Gentile will be loyal to all the laws of the Torah?"[35]

Jewish legal decisors, Uziel insists by implication in this passage, must keep in mind the broadest possible goal of halakhah and must ensure that their rulings are appropriate and reasonable to the world in which they live. If a rabbinic court issued a ruling that Uziel thought made no sociological sense, he did not hesitate to say so. Thus, in a responsum regarding the edict that had been issued by the Syrian Jewish community in Buenos Aires banning all conversions, Uziel seeks to defend some rabbis who have consciously violated the ban.[36] He wonders aloud whether the ban is genuinely likely to protect the Torah. Though it is important to defend the Torah, he notes, it is also critical to ensure that we do not bolt the door in the face of those who would like to repent. "It is our responsibility to bring them closer to Judaism and not to distance them from the Torah of Israel and from the Jewish people forever. And I am very dubious as to whether this fence will really result in people not intermarrying. Perhaps, quite the contrary, [these people] will despair of [marrying] with permission, and will then do the same thing in violation [by marrying a person who has not converted]. And they and their children will be drawn to leave the Torah of Israel and the Jewish people."[37]

Uziel's perspective was informed by a full awareness of social realities and an appreciation of the limited power of rabbinic courts in his time. In another lengthy responsum, cited here only in part, he effectively acknowledges that his permissiveness in these cases does not necessarily reflect his conception of halakhah in ideal circumstances:

> It seems to be obvious that as long as the court has genuine power, it is a commandment and [therefore] incumbent upon us to prevent with full force intermarriages such as these, and not to accept any woman or man as converts once they have married and not even before their marriage if it is clear that this is why they are converting. But an instruction has already been issued to accept the conversion of a man or woman, before or after they have married, because we have no power to forestall this serious transgression. [It is thus our responsibility] to choose the avenue of the least offense [that is, conversion rather than intermarriage].[38]

Note Uziel's sense of the religious establishment's powerlessness, even in the Israeli context.

In a similar vein, Uziel responded to a rabbi who urged him to use his office to prevent Jews from bringing non-Jewish wives with them to

Israel. Uziel's response is uncharacteristically harsh. He even begins his responsum by correcting an error in the question itself.[39] He seems impatient with what he considers unnecessary and unproductive halakhic stringency. He says, quite bluntly, "I suspect that we have no power, and these sinners who have married non-Jewish women have no intention of answering 'as your word, so shall we do.'[40] Therefore, we must simply take the lenient position and convert these people."

Rabbi Uziel's unique sociological perspective, coupled with his profound commitment to the inestimable dignity and worth of all those whom his rulings might touch, resulted in a series of rulings quite unlike those of many of his contemporaries. Could it be that working in the still-emerging State of Israel informed his understanding of Jewishness in a way that was distinct from the perspective of his colleagues in the Diaspora? Did his views reflect a sensibility that would also inform the positions of other rabbis living in the Land of Israel? We turn now to other respondents to answer these questions.

Rabbi Ovadiah Yosef: Sephardic Chief Rabbi, 1973–83

Rabbi Ovadiah Yosef was born in Baghdad in 1920, immigrated to Israel at the age of four, and studied in yeshivot in the Old City of Jerusalem. He was ordained at the age of twenty by the Sephardic chief rabbi of Israel, Ben-Zion Uziel. In 1947, Yosef was invited to become chief rabbi and head of the rabbinic court of Cairo. A maverick, he demonstrated great courage during his tenure in Egypt when he refused to issue proclamations against the Jewish State, forbade contributions to the Egyptian army, and insisted on his right to preach in Hebrew. In 1950, he returned to Israel, where he served as rabbi of Tel Aviv and, later, as Sephardic chief rabbi of Israel. The phenomenal breadth of his knowledge and his total recall of relevant material from rabbinic and post-rabbinic literature endow his responsa with an encyclopedic quality.[41]

A prolific writer of halakhic material, Yosef earned a reputation as a profoundly learned, moderately lenient figure.[42] However, in his responsa on conversion, such leniency does not generally appear. In fact,

Bar-Ilan University scholar Ariel Picard labels his writings as "exclu-sionary" on matters of conversion and notes that his rulings on this topic are marked by a stringent tendency.[43] In one responsum, Yosef is asked whether a *kohein* who had previously married a Gentile woman in a civil ceremony could now be granted permission to have her con-vert.[44] In a decision that cites dozens of authorities on both sides of the question, Yosef examines the precedents with great care. Ultimately, based on a close textual reading of talmudic sources and commentators on those sources, he decides that there is not adequate justification for permitting the conversion when it would simply result in a *kohein* then marrying a convert, a relationship that is forbidden, according to Jew-ish law.

Particularly interesting is the series of extratextual justifications that Rabbi Yosef offers for this decision. He cites one authority who notes that in such cases, the Gentiles would, regardless of their motivations and levels of subsequent observance, be considered full converts after the fact. But Yosef then approves the view of another *posek* who argued that such conversions should not be permitted, even if it would serve *lehatzil et haba'al me'isur* (to save the husband from forbidden behav-ior) by making his wife Jewish because the precedent-setting social implications of such a move would be negative. This authority argued that to allow such a conversion would be to encourage men to marry non-Jewish women in civil ceremonies, believing that they could al-ways later induce their wives to convert to Judaism. Though Yosef does not overtly say that he prefers the second opinion to the first, this seems to be the implicit point he seeks to make. His responsum is not only a matter of close textual analysis; it is also a statement about social policy.

Toward the end of the responsum, Yosef makes it clear that he dis-agrees with those such as Hoffmann or Uziel, who would have per-mitted the conversion. Speaking this time in his own words, he as-serts that these potential converts can in no way be considered converts "for the sake of heaven." Ultimately, he suggests, the woman in this case is converting because the husband is pressuring her on account of his own embarrassment, and she is acquiescing only because of her love for him. This, he rules, is not a legitimate reason for conversion. Evincing a sense of community and responsibility that is very different from that of Hoffmann and Uziel, Yosef asks, *Velamah lanu lehakhnis et atzmeinu lezeh*, "And why should we get involved in all this"? If the woman wishes to be converted, Yosef insists, the man should leave her first with no expectation that he will return to her. If she converts under those circumstances, the conversion could be considered one "for the sake of heaven."

In his next responsum, Rabbi Yosef addresses the plight of children already born of such a union.[45] Here, too, his fairly rigorous definition of "for the sake of heaven" emerges clearly. In this responsum, Yosef is asked whether, in the absence of the mother's conversion, the children can be converted, and, if so, whether this can be done without her knowledge. Following an exacting halakhic analysis, he determines that the conversion can be permitted, but only if the mother herself brings the children and attests that no pressure has been brought to bear on her to permit it. Yet after constructing a clear set of parameters that would make the conversion permissible, Yosef adds that if the *beit din* foresees that after the children convert, they will still desecrate Sabbaths and holidays when they are adults, it is best not to convert them. Retroactively, though, he admits, once they are converted, they are Jews, even if it is revealed that the court made an error in judgment.

For Rabbi Yosef, the critical prerequisite for a *beit din* to accept a prospective convert is the observance of mitzvot. On that issue, he was unwilling to compromise or to pretend that matters would be other than they were. This is why he ruled in another case that one could not convert someone who planned to live in a nonreligious kibbutz.[46]

In some instances, Rabbi Yosef took a more lenient stance. When asked whether a woman's having married a man in a civil ceremony should prevent her from later converting and marrying him in a Jewish ceremony because of the prohibition on converting for an ulterior motive, Yosef follows many lenient authorities (citing dozens) in saying that, since she is already married to him, the conversion cannot, by definition, be for the purpose of marriage and should be considered "for the sake of heaven."[47] The conclusion of his responsum indicates that he is comfortable being lenient on one matter but not on another:

> If it appears to the *beit din* that this Gentile women intends a
> complete conversion with the acceptance of the yoke of Torah

and commandments with a full heart, to perform the laws of the Torah . . . and to teach her children Torah after her conversion as is appropriate, we should permit her to convert a priori, and permit her to be married to him with a *ḥuppah* and with *kiddushin* according to the laws of Moses and Israel. This is in accordance with most of the later authorities [*aḥaronim*] who have written in our time that it is appropriate to be lenient. And even if you wish to say that we are still enmeshed in a rabbinic dispute [on the matter of conversion for an ulterior motive], this is a rabbinic matter [and not one based on the Torah], and in rabbinic matters, we tend to leniency.

In matters relating to conversion, Rabbi Yosef's encyclopedic responsa reflect a distinctly positivist orientation, relying almost exclusively on the explicit precedents before him, without acknowledged recourse to the social and contextual circumstances of the day.

Rabbi Isaac Halevi Herzog: Second Ashkenazic Chief Rabbi of Israel

Rabbi Isaac Herzog was born in Lomza, Poland, in 1888. When he was nine, his family moved to Leeds, England. While in the United Kingdom, in addition to being an outstanding rabbinic scholar, he acquired a broad general education, including a doctorate from the University of London. After serving as rabbi of Belfast and Dublin, he was invited in 1936 to serve as the second Ashkenazic chief rabbi of Israel, after Rabbi Abraham Isaac Kook. Taking an active part in rescue operations in Europe during the Holocaust and afterward, he was instrumental in saving many Jews and bringing them to Israel. He was also actively involved in the affairs of the newly established State of Israel until his death in Jerusalem in 1959.[48]

Rabbi Herzog's responsa on conversion place him on the more conservative side of the spectrum. He insisted that genuine acceptance of the commandments was necessary and ruled in a number of instances that the compromises entertained by some Orthodox rabbis were inappropriate. Most often, Rabbi Herzog's dismissals of those leniencies were based on his contention that they were created for a world that no longer existed—a traditional Jewish world in which halakhic observance on the part of most Jews could be assumed. However, the changed sociological, cultural, and demographic realities of the modern era had diminished the power of Jewish communities to influence the practice of newly converted Jews. The now-porous boundaries of Jewish communities in Europe had weakened Jewish commitment and practice among countless Jews, and the larger Jewish community was no longer predominantly observant. The community could not realistically be expected to have the positive impact on converts that it might once have had, and no assumption could be made that the convert would likely adhere to the commandments. Consequently, a more stringent attitude regarding conversion to Judaism was required.

In a responsum issued in 1940,[49] Rabbi Herzog deals with the issue of a Gentile woman, already civilly married to a Jew, who desired to convert to Judaism. Rabbi Herzog, asked whether it was permissible to convert this woman, begins his response by noting that Maimonides, in the twelfth century, had permitted this on the grounds that "it is better that one should taste the skim of the forbidden than its essence." The Rambam thought that such conversions did not represent the halakhic ideal but that there was room for leniency and, as a matter of community policy, it was probably wise to adopt a more flexible position. After noting this source, Herzog dismissed it as inapplicable in the contemporary setting. In the past, he suggested, Jews were not sinners. "But in our days, to our great sorrow . . . many sinners among the people Israel are leaders of the community, even leaders of the nation." He asked, "Why should [converts] observe the mitzvot when so many Jews do not observe?" The validity of their pledge to accept the commandments must perforce be in doubt, "as the reason for their conversion is [in most instances] externally motivated."

The reason for Herzog's rejection of the Rambam's precedent is important. He stated that the Rambam was able to rule in the way that he did only because of the sociological particularities of his time. In an implicit recognition that the role of the *posek* is not only to adjudicate halakhah but also to set public policy and rule appropriately for his particular Jewish community, Rabbi Herzog argued that the Jewish community had changed too much for the Rambam's responsum to be the basis of good public policy so many centuries later. As we will see below, Rabbi Herzog was not the only authority to make this argument.

Herzog's sense that good public policy required a suspension of some of the leniencies of the past must have pervaded his thinking, for he makes this argument even in responsa to which this issue is not particularly central. At the end of a responsum on converting non-Jews who wish to move to Israel (which we shall review in more detail below),[50] he appended a comment that was not germane to the question before him, suggesting that not only the Rambam but also the tannaim (scholars of the Mishnah, from about 10 to 220 C.E.) had lived in such different times for Jewish communities and Jewish life that the applicability of their positions was now limited:

> Even though in the days of the tannaim of blessed memory, the law was that, a posteriori, they should all be considered converts, I have a serious concern in this age. Formerly in Israel, the transgressor was despised and embarrassed among his people, and thus, when he accepted upon himself *goi yahadut* [Jewish peoplehood], even if the original reason that motivated him was for marriage, he knew that his condition in Jewish society would be problematic . . . if he did not live according to the Torah. That is not the case today, when there are many "free" [unobservant] Jews, and not only do they not encounter difficulties because of this, but they often stand at the head of the nation and [their] communities.

Though this comment is not radically different from the sentiments quoted above, it is instructive in two ways. First, it adds the sages of the mishnaic period to the list of those whose rulings might no longer be applicable. That Rabbi Herzog thought that he could dismiss tannaitic rulings for reasons of inapplicability to the modern setting is noteworthy and demonstrates how important sociological considerations can be in a Jewish legal system where halakhic rulings function as public policy guidelines.

Second, Herzog seems to have been so consumed with this consideration that he added it to discussions of conversion, even those not relevant to the question addressed in the responsum. That Herzog believed that the halakhah on conversion needed to respond to the times is evident from yet another of his responsa, discussed above in chapter 4. This ruling, cited in the collected responsa of Rabbi Yaakov Breisch, was issued in reply to a responsum delivered by the Agudath Harabanim (Rabbinical Union) in Switzerland regarding a teacher whose wife's father was a non-Jew and whose mother, though born a Jew, had apparently converted to Christianity prior to her marriage. Because the Agudah, as we noted above, considered itself to be engaged in *milḥamah keveidah* (intensive war) against conversion to Judaism in Switzerland (presumably because most were done for the purpose of intermarriage), it decreed that this Jewish man could not be accepted as a teacher in the Jewish community's school. The Agudah wrote to Herzog, telling him of the decision and requesting his reaction.

Herzog responded: "You have done according to the Torah and the commandments. May your hands be strengthened as you have erected a fence against lawlessness. For this type of conversion, not conducted for the sake of heaven, is like a rot in the household of Israel. And the obligation is upon every *beit din* in every generation, and especially upon the *beit din* of an entire country, to fence in lawlessness against our holy faith and against the people of God."[51]

What is particularly interesting about Herzog's corpus is the degree to which—in other responsa—he is conscious of the impact of Israeli statehood on some elements of conversion law. Herzog is sensitive to the difference between his own era and that of the tannaim and the Rambam; and he is also deeply sensitive to variations among places. He speaks of the differences in the worlds of Israel and the Diaspora and, in a number of situations, even allows those dissimilarities to affect his decisions.

In a responsum regarding whether a *kohein* living with a non-Jewish woman should be allowed to marry her if she converts,[52] Herzog concludes that although he could find halakhic justification for permitting this conversion, sociological conditions make such a step inadvisable. Herzog expresses his wariness of communicating to Jews at large that Jewish courts are willing to be lenient on the matter of *kohanim* marrying converts (even if she only converts, without actually marrying the *kohein*), and he fears that the court would also convey that it condones couples living together without having had a traditional Jewish wedding ceremony. But these particular concerns, he suggests, are a Diaspora matter. "And after studying the matter, I inform [my colleague who asked the question] that in the Diaspora, in a place where such cases are prevalent," this conversion should not be permitted. Would Rabbi Herzog have ruled differently had the same case arisen in Israel, where the number of such instances was dramatically smaller? We cannot be certain, but Herzog's language suggests that this is, indeed, a possibility.

Herzog explicitly states that Israel's existence can have profound implications for rulings in conversion cases.[53] The language of the question submitted to him by an anonymous rabbi in the Diaspora on December 23, 1948, is fascinating in itself:

> Lately there has been an increase in the number of cases in which Jewish people of our country are married to non-Jewish women in their courts, and they now seek to convert them and marry them with *huppah* and *kiddushin* because they wish to immigrate to Israel.
>
> In general, these Gentile women have special rights, since they saved their husbands from death during the Holocaust by their refusal to obey the Nazis' demands to divorce them; by doing so, they placed themselves in grave danger and were sent to concentration camps. . . .
>
> Until now, I have refused to bring these people under the wings of the Jewish people because their intention is not [to convert] for the sake of heaven, but rather, for the sake of aliyah [immigration to Israel] and in this, I followed the ruling of the *Shulḥan Arukh*. . . . I see the magnitude of the horrific tragedy for hundreds of families who wish to make aliyah, but at the same time, my heart hesitates to take such responsibility upon myself.

In considering the questioner's dilemma, Rabbi Herzog addresses a few technical textual issues and proceeds to the case at hand. Though he unhesitatingly assumes Rabbi David Hoffmann's position that those already married in civil courts cannot, by definition, be converting for the sake of marriage,[54] Herzog points out that these converts are also not converting for the sake of heaven. Rather, they are converting simply because they wish to immigrate to the Land of Israel. To solve this problem, he offers a redefinition of "for the sake of heaven" unlike anything we have seen thus far:

But here there is another concern—that their intention is [to convert] for the sake of making aliyah to Israel. But this depends on the situation in your country. If the conditions are such that as foreigners they could not stay in your country, then it is obvious that their intention is not for the sake of heaven. But if it were possible for them to remain in [their current] country, but they desire Eretz Yisrael, this can be seen as an intention "for the sake of heaven." For they are uprooting their dwelling places and abandoning their sources of income to migrate to another land, and specifically, the Land of Israel. Thus, it becomes clear that their desire is to cling to the Jewish people, in its Land. . . . And this is a good intention, and there is no need to prevent their conversion.

Herzog was responding to the questioner's sense that a human tragedy was unfolding. Herzog, of course, never said that the enormity of the human tragedy trumps the authority of the *Shulḥan Arukh*. Yet he seems moved by the human dimension of the problem and responded by radically reconceptualizing the concept of "for the sake of heaven" in light of Israel's recent creation. To join the Zionist enterprise, Rabbi Herzog essentially says, is to serve heaven, whether or not the convert's intention is to observe the commandments, as traditional definitions of the notion would ideally demand. Seemingly overwhelmed by the momentousness of Israel's creation just a few months earlier, Herzog concludes the responsum almost poetically, by writing to his correspondent, "Signed with the blessing of Zion and Jerusalem, hoping to see him shortly in our holy city, May it be speedily rebuilt."

The daring and creative language of this responsum is noteworthy. And Rabbi Herzog was not the only authority to address new issues regarding conversion and intermarriage after the creation of the State.[55] Nor was he the only modern *posek* who saw matters in this light. Rabbi Isser Yehuda Unterman (1886–1976), in an article in the early 1970s, wrote that as a rabbi in England, he had been strict in not accepting converts of dubious motivation.[56] However, Unterman believed that there were two reasons to distinguish the proper rabbinical response in the Diaspora from the response that would be appropriate in Israel: the sheer number of such cases in the Diaspora; and the fact that converts to Judaism in the Diaspora remained in a Christian setting and were thus less likely to make a full transition to committed Jewish life. Like Herzog, he seems to have believed that the profundity of the Jewish experience in the Land of Israel, and even the theological significance of living there, provided justification for being more lenient and welcoming than would otherwise have been the case.

Rabbi Shlomo Goren: Ashkenazic Chief Rabbi of Israel

Another authority whose pedigree is virtually unquestioned in Orthodox communities but who nonetheless issued some surprising rulings on conversion issues is Rabbi Shlomo Goren (1917–94). Goren, born in Poland, immigrated to mandatory Palestine in 1925. As a yeshiva student in Hebron, he was quickly recognized for his brilliance, and he published his first work, a commentary on Maimonides' *Mishneh Torah*, at the age of seventeen. A committed Zionist, Goren joined the Haganah in 1936 and was later appointed by then–Chief Rabbis Herzog and Uziel to be the first chief rabbi of the Israel Defense Forces (IDF). He became Ashkenazic chief rabbi of the State in 1972.[57]

Goren addressed the issue of conversion in several celebrated cases. One of the most interesting for our purposes is the famed case involving Dr. Helen Seidman (1930–80). Seidman, a Unitarian, came to Israel in 1964 from Bethesda, Maryland, as a tourist. Accompanied by her daughter, Seidman was drawn to Israel and kibbutz life and settled in Kibbutz Naḥal Oz. Eventually, she met a Jewish man and married him in a proxy marriage in Mexico.[58]

Seidman later wished to convert to Judaism. However, as she was living in a nonreligious kibbutz where the laws of kashrut and Shabbat were not observed, it was obvious that she did not intend to become halakhically observant, so her conversion could not fit the traditional definition of "for the sake of heaven," as Orthodox authorities would have required. Thus, Seidman decided to convert under Reform auspices.

After her conversion ceremony, which was performed by Rabbi Moshe Zemer of Tel Aviv, the Reform Movement's leading halakhic spokesman in Israel, Seidman applied to register as a Jew with the Ministry of the Interior, which refused her request. A court battle ensued, with the country's highest secular courts ruling that there was no legal basis for the Ministry's actions. Ultimately, the Ministry was instructed to register Seidman as a Jew. The Orthodox establishment was unwilling to accede to this demand, and a political struggle erupted that threatened to topple a fragile governmental coalition between Orthodox and secular political parties. Against the background of this impending political crisis, Rabbi Goren, then chief chaplain of the IDF, met with Seidman for about three hours, after which he assembled a *beit din* and hastily converted her. As Goren was an Orthodox rabbi of unquestionable stature, Seidman's conversion was now recognized by the Ministry of the Interior, and the political crisis was averted. Goren's decision was surprising, given his general position that Reform conversion was not considered conversion at all.[59]

Not surprisingly, the decision unleashed a storm of criticism from numerous Orthodox rabbinical colleagues. They claimed that Goren's decision to convert Helen Seidman was virtually incomprehensible, given that Jewish law required *kabalat ol mitzvot* as a sine qua non for conversion. Some of Goren's Orthodox critics suggested that behind the decision lay the belief that the standards for conversion could be different in Israel from what they were in the Diaspora. Rabbi J. David Bleich offers an explanation for Goren's motivations:[60]

A feature article appearing in the weekend supplement of *Ha-Tzofeh*, 15 Sivan 5730 [June 19, 1970], purports to give the rationale governing Rabbi Goren's actions in this case. It is reported that Rabbi Goren is of the belief that in Israel, prospective proselytes are to be viewed differently from the way in which they are regarded in the Diaspora. . . . It is suggested that proselytization was frowned upon by the Sages in the Diaspora but welcome in Israel. It is reported that Rabbi Goren, going a step further, asserts that in Israel, sincerity of motivation may be dispensed with as a prior requirement for conversion.[6]

In the Diaspora, converts motivated by reasons other than religious conviction cannot be accepted since doubts remain with regard to their future comportment; in Israel, where conversion entails not merely religious affiliation but national identification as well, such fears do not exist, contends Rabbi Goren. Hence, in his opinion, even converts prompted by self-serving motives may be accepted in Israel.

According to this interpretation, the decision that Rabbi Goren rendered in the Seidman case indicates that he believed residence in the State of Israel to be a decisive factor that allowed a prospective convert to be accepted into the Jewish fold, even when it appeared unlikely that the convert would observe the commandments following her conversion. Those explaining Goren's actions in this way concluded that, like his predecessors Rabbis Herzog and Unterman, Rabbi Goren felt that the decision on the part of the convert to live in the Jewish State meant that she would be part of Jewish destiny. Her decision to live in Israel, a setting in which her identity as a Jew would be reinforced by her surroundings, was sufficient to justify her acceptance as a convert despite her level of observance.

How, then, shall we explain Goren's actions? The perspective offered in *Ha-Tzofeh*—that Rabbi Goren viewed conversion differently in Israel from how he might in the Diaspora—finds support in his published views regarding another situation: that of Paula Cohen, a woman whom Rabbi Goren converted, despite the fact that she had married, in violation of Jewish law, a man of priestly descent who was a member of a nonreligious kibbutz. When, after a number of years in Israel, the Cohen family moved to Manchester, England, and sought to register their children there in a school under Orthodox auspices, they were told that the conversion that Mrs. Cohen had received from Rabbi Goren was valid only in Israel. The British *beit din* based this ruling on the conversion certificate, which declared: "This document has no legal validity in the Diaspora." Thus, ironically, and in contravention of the usual difficulties that people encounter, Mrs. Cohen was considered Jewish in Israel by the chief rabbinate but not outside of Israel.[62]

In "Conversion in the Land of Israel and Outside the Land of Israel," Goren explained the reasoning and sources supporting his decision. He said that during his tenure as chief rabbi, all certificates of conversion stated that these conversions were valid in Israel alone.[63] He insisted that all conversions that occurred under his authority as chief rabbi required the convert to take up permanent residence in the State and asserted that this decision had a "significant halakhic foundation." Goren noted that while the Babylonian Talmud was negatively disposed toward conversion, the Jerusalem Talmud had nothing to say against "converts or those who converted them": "The Jerusalem Talmud adopts a positive and sympathetic approach to the institution of conversion," even when the conversion is seemingly motivated by love for a Jewish man or a Jewish woman.[64]

Goren claimed that the differences between the views of the Babylonian and Jerusalem talmudic traditions were logical. The rabbis of the Jerusalem Talmud believed that when a conversion took place outside the Land of Israel, the "convert would still remain within the bosom of his Gentile family, and a serious fear existed that the male or female convert and their children would not sever themselves from their family, from their holidays, their festivals, and their ritual. They would continue to live as one family, and . . . [t]heir children would thus be raised in a Gentile atmosphere. Therefore, no conversion there could be regarded as authentic."

In Israel, the situation was completely different. In contradistinction to the associational and kinship patterns that attached converts in the Diaspora to their family of origin, Rabbi Goren contended, converts to Judaism in Israel "were cut off completely from their Gentile family and from their Gentile existence. Their children did not even know that they came from a mixed family. Here the conversion is authentic and more certain from the standpoint of Judaism." From this perspective, it is "easy to understand why Massekhet Geirim 4 [the tractate on converts] states, 'Beloved is the Land of Israel, *shemakhsheret geirim* [as it legitimates converts].' " In Israel, it is certain that converts "will live as Jews in every way."[65] It could not be clearer that Goren saw the Israeli context as a key factor in judging conversion cases.

It was this same Israeli context that apparently led Goren to rule in a much more strict fashion in what may have been the most controversial case of his colorful career: the Langer case, which came before the Tel Aviv religious court in 1956 but was not resolved until 1972. The facts of the case were relatively simple. In 1943, Borokovsky, a non-Jewish Polish man, married a fifteen-year-old Jewish girl, Hava, who came from a very religious family. Her devastated family pressured Borokovsky to convert, which he did. Hava later left Borokovsky without getting a religious divorce, and later married a Jewish man, Otto Langer, with whom she had two children, Hanoch and Miriam, in 1945 and 1947.

The Tel Aviv religious court, which found out about the situation in 1956, ruled that the two children were *mamzeirim* (illegitimate children) because Hava's first marriage had not been dissolved with a get. Consequently, she was not free, under Jewish law, to remarry. Therefore, the court ruled, she remained married to Borokovsky. Her union with Langer was legally an extramarital affair, and her children, as the offspring of an adulterous relationship, were illegitimate. At the time, this ruling received no public attention. But when Hanoch applied for a marriage license in 1966, he was refused permission to marry on the grounds of his illegitimacy. Miriam suffered the same fate when she became engaged to an Israeli Jewish man and attempted to obtain a marriage license.

The plight of the Langer children, who, as *mamzeirim*, could not marry "kosher Jews,"[66] according to Jewish law, captured the attention of the country. Several unsuccessful attempts to solve the problem questioned the validity of the Borokovsky conversion. After all, if the Borokovsky conversion were declared invalid, the original marriage of Mrs. Langer would be legally null and void, and the stigma of *mamzeirut* removed from the Langer children. However, various Israeli rabbinic courts repeatedly ruled that the conversion was legitimate and affirmed Borokovsky's standing as a Jew.[67] The irony of the situation was lost on very few. Leniency in one aspect of the case meant stringency in the other. If a rabbinic court affirmed the legitimacy of the Borokovsky conversion despite his ignorance of Jewish tradition and nonobservance of Jewish law, it would have to recognize Hava's first marriage as valid and require a get to dissolve it, thus declaring the Langer brother and sister *mamzeirim*. If, on the other hand, the court was strict and ruled that the conversion was null and void because Borokovsky had not been observant and had never intended to be observant, it could invalidate the first marriage on the grounds that it was a forbidden union, thereby removing the stigma of *mamzeirut* from the Langer children and allowing them to marry within the Jewish people. However, a single court could not be strict and lenient on both issues.

Because of the enormous and enduring negative stigma surrounding the classification of *mamzeirut* and the seriousness of its status as a *mitzvah de'oraita* (law from the Torah), as well as a reluctance to retroactively annul a conversion that had been recognized by the Israeli rabbinical court system, most of Israel's halakhic authorities affirmed the 1956 decision of the Tel Aviv rabbinical court that had declared Borokovsky's conversion valid. They insisted that the children were *mamzeirim* and could not marry into the nation of Israel.

What would have seemed to be an exclusively religious issue quickly took on political significance as well. General Moshe Dayan, hero of the Six-Day War, became an advocate for the Langer children. A bill was even introduced into the Knesset that would have permitted civil marriage in Israel, thus allowing the children to marry without Orthodox rabbinic sanction. In response, religious parties threatened to withdraw immediately from Prime Minister Golda Meir's coalition and thus bring down the government. Golda Meir threatened to resign if a solution could not be found.[68]

It was into this thicket that Goren stepped in 1972, when, at the age of fifty-four, he retired as chief rabbi of the IDF and was elected chief rabbi of Israel. Goren immediately took steps to resolve the situation. He convened a court of ten people (himself and nine other rabbis whose names were never released), which ruled that Borokovsky's original conversion was not legally valid and that he was not Jewish. Because Jewish law does not recognize the possibility of marriage between a Jew and a non-Jew, Hava was no longer seen as ever having been married to Borokovsky. Consequently, her second marriage was not adulterous, and the children of that marriage (Hanoch and Miriam) were not *mamzeirim*. Immediately after Goren issued his ruling, the brother and sister each got married. Golda Meir and many other political leaders expressed satisfaction at the resolution of the case, but many authorities in the rabbinic establishment were aghast.

In Goren's summary of the case,[69] he reviews his legal reasoning, none of which breaks any new ground. He notes evidence that Borokovsky was never a serious convert, that there was no solid information about the "quality" of his conversion ceremony, and that his level of Jewish knowledge indicates that he was not a practicing Jew. He used these purely halakhic reasons to declare the conversion void, although he himself had disregarded such reasons in the Seidman and Cohen cases discussed above. The conclusion that the political dimension was central in influencing Goren's ruling in the case of the Langers is inescapable.

Goren was explicit about his desire to resolve the case for the Langer children: "The emotional state of these two young people was becoming very weakened, and in my office at army headquarters, they found in me an outlet for their emotions and a source of comfort and hope. Whenever they were feeling overwhelmed by their situation, they would come to me to shed tears . . . over the bitterness of their fate."

It was a combination of his concern for the Langer children—the perceived unfairness of their situation and the threat to their emotional well-being—and the unambiguous political overtones of the case that surely led Goren to rule as he did. This was the source of the vociferous objections from those on the right, who claimed that his ruling was not halakhic but political, and that in ruling in this fashion, he had opened the floodgates to impure lines of reasoning.

Moreover, in being lenient for the Langer children, Rabbi Goren established that a conversion could be retroactively annulled on the basis of a convert's failure to observe Jewish law fully subsequent to conversion. His compassion and concern for the fate of the Langer children earned him the approbation of the Israeli public. However, Rabbi Goren also established a virtually unprecedented standard of "stringency" that had to be met before a conversion could be deemed permanently irreversible.[70] This creeping restrictiveness in the area of conversion manifests itself perhaps most clearly in the experience of the Ne'eman Commission, an experiment similar in some ways to that of the Denver community.[71]

The Ne'eman Commission

In the late 1990s, Israel was facing a dramatically shifting demographic reality. Between 1987 and 1997, some 700,000 immigrants from Russia and other parts of the former Soviet Union immigrated to Israel.[72] Of them, about 150,000 were thought to be children of intermarried Jewish fathers or in some other way not halakhically Jewish. At the same time, the Reform and Conservative movements began to press for their own conversions in Israel to be recognized by the State. The Orthodox establishment, well represented in then–Prime Minister Netanyahu's government, sought to invalidate Reform and Conservative conversions. But that move, Netanyahu knew, would undermine his base of support in America, in which liberal movements accounted for about 75 percent or more of the Jewish community.

In 1997, in an effort to avert a political crisis, the prime minister appointed a committee to develop ideas and proposals regarding religious conversion in Israel. He appointed Finance Minister Yaakov Ne'eman, an observant Orthodox Jew, to seek a compromise that might satisfy all parties and avoid a showdown that could bring down the government. (Recall that Rabbi Goren had also seen his intervention in the Seidman case as a way of saving a government from falling, a factor that can arise in Israel but not in Diaspora communities.) After some seventy sessions and 150 hours of deliberations, the commission's recommendations called for the creation of panels of rabbis representing all three movements to prepare the candidates for conversion. The ritual conversion itself would remain within the province of the Orthodox rabbinate alone.

Both camps understood that the impact of the decision would be momentous. For non-Orthodox parties, the commission's recommendations were an opportunity for the Reform and Conservative movements to be at least marginally recognized in Israel. A compromise, they insisted, would also help defuse a looming demographic time bomb created by the large number of Russian immigrants who lived as Jews within Israel but who were not Jewish from the standpoint of halakhah and therefore unable to marry Jewishly within Israel. According to Alex Lubotsky, then a member of Israel's parliament representing a largely Russian party, failure to secure a compromise on the issue of conversion that could recognize these persons as Jews eligible for Jewish marriage could contribute to "a historic rupture among the Jewish people."[73]

The Orthodox rabbinate feared that a crack in the wall might lead to recognition of a fundamentally illegitimate, even dangerous, form of Jewish life. Rabbi Ovadiah Yosef, whose work we have examined in this chapter, denied that his opposition to the compromise was designed to encourage hatred of Reform Jews. He sought only "to distance their priests, who call themselves rabbis."[74]

Realizing that the Ne'eman Commission's proposal was headed for defeat at the hands of the chief rabbinate, Avraham Burg, a onetime Speaker of the Knesset who was then chairman of the Jewish Agency, proposed a compromise that would allow persons converted by Reform and Conservative rabbis to be recognized as Jews for the purpose of citizenship in Israel but not for religious purposes (such as marriage).[75] Burg's proposal cast a spotlight on what is unique about the conversion issue in Israel, namely, that "Jewishness" in the Jewish State is a matter both of religion and of nationality, a factor that we have seen in a number of the responsa that this chapter has examined.

As expected, the chief rabbinate rejected the Ne'eman Commission's proposal in 1998; since then, little has changed with regard to the status of conversions in Israel performed under non-Orthodox auspices.[76] Israeli courts have ruled periodically on conversion, and the non-Orthodox movements have made small gains. For our purposes, what is perhaps most significant is the similarity of the final disposition of the Denver experiment and that of the Ne'eman Commission. The participation of Orthodox personalities, many of them scholars, saved neither endeavor from rejection by the larger Orthodox community.

Ultimately, it is not halakhah that has divided the Jewish people regarding the issue of conversion. Halakhic standards, as we have seen throughout this book, have proved themselves malleable in the hands of many Orthodox authorities. What has often determined the final disposition of matters of conversion is not only Jewish law but conflicting viewpoints about Jewish social policy, for which Jewish law can often serve as a powerful and creative tool. What has usually separated adherents of the different positions on conversion is a sense of what is good for the Jewish people—a vision of thriving Jewish life, of which conversion policy has always been a reflection.

Recent and Contemporary Developments

It is surely no surprise that in the State of Israel, where religious decision-making and policy inevitably affect the entire Jewish nation, recent and contemporary Orthodox discussions of conversion have reflected halakhic and sociological elements as well as explicit policy claims. Some of these emphases have to do with the ways in which the modern world has altered the tone of Jewish religious discourse. Even beyond this consideration, the responsibility of Israeli religious leadership for the entire people has forced a number of authorities into openly recognizing that their halakhic decision-making is also a matter of policymaking for the Jewish State and, ultimately, for the Jewish people as a whole. Menachem Finkelstein (1951–), a brigadier-general in the Israeli army (heading the IDF's legal arm until 2003) and author of a scholarly work on conversion that we have cited previously in this book,[77] exhibited this concern when he suggested to the Ne'eman Commission that the time had come for greater halakhic creativity in the face of the sociological challenges that Israel confronted: "In my opinion, the principal problem in Israel today pertaining to matters of conversion ensues from the existence of thousands, and perhaps hundreds of thousands, of immigrants from the former Soviet Union, who, from the point of view of the *Halacha*, are not Jewish or whose Jewishness is doubtful. . . . It seems to me that we are facing a *new situation* which requires a fresh look and courageous new handling. . . . The goal must be to admit larger numbers of converts than have been admitted to date."[78]

The degree to which sociological reality affected Israeli rulings on conversion could be seen, Finkelstein added, even from the comments of Justice Moshe Zilberg, who was then deputy president of the Supreme Court, regarding a petition that the court make more flexible requirements for the conversion of Russian immigrants.[79] Zilberg declined to do so, arguing that a massive immigration from Russia was "still a closed vision, hope, dream" but that should such a massive immigration transpire, he was confident that "wise men will be found who will use their full authority, and will ease the absorption of the remote Russian peoples, among our people and in the country. The values of the *Halacha* have always unified the people, but they did not suffocate them."[80]

For Finkelstein, the sociological reality of Israel demanded flexibility so that an ever-greater number of potential Jews could be brought into the fold. Finkelstein's boldness is evident in the closing passage of his article: "[In some cases], the 'possibility' that a certain convert would accept the Commandments prevented the Posek from negating the decision of the Rabbis admitting the converts to Judaism. In my opinion, [this] may provide an opening for considering a certain 'leap forward' in relation to the conversion in Israel of immigrants from the former Soviet Union."[81]

Finkelstein makes an interesting, though unsubstantiated, claim regarding Israeli society: "There are increasing numbers of people keeping the Commandments among the population absorbing converts in the State of Israel. The cases in which it becomes clear that acceptance of the Commandments is real are not few but are rather on the increase. . . . The former Sephardi Chief Rabbi, Rabbi Uziel . . . did not see any obstacle or difficulty to admitting converts, even when it was known that they would not abide by the Commandments (*The Decisions of Uziel in the Questions of the Time*, Para. 65)."[82] Finkelstein suggests that the fact that the State of Israel is a Jewish society is bound to have a distinct impact on the behavior of its citizens and, like Goren and others we have cited, believes that this offers a potential halakhic justification for greater leniency in the conversion of Gentiles who might otherwise be inadmissible because of their still-unformed commitments to religious observance.

This tendency toward expansion and inclusion can be seen in the writings of an increasing number of contemporary Israeli Orthodox respondents. In the Israeli journal *Eretz Acheret*, a publication devoted to contemporary cultural and religious issues in Israel, two such articles appear in an issue devoted to the subject of conversion. In one article, Zvi Zohar, a professor at Bar-Ilan University and an authority on Jewish law as well as coauthor of a heralded book on conversion,[83] argues that a dramatic change in the standards demanded for conversion had taken place as the result of a relatively unknown 1876 responsum by Rabbi Yitzḥak Schmelkes.[84] Zohar reports that Schmelkes maintained that the convert had to agree to observe the totality of Jewish law at the moment of his conversion. If a conversion ceremony takes place but the person does not genuinely intend to observe Jewish law, the conversion is invalid.

Until this responsum was issued, Zohar insists, motivations for conversion (and the expectation that the prospective convert would observe Jewish law) were not seen as a sine qua non for conversion. Citing the well-known talmudic story about Hillel and the prospective convert,[85] Zohar observes: "Hillel first performed the conversion, and then gave [the convert] instruction about Judaism. Thus, not only did [Hillel] not disqualify him because of dubious motivations, but he even converted him without his knowing anything about Judaism."[86]

Zohar accepts that talmudic story at face value and stresses the radical difference between the leniency and acceptance that marked Hillel's actions and the more stringent and less inclusive tradition regarding the demands made of converts that he claims emerged, beginning with Schmelkes, in the modern period. Zohar summarizes his reading of the rabbinic tradition: "We found that the Mishnah, the Babylonian Talmud, the geonim, medieval authorities and later halakhic authorities determined unambiguously that even if a prospective convert has no religious motivations and is converting for some other purpose, the conversion ceremony is absolutely effective and binding. Indeed, among halakhic authorities, there was disagreement as to whether the converting *beit din* had to take any interest in the motivations of the convert."[87]

The approach taken by Schmelkes, Zohar argues, was "revolutionary."[88] In making this claim, Zohar notes: "[These rabbis] could not deny these [secular] people, who to their minds had betrayed authentic Judaism, the title 'Jew,' since even traditional Judaism insisted that 'a Jew who sins is still considered a Jew.' But there was, still, one human group [that] those who held this worldview could seek to force to live in accordance with their Orthodox perspective—the group of Gentiles who were seeking to convert. Thus, a view from which those born Jewish were de facto exempt, was brought to bear with excess rigidity on those who sought to become Jews by volition."[89]

Of course, many authorities such as Feinstein, Breisch, and Kook would disagree with Zohar. For them, as for others, the position that

Schmelkes adopted and that they championed in their demand for a full "acceptance of the yoke of the commandments" as a prerequisite for conversion represents the plain time-honored thrust of the halakhic tradition. They would assert that the Schmelkes reading should thus not be deemed "revolutionary." In making this observation and in citing Zohar, we do not purport to resolve this debate; we leave that judgment to others. However, what is unmistakable is that the Zohar claim—that the policy initiated by Schmelkes and that was adopted by others embodied a novel level of strictness on the part of Orthodox rabbis and that this change was due to the rabbis' desire to maintain boundaries in the face of the rapid secularization of Jews—is proof that a significant Israeli Orthodox spokesman and scholar thought that a stringent and exclusionary attitude toward conversion was a symptom of social and political weakness not demanded by Jewish law, with horrific consequences for the Jewish people in Israel.

Rabbi Yoel Bin-Nun, one of the leading rabbinic figures in the Religious Zionist movement, arrives at the same policy conclusion as Zohar and advances a unique resolution for the questions surrounding conversion in Israel for the Israeli Jewish body politic. Though recognized more as an exemplary teacher of Bible than as a *posek*, Bin-Nun is a charismatic leader with a huge following in Israel, particularly among young people who see him as their primary religious authority. In an article in *Eretz Acheret*,[90] Rabbi Bin-Nun makes the familiar argument that the existing legal structure in Israel was thoroughly unprepared to deal with the hundreds of thousands of Russian immigrants who were halakhically non-Jewish. As long as conversions are handled on an individual basis with the classical standards traditionally employed in cases of conversion, he argues, the system will never keep up with the number of persons who desire to convert, and the Jewish State will eventually absorb a significant number of non-Jews into its ranks. Like his colleagues cited above, Bin-Nun believes that such a policy undermines the very purpose and nature of the Jewish State. He makes the extraordinary proposal that a centralized mass conversion be instituted to bring these people formally into the Jewish fold.

By advocating a mass conversion ceremony, Bin-Nun sidesteps altogether the level of observance of the prospective convert. In his mind, the national needs of the Jewish people residing in their sovereign state require a radical approach to conversion. Mindful of this revolutionary posture, he nevertheless advocates this stance and concludes his article with "Courage, my colleagues, courage."

This same view of Jewish nationalism as a determinative factor in causing rabbis to accept converts into Judaism can be seen in an article by Rabbi Yigal Ariel, rabbi of the northern settlement of Nov in the Golan Heights, on the challenge posed by the large number of Russian immigrants, many not halakhically Jewish, who have come to Israel in recent years.[91] Though Rabbi Ariel explicitly states that he sees himself as writing an exploratory study and not a formal responsum, the halakhic style that he employs has significant legal overtones and suggests that he is describing what he regards as the optimal way to handle this problem.

Ariel contends that, for the massive Russian immigration to Israel, "even those approaches and arguments that have not heretofore been the basis of law might now, in this urgent time, be a basis for lenient rulings, using a posteriori justifications as ex ante solutions."[92] Ariel observes that these Russian *olim* are mostly not observant and that there is little chance that they will become so. On the other hand, they are living as "Jews" in the Jewish State, and their lot is intertwined with the Jewish people. His challenge is to justify the conversions of such people from the standpoint of Jewish law, for, as he points out at the conclusion of his article, "Conversion [of these immigrants is] not the problem of the immigrants but the interest of the rabbinate, which is charged with saving Israeli society from a 'stumbling block' [wherein "Jews" of non-halakhic status would marry Jews of unquestioned status in possible intermarriages]."[93]

Rabbi Ariel is determined to provide a solution to this dilemma. For him, as for the authorities we cited above, conversion is more than a religious act; it is a national act. Indeed, he suggests, two paradigms for conversion exist in the Jewish tradition: Abraham and Ruth. Ariel describes the "conversion" of the biblical patriarch Abraham as "theological" in nature, contrasting it with that of the biblical Moabite Ruth, which he regards—on the basis of her pledge, "Your people will be my people"—as "national." Ariel argues that there is precedent for conversion based on "national" rather than "theological" commitments. While he observes that "the Russian immigrants do not know very much about Judaism," he also insists that "there is no doubt that they wish to become integrated into the nation and its land." Those who join the Jewish people, as these immigrants have done by virtue of their becoming Israelis, are then eligible for conversion to Judaism.[94]

Of course, Ariel expresses the hope that these Russian immigrants will one day come to embrace the tradition and its practices; he does not see "conversion without acceptance of the mitzvot" as optimal. Nonetheless, the strength of the "nationalist dimension" that marks Judaism can allow for conversion of these people and "through this gateway to the Jewish people, the convert makes his way to Torah."[95]

Rabbi Ariel argues that the famous *baraita* from Yevamot 47a provides a warrant for this stance. In this passage, the prospective convert is asked, "What reason have you for desiring to become a proselyte? Do you not know that Israel at the present time is persecuted and oppressed, despised, harassed, and overcome by afflictions?" Ariel states that this passage indicates that conversion to Judaism must be understood primarily from the perspective of nationhood, not theology.[96] While he apparently remains troubled that these Russian immigrants are unlikely to become observant Jews, he does not allow this concern to trump his determination to make them eligible for conversion. For theirs is "not an intentional [violation of the commandments]." They are to be considered as "infants who were kidnapped,"[97] and thus are not responsible for the sins that they would commit as Jews after their ceremony of conversion inasmuch as "they [mistakenly] believe that a Judaism of the sort practiced by the majority of the people is sufficient."[98]

Ariel's stance is reflected among other contemporary Israeli rabbis who view residence in the State as a decisive factor for admitting persons into the Jewish fold as converts. Rabbi Shlomo Rosenfeld, head of the Hesder (religious Zionist) Yeshiva Shdemot-Nerya, asserts that current realities in Israel require a fresh look at conversion policy. While his recommendations are not as far-reaching as those of Ariel, he states that the central challenge confronting the rabbinate is to honor halakhic precedent while recognizing that rabbis have a responsibility to all of Israeli society. Rosenfeld contends that life in the Jewish State makes a difference in how the laws of conversion ought to be applied and that the "complex situation is only growing more urgent. From a legal perspective, almost all these [nonconverted people] can be citizens of the State. This state of affairs requires that we adopt an attitude of 'it is time to act.'"[99] Rabbi Rosenfeld is concerned for the entire nation of Israel, not just the observant sectors of the community: "[We must] attend to [the converts themselves] and thereby assist the entire Jewish nation. This is because mixed marriages and people's distancing themselves from the Jewish religion are likely to gnaw deeply into our collective."[100]

As for the converts' motivation and the centuries-old resistance to performing conversions for those already civilly married to nonobservant Jews, Rosenfeld states that immigration to Israel is a factor that distinguishes these potential converts from others: "Their immigration to Israel and their desire to integrate into the life of the Jewish people here are reasons for greater consideration in the process of their conversion . . . as distinguished from other Israelis who met non-Jews in Israel or abroad [whose conversion was motivated by a desire to marry]."[101] Rosenfeld's position is undoubtedly colored by his awareness that legal arbiters are engaged in public policymaking and by his commitment to the broader body politic of Israeli society. For him, the Zionist commitments of these immigrants justify allowing their entry as converts into the Jewish people and religion.

Other contemporary Israeli Orthodox authorities reflect very different attitudes regarding conversion policy in the Jewish State. For Sephardic chief rabbi Shlomo Amar, a concern with an exacting standard of halakhic practice led to a 2006 ruling that rejected conversions from abroad conducted even under Orthodox auspices. Amar demanded that the government's rabbinic courts stop recognizing as Jews those who were converted by most Orthodox rabbis outside Israel.[102] Rabbi Amar (1948–) has been the Sephardic chief rabbi of Israel since 2003. Born in Casablanca, Morocco, he immigrated to Israel in 1948. Closely connected with Rabbi Ovadiah Yosef, Amar was chief rabbi of Tel Aviv prior to his election as Sephardic chief rabbi of Israel, and earlier served as head of the Petaḥ Tikvah Rabbinical Court. His writings on conversion have consistently been marked by stringency.

In this case, his stringency went beyond what previous Israeli chief rabbis had insisted upon. Prior to this ruling, the chief rabbinate had disqualified conversions performed by Reform and Conservative rabbis in the United States but had regularly accepted the conversions of rank-and-file American Orthodox rabbis. With this step, most Orthodox rabbis living in North America were not deemed sufficiently reliable to conduct conversions for Israeli purposes. Amar's ruling echoes decisions that Rabbi Moshe Feinstein had rendered years earlier. However, the implications of Rabbi Amar's decision—because of his Israeli venue and the central role that Israel occupies in the modern Jewish psyche—were clearly greater than those of Rabbi Feinstein's.[103]

Amar's ruling suggested that he, as Sephardic chief rabbi of Israel, was content to disenfranchise mainstream elements of American Orthodox Judaism, and he demonstrated that an increasingly ultraorthodox chief rabbinate was prepared to impose stringencies that previous Israeli Orthodox rabbis had not expressed on the matter of conversion. Rabbi Amar seemed to have little concern for a sense of shared enterprise with American Orthodox Jews, which might have caused him to relax what he regarded as the stringent standards halakhically demanded for the acceptance of converts. The important new element here is that Amar's attempt to maintain ultraorthodox control over the standards for determining the legitimacy of converts in the Jewish State transformed the issue from one of denominational divides between Orthodox and Liberal streams of Judaism to divisions between Israeli ḥaredi and Modern Orthodox Judaism as well. Concerns for the inclusion of these converts as Jews in the Jewish nation had no impact upon his ruling.

A dramatic decision reflecting an even more extreme sensibility on conversion was issued in 2008 by Rabbi Avraham Sherman, head of Israel's High Rabbinical Court, regarding conversions conducted in Israel under the authority of Rabbi Haim Druckman. Druckman, a charismatic Orthodox figure, was appointed director of the State Conversion Authority in 1990, at the time a new governmental body designed to provide services to prospective converts to Judaism. Druckman was suddenly dismissed from that position in May 2008, after Sherman ruled that all conversions performed under his authority were invalid, thus leaving up to fifteen thousand Israelis who had converted to Judaism under Druckman's system unsure about their religious status.[104]

Subsequently, the Israeli chief rabbinate issued a document reserving the right to revoke any conversion at any time. Israel's Ashkenazic chief rabbi, Yona Metzger, announced in June 2009 that he supported Sherman's decision to invalidate the thousands of conversions performed under Druckman's aegis, arguing that the draconian step was necessary to "fortify the walls of conversion."[105] The exclusion of converts as a result of Sherman's ruling not only contrasts sharply with the expansiveness advanced by the rabbis and scholars cited at the beginning of this section; it also bespeaks the character and evolution of contemporary *haredi* Judaism.

Metzger's biography could be a metaphor for the shift toward stringency and exclusion increasingly exhibited today in ultraorthodox Israeli circles. Born in Haifa, Metzger served in the IDF as a chaplain, fought in several wars in an armored brigade, and earned the rank of captain. Rabbi Metzger received his ordination from Yeshivat Kerem Be-Yavne, a leading yeshiva in the Hesder movement. He served as rabbi of the Tiferet Zvi Synagogue in Tel Aviv and was later appointed regional rabbi of northern Tel Aviv. Intellectually distinguished, Metzger has seen two of his ten published books awarded prizes by the president of Israel. He has gradually shifted to the religious right, distancing himself from the religious Zionist camp that spawned him, even while serving as chief rabbi of the State of Israel. His decision to uphold the ruling issued by Rabbi Sherman invalidating the conversions conducted under the authority of Rabbi Druckman is reflective of this shift. It also indicates a move toward greater isolation from the larger Jewish world in ultraorthodox precincts.

This last point is highlighted when we compare the career and decisions of Rabbi Metzger with those of an early founder of the *haredi* non-Zionist Agudath Israel movement—Rabbi Judah Leib Zirelson—whom Metzger admires. Zirelson, the widely revered chief rabbi of Bessarabia whom we mentioned in chapter 4, issued a landmark lenient ruling on conversions in 1922, though he was an unlikely candidate for maverick positions on this subject. He formally quit the Zionist movement during the heated controversies about the role of the World Zionist Congress in cultural education, and he went on to become a founder of the non-Zionist Agudath Israel movement in 1912. Nevertheless, Rabbi Zirelson remained a passionate supporter of the Zionist cause and maintained his outspoken support for it.

Zirelson's 1922 decision on conversion was not terribly different from a number of the responsa that we have seen in this volume. Addressed to a Jewish communal leader in Pernambuco, Brazil, the responsum dealt with Russian Jewish immigrants who had married local Brazilian women in civil marriages and, in many cases, had had children with them.[106] These Gentile wives were reported to have expressed an interest in converting to Judaism and had even begun studying Hebrew. This posed a problem with which we are now familiar: many classic halakhic sources tend to rule against converting a Gentile who had already married a Jew, out of suspicion that the conversion would not be for the sake of heaven. But Zirelson was compelled by the personal urgency of the situation and its national implications to adopt a flexible stance regarding these sources. He wrote a lenient and inclusive responsum in which he allowed the conversions to take place.

In 1920, when Bessarabia became part of Romania, Rabbi Zirelson studied Romanian and, in 1922, was elected a deputy to the Romanian Parliament. In 1926, he was elected senator. For a certain period, Zirelson even served as mayor of Kishinev.[107] He was thus a full participant in the secular world and conscious of the larger social frameworks that informed and shaped the Jewish world. Zirelson constituted a radically different model of religious leader from those *haredi* leaders today who seek to ignore secular Israeli and American Jewish realities and who insist that their own standards should be the standards for all. Their decisions indicate that they are informed by their own religious commitments and proclivities alone, apart from a sense of shared destiny with and responsibility for the nonobservant community. They demonstrate no network of interrelationships with other Jews in Israel or abroad that would temper or redirect their rulings.

The communal paroxysms resulting from this change in *haredi* attitudes from Zirelson to Metzger are evident in Israel. Subsequent to the

Druckman affair, Knesset member David Rotem, from the secular and largely Russian Yisrael Beiteinu Party, proposed a bill in 2009 designed to facilitate the conversion of thousands of non-Jewish immigrants living culturally and communally as Jews in Israel. In response to the attempts by Rabbi Sherman and Rabbi Metzger to overturn thousands of conversions that had already taken place, Rotem proposed that once a conversion is recognized by the State, no religious body would have the right to overturn it.[108]

As often happens in Israeli politics, the Rotem bill created strange bedfellows. The secular Russian Yisrael Beiteinu Party's Avigdor Liberman, at that time the foreign minister, and Eli Yishai, the *haredi* head of the Shas Party, agreed to work together in support of the bill. The secularists received support for civil marriage in exchange for surrendering exclusive control over religious conversions to the Orthodox rabbinic establishment. This latter provision of the bill meant that non-Orthodox conversions to Judaism, which had formerly been recognized as legitimate for purposes of the Law of Return and for the determination of Israeli citizenship by Knesset legislation and by the Israeli Supreme Court, might no longer be viewed as valid for these purposes. This proposed legislation would have had the state annul the legitimacy of conversions conducted under Reform, Conservative, Reconstructionist, and, to some extent, even Modern Orthodox rabbinical aegis, effectively granting exclusive control over conversions to the *haredi* parties.

What seemed a panacea to people concerned with affirming the inclusion of Russians of dubious or non-Jewish halakhic status living in Israel who nevertheless participated in Israeli life as "Jews" struck others as dangerous and needlessly divisive. The American leadership of the Reform, Conservative, and Reconstructionist movements were outraged by this proposed section of the Rotem bill and argued that passage of such a law could sever the relationship between Israel and Diaspora Jewry and thereby endanger the State itself. Rabbi Eric Yoffie, president of the Union for Reform Judaism, insisted that the ultimate impact of the bill would be "to prevent [the Reform and Conservative movements] from either having [the benefits of] the Law of Return or from using current law to gain full recognition for conversions in Israel. The American Jewish leadership feels that this would be a significant blow to our standing in Israel and our ability to even maintain our current position under existing law. . . . Is this bill good for the state, does it advance the cause of religious freedom and advance the cause of the Reform and Conservative movements? The answer is no."[109]

Similarly, Steven Bayme, director of the Contemporary Jewish Life Department at the American Jewish Committee, opined that although the bill was "well-intentioned," it would do more harm than good. Bayme continued: "At a time when American Jewish leadership is deeply concerned about inspiring American Jews to identify with Israel as a Jewish state and a state of the entire Jewish people, this sends a wrong message. . . . Initiatives such as this threaten to drive a wedge between American Jewry and Israel, and that is bad for the Jewish people."[110]

Even some Modern Orthodox rabbis bemoaned the bill and complained that the *haredi* world was assaulting the unity of the Jewish people by supporting this and similar legislation. Orthodox rabbi Allan Nadler, professor of Jewish studies at Drew University, stated: "Sadly, the U.S. mainstream Orthodox rabbinate, represented by the Rabbinical Council of America, lamely caved to the outrageous new conditions imposed on them by the Israeli Chief Rabbinate. With very few exceptions . . . this country's modern Orthodox rabbis demonstrated a shameful failure of courage to express righteous outrage, let alone to assert their own authority."[111]

The Rotem bill is a prime example of the ways in which both Israel and the Diaspora community are affected by Israeli legislation. It also demonstrates that conversion is a bellwether issue for the Jewish world. These responses as well as the diversity of opinions that Israeli authorities have expressed in their rulings and articles on conversion indicate that Orthodox *posekim* do not possess a monolithic viewpoint on conversion. Their rulings are influenced by sociological and political reality, as confirmed by Rabbi Nadler:

> In my own previous career as a congregational rabbi in Boston and Montreal, I officiated at dozens of conversion ceremonies with both immigrant Lithuanian Sages and native Modern Orthodox rabbis of great stature, in which the observance of the mitzvot, while always emphatically stressed, was an ideal goal, and never an absolute

prerequisite, for our converts. And we certainly never followed, or spied upon, our converts to assess their level of halakhic observance. Like all good legislation, cogent adjudication of Jewish law requires not only a technical mastery of the Talmud and medieval codes, but sensitivity to one's political and social reality.[112]

The classic tension between boundary maintenance and constituency retention has arisen once again, indicating how conversion has become both the barometer and the lightning rod—the central issue—for measuring and absorbing issues of "Jewish belonging" and Jewish peoplehood in the modern world.

Concluding Thoughts

Our analysis of the responsa of the chief rabbis and other representative authorities and scholars who followed them indicates that their attitudes toward conversion have been palpably affected by the return of Jewish statehood. Some of Israel's leading halakhic authorities have taken surprising positions on these matters. Some clearly understood their roles as public policymakers and not merely as halakhic decisors. They have acknowledged the possibility that halakhic policy in Israel might have to be different from that in the Diaspora and have asserted that Jewish national independence makes manifest an entirely new way of legitimating conversion to Judaism. Jewish sovereignty appears to be so profound a factor that several of these men have suggested that factors involved in allowing for conversion in Israel might lead to a policy that is distinct from what should be adopted in the Diaspora.

These Orthodox authorities, aware that they are not writing only for a narrow community of adherents who subscribe to their theologies and way of life, view themselves as addressing a much larger Israeli Jewish community comprising many nonobservant and religiously uninterested Jews. In the face of Jewish sovereignty, many of these Jewish leaders regard conversion as more than a theological affirmation on the part of those whom they convert. They assert that there is now a national component to the decision to become Jewish that they cannot ignore. These men are shaping public policy for the first fully sovereign community that the Jews have had in two thousand years. But these same conditions have led others, such as Rabbi Amar and Rabbi Metzger, to "fortify the walls against conversion." This chapter, like those that have preceded it, demonstrates that Orthodox opinions on conversion policy in the modern world are no more monolithic in Israel than they have been in the Diaspora.

Conclusion

This volume has presented and analyzed a wide array of decisions rendered by Orthodox legal authorities throughout the world on the topic of conversion during the past two centuries. It would be disingenuous of us to claim that we have no opinions regarding the normative implications of the diverse rulings that these men have delivered on this matter. We are both activists on the contemporary Jewish scene, and each of us has his own viewpoint concerning the policy implications that flow from the materials and directions discussed in these pages. Nonetheless, we have avoided policy as such in this volume. We have sought to be as fair and objective as possible in our description and analysis of the stances of the many *posekim* we have examined, seeking to elucidate *their* approaches to Jewish law and Jewish communal life. In order to focus on an analysis and understanding of their work, we have refrained from providing our own policy position(s) on the many questions surrounding conversion to Judaism in the modern world.

We believe that our book reveals a great deal about legal adjudication within halakhic Judaism and that the rabbis whose work we have presented employed their legal writings on conversion to establish public policy for the Jewish people in the modern era on this most crucial of Jewish concerns. Through their decisions, the rabbis we have investigated have expressed conceptions of the essence of Judaism and have, as well, defined the borders of the modern Jewish community. These *posekim* should not be regarded as mere legal arbiters deciding individual cases; they must be viewed as framers of public policy for a Jewish community that has struggled during the last two hundred years to address the overarching issues of Jewish identity, status, conversion, community, and religion in a period when intermarriage and religious nonobservance have been (and are likely to remain) rife.

Through the legal decisions they have rendered, these Orthodox men have strived to be faithful to a tradition that they honor and revere. They have also sought in these holdings to guide Judaism and the Jewish people toward the future even as they direct their religion and their community in the present.

Many people tend to conceive of law in general and Jewish law in particular as utterly dispassionate, claiming that the Jewish system of jurisprudence is unchanging and impervious to time and setting. They seek an ideal of objective truth, not subject to changing circumstances, in the Jewish legal process. Their worldview is reflected in the classic comment of Rabbi Samson Raphael Hirsch, in his philosophical work *Horeb*, where he argued on behalf of the timeless and unchanging nature of Jewish law: "The Law, both Written and Oral, was closed with Moses."[1] Similarly, Rabbi Moshe Feinstein, in his *Igerot Moshe*, declared: "It is necessary to know that among the foundational principles of our holy faith [is the belief] that all the Torah, whether Written or Oral, was given at Mount Sinai by the Holy One, Blessed be He, Himself to Moses our Rabbi, peace be upon him. *And it is impossible to change even a single jot, either to be lenient or stringent.*"[2]

Our study forces us to reject such assertions, and we believe that this book calls such claims about the objective and singular character of Jewish law into serious question. We have demonstrated that it is surely beyond the reach of rabbis to attain such absolutism and finality in this area of Jewish legal opinion—and, we suspect, in most other areas of halakhah as well. If anything, our work indicates that the parameters of the law and its holdings are forged in the crucible of life by human beings who bring intense convictions in specific historical contexts to the cases that come before them. Legal decision-making is unavoidably malleable and varied, and a spectrum of positions emerge even when persons devoted to the same canon of law make decisions in difficult cases. There is an inescapable hermeneutical circle that involves, on the one hand, texts containing diverse principles and postures and, on the other, human and therefore finite interpreters who understand and weigh these texts and principles in distinct ways in distinct settings.

Jewish law is no exception to this process, and halakhah undeniably speaks in different ways through the human voices of its legal exemplars—its *posekim*. The Sephardic chief rabbi Ḥayim David Halevi (1924–98) of Tel Aviv described the dynamic nature of halakhic adjudication in his responsa collection, *Aseh lekha rav*, in a way that contrasts with the view expressed by Rabbi Feinstein: "Whoever thinks that the halakhah is frozen, and that we may not deviate from it right or left, errs greatly. On the contrary, *ein gemishut kigmishuta shel hahalakhah* [there is no flexibility like that inherent in the halakhah]."[3]

The notion that Rabbi Halevi put forth in his characterization of the Jewish legal process—that halakhah is multivalent and elastic—has been borne out by the research reflected in this book. For example, Rabbi Jacob Ettlinger could write that the rabbis should not allow a woman who had already been married in a civil ceremony to a Jewish man to convert, yet he could acknowledge "justification for those rabbis in our community who are lenient and adopt the position that a [Gentile] may be converted ab initio and then permitted to marry a Jew."[4] Ettlinger issued his ruling even as he recognized that another position on this question was acceptable from a Jewish legal standpoint. Given two legally legitimate options, Ettlinger made his decision believing that a lenient ruling on this matter would lead to lenient rulings in other areas and thereby lessen the ability of those Jews who were *gesetztreuer* (faithful to the Law) to preserve standards of traditional Judaism in the social and cultural context of the modern world. These contextual factors led him to conclude that it would be unwise for the future of the Jewish community for a relaxed ruling to be issued.

Rabbi David Tzvi Hoffmann was asked if it was permissible to accept a woman as a convert if she was converting in order to marry a Jewish man. He knew that the default conclusion was that it was not permissible, but that a more profound and nuanced attitude toward Jewish law suggested that halakhah could accommodate either a lenient or a stringent decision. His assessment of the modern milieu led him to a ruling substantively at odds with that of Rabbi Ettlinger. He cited the halakhic principle of *hakol lefi re'ut einei habeit din* ("everything depends upon the judgment of the rabbinic court") to justify accepting this woman as a candidate for conversion despite traditional laws that

forbade acceptance of converts with ulterior motives who were unlikely
to observe the commandments after conversion.

Rabbi Hoffmann was explicit about some of the extralegal reasons
for his ruling. He feared that if an Orthodox rabbi failed to accept this
woman, she might go to *eḥad meihaḥadashim* (non-Orthodox rabbis)
who would convert her, which would be tragic in a Jewish world where
Orthodox and non-Orthodox comingled socially and where inspec-
tion of the pedigree and lineage of converts could well be lax. While
he indicated that the ideal standard of conversion included practice of
the commandments, he thought that the need for constituency retention justified a lenient decision that would promote inclusion for such
a woman and her Jewish husband and their children. In this way, "the
evil would be kept to a minimum."[5]

These examples from Ettlinger and Hoffmann are hardly exceptional; indeed, they are representative of the many responsa that we
have presented in this work. Rulings issued by these rabbis, as for jurists in other systems of law, are based on principles and precedents
drawn from the Jewish legal tradition. Nevertheless, cases can still be
decided in a multiplicity of ways. Plausible reasons are given to justify
different rulings and postures. What is decisive in analyzing how these
rulings emerge are the subjective postures and judgments that each decisor makes as he considers the policy implications of his rulings for the
welfare of Judaism and the Jewish community.

This is not to say that *pesak* is arbitrary. There is a panorama common to the landscape of rabbinic adjudication, wherein competent *posekim* appeal to an identical canon and affirm a shared method of rational
discourse—*even as they disagree*. Pluralism remains a vital feature of the
Jewish legal process; the view of any one *posek* in any given instance is
not the only valid ruling. Colleagues may, and often do, advance contrary claims.

None of the rabbis we have discussed in this book ignores precedent.
Stare decisis remained at the heart of all their rulings. After all, judi-
cial opinions can only attain normative status if they have recourse to
some sort of legal argumentation. A *posek* must justify his conclusion
as a conclusion of law. Each rabbi maintained that the rulings he issued
were consistent with established and binding elements of the law and

that his decisions instantiated an accepted legal principle or rule. This does not mean that "objective standards" can be seen as pertaining in an a priori way to an instant case. Nor does it suggest—as we have seen—that individual rabbis can prevent personal judgments from influencing the decisions that they render.

Ultimately, by the very nature of the way that law works, *posekim* must employ discretion. Two responses that are contrary to each other can both be reasonable. In difficult cases, there is no "right answer" waiting for the judge to unearth, nor does precedent provide a narrative fit that can provide unequivocal and clear direction to every rabbi. As Rabbi Ettlinger realized, opponents cannot be said to have somehow failed to see the truth. The "right answer" is what the rabbi as judge believes to be the right answer, after dealing with all the complexities of a problem. The *posek* cannot shirk personal responsibility; he must render judgment in light of standards set by the authority of the legal tradition. At the same time, he cannot escape a host of logical, contextual, and personal factors that influence his determination of the law in an instant case.

Controversy thus turns not upon the rule of law but upon how the law is applied to the facts in a given decision. Again, this does not mean that a rabbi wills at the beginning the results that emerge from his judgment and that he discovers principle only afterward. Rather, it indicates that no judgment that a rabbi offers can fully transcend the limitations that hedge human nature. Every time a rabbi offers an interpretation of law, he necessarily enacts into law parts of his own theological beliefs, his assessment of the particular challenges facing the Jewish people, and his philosophy of halakhah. The personal measure of the interpreter cannot be eliminated. Rabbis devoted to the Jewish legal tradition surely owe their fidelity to God and to the people Israel as they seek to frame policy that will guide the Jewish community in a world of exceptional opportunity and extraordinary challenges. Our book has shown that much reasoning within the law is not distinctively legal but is both profoundly relevant to decisions that are made and a legitimate dimension of the legal process.

All the rabbis we have studied performed their halakhic work with an eye to the demands of the law as well as the realia of the rapidly metamorphosing world in which they lived. Social and cultural conditions caused one group to apply the precedents containing the rules and principles of the Jewish legal tradition stringently so as to promote a restrictive policy regarding conversion—one that they believed would protect the community and the religion from dissolution. These same conditions led another faction to assert that the legal sources should be read to legitimate lenient decisions that would advance an expansive policy—one that allowed for the acceptance of numerous candidates for conversion. Each group of rabbis regarded their approach as the optimal policy direction for guiding the Jewish community in the present and toward the future.

It is perhaps ironic that conversion should have such a pivotal bearing on the unity of the Jewish people. In its debates about conversion, the leadership of the Jewish community defines the essence of belonging to the Jewish people, shapes public policy to further that essence, and imagines the nature of the Jewish future. Debates about conversion in a world where intermarriage and conversion are more and more common are unlikely to subside.

While the focus of this book has been on the writings of representatives from the Orthodox denomination of Judaism, our aim—as we stated at the outset—has been to show that these writings illuminate the larger and more complex task that all Jewish leaders undertake as they seek to establish borders and define commitments and obligations for Jews and the Jewish community in the modern period. We hope that we have succeeded in illuminating issues that extend beyond the specific focus of the responsa we have examined and that suggest potential avenues for thinking about the challenges that modernity in all its complexity poses to Judaism and to the entire Jewish people.

Notes

Introduction

1. The outlines of the case are most clearly described in Shaviv, "Loved in Life [II Sam. 1:23]—and in Death?" See also the discussions online that confirm this version of the story, including http://www.peopleil.org/details .aspx?itemID=7676 (Hebrew) (accessed July 8, 2011); and http://www .mixedfamilies.org.il/hebrew/index.php?subaction=showfull&id=1289917682&a rchive=&start_from=&ucat=27& (Hebrew) (accessed July 8, 2011), which notes the huge public outcry. Readers who search for the case in the literature will note that some articles relate the story differently, claiming that Paschov was first interred in a regular Israeli military cemetery, but after it was discovered that his mother was not Jewish, the Israeli army's rabbinate insisted that his body could not remain in a cemetery consecrated for the burial of Jews. Paschov's corpse was therefore exhumed, and he was buried a second time, in a cemetery for non-Jews. This version is found in Stuart Cohen, *Israel and Its Army*, 118; and Cohen, "Relationships between Religiously Observant and Other Troops in the IDF." We have confirmed that the version by Shaviv is the correct one.

2. Berger, *Heretical Imperative*, 79. The discussion of status and identity, above, is indebted to Berger's analysis.

3. For concepts of "coercive legal authority" and "influential authority," see Carlin and Mendlovitz, "American Rabbi."

4. Ellenson, "Jewish Legal Interpretation."

5. Hume, *Enquiry Concerning the Principles of Morals*, 195–96, 210, 308–9.

6. See Gordis, "David Zevi Hoffmann on Civil Marriage," where the term "constituency retention" is employed.

7. Hartman, *Boundaries of Judaism*; and Sagi and Zohar, *Transforming Identity*.

8. Finkelstein, *Conversion: Halakhah and Practice*.

Chapter 1

1. BT Yevamot 47b.
2. BT Bava Metzia 59b. The Babylonian Talmud records some disagreement regarding the precise number of commandments that are violated. The first opinion introduced says that one who derides the *geir* (convert) violates three negative commandments. Rabbi Eliezer insists that the number is actually thirty-six; yet another opinion goes as high as forty-six.
3. M. Bava Metzia 4:10.
4. M. Bikurim 1:4.
5. Recall the example of Lev Paschov discussed in the introduction to this volume. See also, as one of many examples, the discussion of a young man killed in the 1997 bombing in a Jerusalem market whose parents could not find a cemetery that would accept his body because he had not undergone an appropriate religious conversion (Daniszewski, "No Place to Bury Teen Bomb Victim").
6. No treatment of this length could begin to address all the relevant sources. This chapter looks at the sources of prime importance but, of necessity, omits many, particularly those from the post-talmudic periods. Those interested in a more comprehensive listing of sources should examine Finkelstein, *Hagiyur, halakhah uma'aseh*; Finkelstein, *Conversion: Halakhah and Practice*; and the *Talmudic Encyclopedia* entries *geirut, geirim*, etc.
7. Shaye Cohen, "Conversion to Judaism in Historical Perspective," 31.
8. For an interesting discussion of these marriages, cf. Shaye Cohen, "Origins of the Matrilineal Principle in Rabbinic Law," 21.
9. Ruth 1:16–17.
10. Shaye Cohen, "Origins of the Matrilineal Principle in Rabbinic Law," 21.
11. BT Yevamot 22a. The Talmud notes, incidentally, that this perspective should have allowed the convert to marry a relative, such as a brother or sister, since he or she is no longer related to those who were previously family members. But on this same page, the sages declared that one should not do so, so that people should not say that "we have exchanged a religion of greater sanctity for a religion of lesser sanctity." The same position is codified by Maimonides in *Mishneh Torah, Isurei Bi'ah*, 14:12.
12. M. Bava Metzia 4:10, based on the verse in Exod. 22:20.
13. Exod. 12:49, Lev. 24:22, and Num. 9:14.
14. Exod. 22:21 and 23:9; see also Lev. 9:13 and Deut. 10:19.
15. Num. 15:15.
16. Deut. 24:17.
17. Deut. 28:43–44.
18. Exod. 23:12; cf. also Deut. 5:14.
19. Exod. 12:43–49. Cf. also Num. 15:14.
20. Deut. 10:18.

21. Lev. 19:10 and 23:22; and Deut. 24:19–21.

22. Shaye Cohen, "Conversion to Judaism in Historical Perspective," 35.

23. Cf. Ezra 9:1–10:4, esp. 10:3.

24. Shaye Cohen, "Rabbinic Conversion Ceremony," 195.

25. A *baraita* is a tannaitic rabbinic text (meaning that it is no later than the codification of the Mishnah in 220 C.E.) that was not included in the Mishnah or the Tosefta, the two most important collections of tannaitic material.

26. Because Jewish law ultimately held that circumcision and immersion were absolutely required, those texts that still debate this issue are obviously an early stage of the ritual's development. Nonetheless, the *baraita* on Yevamot 46b is fascinating. The salient section reads: "All [i.e., even Rabbi Eliezer] agree that ritual ablution without circumcision is effective; and they differ only on circumcision without ablution. R. Eliezer infers from the forefathers, while R. Joshua [maintains that] in the case of the forefathers also ritual ablution was performed."

27. BT Yevamot 47a–b.

28. As we will discuss below, the classic talmudic locus for this claim is BT Bekhorot 30b.

29. BT Yevamot 48a.

30. BT Bekhorot 30b.

31. Shaye Cohen, "Rabbinic Conversion Ceremony," 198.

32. Ibid., 201–2.

33. M. Bikurim 1:4.

34. Deut. 26:1–10.

35. This attitude is apparently similar to the one that must have given rise to the Qumran text that prohibits a convert from entering the Temple. In a Qumran text known as 4Q Florilegium, the sect prohibits "the Ammonite, Moabite, *mamzeir*, Gentile [*ben neikhar*], and proselyte [*geir*] from entering the Temple to be built in the messianic future." This text is cited in Shaye Cohen, "From the Bible to the Talmud," 32.

36. M. Yevamot 2:8.

37. Dating Geirim is not simple. Some scholars date the composition of the text at around the time of the geonim, which is very possible. Regardless of the date of Geirim's composition, it is likely that the tradition reflected here is a very early one. Some views in Geirim, however, were already dismissed in the tannaitic period. It is thus difficult to pinpoint a date for the composition as a whole. An example of a view in Geirim that is subsequently dismissed by the Talmud is Geirim 2:4, which claims that acceptance of converts on the wings of the Divine Presence is akin to Israel's entry into the covenant, with circumcision, immersion, and offering a sacrifice. But BT Keritot 9a quotes Rabbi Yoḥanan b. Zakkai's ruling that once sacrifices at the Temple were annulled because of the Temple's destruction, the convert did not have to set aside that money any longer. Would

Geirim have made the claim in 2:4 if it knew of Rabbi Yoḥanan's view? Would it have made that claim after the destruction of the Temple? It is difficult to know.

38. Geirim 1:3, Heiger edition.

39. Note that Geirim 1:1 also has the parallel to the *baraita* in BT Yevamot 47a. See Shaye Cohen, "Rabbinic Conversion Ceremony," for a fascinating comparison of the two texts.

40. PT Kiddushin 4:1; 65b.

41. BT Yevamot 24b. This *baraita* is also quoted in BT Avodah Zarah 3b.

42. Rav's view is echoed by PT Kiddushin 4:1, 65b–d; in Maimonides' *Mishneh Torah* in *Hilkhot Isurei Bi'ah*, 13:17; and in *Shulḥan Arukh, Yoreh De'ah*, 268:12.

43. Cf. 2 Kings 17:24 ff.

44. BT Bekhorot 30b.

45. BT Shabbat 31a.

46. Rashi, Shabbat 31a, s.v. *gairei*. The Tosafot, BT Yevamot 24b, s.v. *lo bimei David*, raise similar concerns about both this narrative and the one from BT Menaḥot 44a (which we cite below) and offer an explanation similar to Rashi's.

47. BT Menaḥot 44a.

48. BT Sanhedrin 99b.

49. BT Sotah 47a and BT Sanhedrin 107b.

50. M. Yevamot 2:8.

51. BT Yevamot 47a–b.

52. BT Yevamot 24b.

53. *Mishneh Torah, Isurei Bi'ah*, 13:4.

54. Ibid., 13:14.

55. Riskin, "Conversion in Jewish Law," 64.

56. *Mishneh Torah, Isurei Bi'ah*, 13:17. On this passage in the Rambam and the implications to be drawn from it, see Sagi and Zohar, *Transforming Identity*, 166 ff. For a sharp critique of Sagi and Zohar and their position on this passage in particular and their argument in general, see Broyde and Kadosh, "Review Essay," 87 ff. Sagi and Zohar, in "Transforming Identity," respond to this critique and defend their position, and Broyde and Kadosh answer their response. Mark Shapiro, "Transforming Identity," 2 ff., provides a detailed exposition of this debate between Sagi and Zohar on the one hand and Broyde and Kadosh on the other as well as a discussion of the Sagi and Zohar book in general. See also Amsalem, *Sefer zera Yisra'eil*, chap. 1, "Kabalat hamitzvot," 1:52 ff., for a full presentation and discussion of this source and others in Maimonides on this issue.

57. *Mishneh Torah, Isurei Bi'ah*, 14:1.

58. Responsa of Maimonides, Bar-Ilan Responsa Project Database, sec. 211.

59. The matter was of relevance to the local magistrate because it was a violation of local law for a Jew to own a non-Jewish slave.

60. M. Yevamot 2:8.

61. For the classical talmudic discussions of *takanat hashavim*, cf. primarily BT Gittin 55a, BT Bava Kama 66a–b, and BT Bava Kama 94a–95a.

62. Responsa of Maimonides, Bar-Ilan Responsum Project Database, sec. 293.

63. M. Bikurim 1:4.

64. PT Bikurim 1:4; 64a.

65. English spellings of the surname vary. Most recent writings use "Karo." The *Encyclopaedia Judaica* and others use "Caro."

66. Joseph Ben-Ephraim Karo, *Beit Yosef, Orah Hayim*, 268:12.

67. BT Shabbat 31a.

Chapter 2

1. Bernays's responsum on intermarriage is included in Duckesz, "Zur Biographie des Chacham Jsaak Bernays."

2. Davis, "Mixed Marriage in Western Jewry," 181.

3. Lowenstein, "1840s and the Creation of the German-Jewish Religious Reform Movement," 255.

4. Ferziger, *Exclusion and Hierarchy*, 92.

5. For a more detailed description of Chajes's fury at Reform as expressed in his polemic, see Ellenson, *After Emancipation*, 161–67.

6. Chajes, *She'eilot uteshuvot* (1850), vol. 3, fols. 8b–9a.

7. Ettlinger's statement can be found in Judith Bleich, "Jacob Ettlinger," 131–34.

8. Ettlinger, *Binyan Tziyon*, no. 149.

9. *Shomer Tziyon Hane'eman* (1847), 56a–b, cited in Ferziger, *Exclusion and Hierarchy*, 98.

10. See the Tosafot on Kiddushin 75b, "*VeRabi Yishma'el savar la. . . . .*"

11. Ferziger, *Exclusion and Hierarchy*, 98.

12. For an excellent description and account of Jewish intermarriage from 1840 onward, see Meiring, *Die christlich-jüdische Mischehe in Deutschland 1840–1933*. Precise statistics for Jewish-Christian intermarriage in all of Prussia and Germany from 1875 to 1933 are found on 94–95.

13. Illowy wrote his letter on October 31, 1864. It appears in Illoway, *Sefer Milhamot Elohim*. See a full discussion and analysis of this entire episode in Ellenson, "Jewish Legal Decision by Rabbi Bernard Illowy of New Orleans and Its Discussion in Nineteenth-Century Europe."

14. Feilchenfeld's article appeared in *Der Israelit* 6, no. 2 (January 4, 1865): 17–20; and Hildesheimer's appeared in *Der Israelit* 6, no. 5 (February 1, 1865): 57–59.

15. Eliav, *Rabbiner Esriel Hildesheimer Briefe*, letter 16.

16. Hildesheimer, *She'eilot uteshuvot Rabbi Azriel, Yoreh De'ah*, nos. 229–30.

17. Ibid., no. 234.

18. *Der Israelit* 12, no. 30 (July 26, 1871): 568–69.

19. The Kalischer responsum is printed in Hildesheimer, *She'eilot uteshuvot Rabbi Azriel, Yoreh De'ah*, no. 229.

20. See Eliav, "*Torah im Derekh Eretz* in Hungary," 127–42.

21. Horovitz, *Mattei Levi*, I.

22. Horovitz, *Frankfurter Rabbinen*, vols. 1–4.

23. This responsum can be found in Horovitz, *Mattei Levi, Yoreh De'ah*, no. 54.

24. Ibid., no. 55.

25. For biographical information on Hoffmann, see Marx, *Essays in Jewish Biography*, 185–222.

26. Hoffmann, *Melamed Leho'il, Yoreh De'ah*, no. 83.

27. Ibid., no. 85.

28. Ibid., no. 87.

29. For an analysis of another responsum in which Hoffmann wrote on *hatafat dam berit*, see Levine and Ellenson, "Jewish Tradition, Contemporary Sensibilities, and Halacha," 49–56.

30. On *kabalat ol mitzvot* in the responsa literature on conversion, see Zohar and Sagi, *Giyur vezehut Yehudit*.

31. Obviously, the child was not Jewish, as Judaism affirms a matrilineal principle that holds that Jewish status is determined by the status of the mother. Circumcision alone is an "enabling act" that facilitates the entry of such a child into the Jewish people; but the boy does not attain Jewish status until he is ritually immersed, in accordance with Jewish law. Nevertheless, the woman appears not to have grasped this law and apparently believed that her child shared the father's status.

32. Hoffmann, *Melamed Leho'il, Even Ha'ezer*, no. 8.

33. According to Maimonides, in *Hilkhot Isurei Bi'ah*, 12:6, and *Shulḥan Arukh, Even Ha'ezer*, 17:2, Jews who have regular sexual relationships with Gentiles are subject to *kareit*. This punishment surely reflects the severity that the rabbis wished to accord intermarriage. Hoffmann wanted the Jewish man to avoid this fate and hence argued that the non-Jewish woman be converted.

34. The following legal considerations appear to have informed and guided Hoffmann in this instance: the *kohein* would no longer be subject to *kareit* once the non-Jew converted. However, Jewish law prohibits a *kohein* from marrying a convert. Such a *kohein* loses his status as a priest (Lev. 21:6–7), and, according to *Even Ha'ezer* 6:1, the *beit din* should compel such a couple to divorce. There was no easy halakhic solution to this dilemma that could address all the concerns that this case raised; Hoffmann chose what he considered the best of the limited options that were open to him.

35. Hoffmann's desire to reach this conclusion and cite respected Jewish precedent for his holding is so strong that even when he admits that the *Beit Yitzḥak* on *Yoreh De'ah* says that one should not permit a conversion for a non-Jewish

woman who previously had intercourse with a Jewish man, he points out that the *Beit Yitzhak* was not addressing a case that involved civil marriage. Had he done so, Hoffmann suggests that the *Beit Yitzhak* might have ruled otherwise. However, nothing in the *Beit Yitzhak* appears to indicate this.

36. Biographical information on Jakob Hoffmann and Menachem Mendel Kirschenbaum is found in Zur, *Rabbi Dr. Jakob Hoffmann*.

37. Kirschenbaum, *Menahem Meishiv*, no. 42.

Chapter 3

1. E.g., see Hamiel, "Hatam Sofer on Reform, Hebrew, and Israel's Fate among the Nations."

2. See *Shulhan Arukh*, *Yoreh De'ah* 268:12.

3. Sofer, *Derushim va'agadot Hatam Sofer*, sermon 37.

4. Sofer, *She'eilot uteshuvot Hatam Sofer*, *Even Ha'ezer*, no. 125.

5. Ibid., *Yoreh De'ah*, no. 253.

6. Ibid., *Hoshen Mishpat*, no. 89.

7. Eger, *Teshuvot Rabbi Akiva Eger*, no. 41.

8. Katzberg, "Hungarian Jewry's War for Equal Religious Rights in the 1890s," 145.

9. The Talmud proscribes the teaching of Torah to Gentiles in Hagigah 13a and Sanhedrin 59a.

10. Ferziger, *Exclusion and Hierarchy*, 80.

11. Guttmacher, *Aderet Eliyahu*, *Yoreh De'ah*, no. 33. The prohibition forbidding a *kohein* from marrying a convert is found in *Even Ha'ezer*, no. 6, subsec. 1. For a concise summary of this prohibition, see Klein, *Guide to Jewish Religious Practice*, 383 and 387–88.

12. In the late 1840s, legislation was enacted by various German states that allowed intermarriage between Jews and Gentiles; in various parts of Hungary during the same period, legislation was enacted that permitted such marriages as well. See Baron, "Aspects of the Jewish Communal Crisis in 1848," 216.

13. Guttmacher, *Aderet Eliyahu*, *Yoreh De'ah*, no. 87.

14. See Katzberg, "Hungarian Jewry's War for Equal Religious Rights in the 1890s," where he mentions in several places that civil marriage between Jews and non-Jews was legal in Hungary during this period.

15. Guttmacher, *Aderet Eliyahu*, *Yoreh De'ah*, no. 85.

16. See Hoffmann, *Melamed Leho'il*, *Yoreh De'ah*, no. 83, and *Even Ha'ezer*, no. 8.

17. Guttmacher, *Aderet Eliyahu*, *Yoreh De'ah*, no. 87.

18. For an identical holding that employs precisely the same wording, see the opinion of Rabbi Zvi Hirsch Kalischer of Thorn, in Hildesheimer, *She'eilot uteshuvot Rabbi Azriel*, *Yoreh De'ah*, no. 229.

19. See Hoffmann, *Melamed Leho'il*, *Yoreh De'ah*, no. 83, where the same reasoning is expressed in an identical case.

20. Kramer, *From Emancipation to Catastrophe*, 4–6.

21. Ibid., 7–12 and 27.

22. Aszod, *Yehudah Ya'aleh*, no. 237.

23. For a superb description of Schlesinger, see Silber, "Emergence of Ultra-Orthodoxy," 81.

24. Schlesinger, *Lev Ha'ivri*, vol. 2, 118b–119a; also in Silber, "Emergence of Ultra-Orthodoxy," 81, where he provides a different discussion on "He'ara al inyan kabalat geirim shenitrabu bedoreinu" [Note on the Acceptance of Converts Who Have Increased in Our Time].

25. Ferziger, in *Exclusion and Hierarchy*, 56, notes that eighteenth-century rabbi Jacob Emden employed the term *eirev rav* to describe contemporary Jewish philosophers whose viewpoints provided fertile ground for deviations from traditional Jewish belief and practice. Ferziger reports that Emden, *Ḥali Khatem* 26b, wrote: "They are surely not of the seed of Israel, only descendants of the mixed multitude [*eirev rav*]." This surely indicates that Schlesinger had respected rabbinic precedent for this polemic.

26. Schick, *She'eilot uteshuvot Maharam Schick*, *Even Ha'ezer*, no. 14.

27. Ibid., *Yoreh De'ah*, no. 249.

Chapter 4

1. Liebman, "Extremism as a Religious Norm," 75.

2. Ibid., 77.

3. Ibid., 80.

4. For a masterful biography of Rabbi Weinberg, see Shapiro, *Between the Yeshiva World and Modern Orthodoxy*.

5. Weinberg, *Seridei Eish*, vol. 3, no. 50. The Bar-Ilan database, which uses a new reference-numbering system for Weinberg, calls this responsum vol. 2, no. 66.

6. Weinberg cites *Peri haSadeh*, by Rabbi Eliezer Hayim ben Avraham Deutsch, as precedent in this instance.

7. Weinberg could have argued the reverse—namely, that the fact that she was pregnant was the real reason that she wished to convert, and thus, a conversion in this instance would clearly not be "for the sake of heaven," since the impending birth of a child might increase the couple's desire for "legitimacy," which itself could be construed as an ulterior motive. (Rabbi Meir Arik makes precisely that claim later in this chapter.) It is instructive that Weinberg did not choose this argument but made the opposite claim.

8. Weinberg, *Seridei Eish*, vol. 2, no. 101; in the new numbering, vol. 2, no. 31.

9. Ibid., vol. 3, no. 100; in the new numbering, vol. 2, no. 99.

10. Feinstein quotes Weinberg on a number of matters, some related to conversion. In *Yoreh De'ah*, vol. 2, no. 132, Feinstein, in discussing whether it is permissible to teach Torah to a non-Jew, begins with a stinging rejection of the validity of Reform conversions. A Jewish man who has married a woman so converted, he asserts, has married a Gentile. Feinstein also cites Weinberg in a responsum dealing with abortion (*Igerot Moshe, Ḥoshen Mishpat*, vol. 2, no. 69) but takes issue with some of his positions. In *Igerot Moshe, Oraḥ Ḥayim*, vol. 2, no. 33, Feinstein refers to Weinberg with the title *shlita*, typically reserved for outstanding authorities.

11. Numerous halakhic sources also stipulate eight *amot* as the minimal distance required to remain to each party so that a space can be divided into two "properties." Cf., e.g., the *baraita* on BT Bava Batra 11a.

12. Weinberg, *Seridei Eish*, vol. 2, no. 95; in the new numbering, vol. 2, no. 60.

13. In general, Weinberg was very strict on matters of circumcision. Cf. ibid., vol. 2, no. 102; in the new numbering, vol. 2, no. 67, where he ruled that a man with a heart condition and diabetes, who could not withstand a circumcision, could not be converted. Weinberg dismissed arguments that the man could be converted without circumcision, while acknowledging that the man's motivation for conversion was pure and selfless. He even ruled that because of the danger to the man in question, he was not to be given the choice of having the procedure. Weinberg was clear: given his medical condition, this man was not to convert under any circumstances.

14. Weinberg wrote another responsum on circumcision, in which he discussed the permissibility of circumcising the son of a Jewish man who declared himself to be without religion. But, of course, since it is the religion of the mother that mattered here (and the mother was presumably Jewish, or there would be no question), Weinberg stated that the boy should have a full religious circumcision.

15. Weinberg, *Seridei Eish*, vol. 2, no. 96; in the new numbering, vol. 2, no. 61.

16. Note that this case is discussed in chapter 2 of this volume.

17. Breisch, *Ḥelkat Ya'akov, Yoreh De'ah*, no. 150, according to the Bar-Ilan numbering system. The responsum itself is undated.

18. Hoffmann, *Melamed Leho'il, Yoreh De'ah*, no. 85.

19. See the writings of Bamberger and Hirsch in chapter 2 of this volume.

20. Herzog's responsum is found in Breisch, *Ḥelkat Ya'akov, Yoreh De'ah*, no. 151, according to the Bar-Ilan numbering system.

21. Responsa of Maimonides, no. 111.

22. Tabak, *She'eilot uteshuvot teshurat Shai*, 3, cited in Sagi and Zohar, *Transforming Identity*, 47.

23. Horowitz, *Imrei David*, no. 124.

24. *She'eilot uteshuvot Atzei haLevanon, Yoreh De'ah*, 63a. Cited in Sagi and Zohar, *Transforming Identity*, 47.

25. *She'eilot uteshuvot aḥiezer*, 3:27. Cited in Sagi and Zohar, *Transforming Identity*, 47.

26. Rabbi Arik here uses the term *bo'eil*, which technically means "one who is having intercourse with her." It is an ironic play on the word *ba'al*, which means "husband."

27. *She'eilot uteshuvot imrei yosher*, 1:176. Cited in Sagi and Zohar, *Transforming Identity*, 50.

28. *She'eilot uteshuvot minḥat Eliezer*, 3:8. Cited in Sagi and Zohar, *Transforming Identity*, 50.

29. Feinstein, *Igerot Moshe, Yoreh De'ah*, no. 160.

30. Ibid., *Yoreh De'ah*, vol. 2, no. 128; *Even Ha'ezer*, vol. 3, nos. 2–3.

31. Ibid., *Even Ha'ezer*, vol. 3, no. 2.

32. Ibid., *Yoreh De'ah*, vol. 2, no. 125.

33. See Ellenson, "Development of Orthodox Attitudes to Conversion in the Modern Period."

34. Hoffmann, *Melamed Leho'il, Yoreh De'ah*, no. 83.

35. Interestingly, Feinstein exhibits an occasional lenient tendency. E.g., he held that, a posteriori, it might be possible to accept such a person as a convert to Judaism, even if she came to convert *lesheim ishut* (for purposes of marrying a Jewish mate). Thus, if the conversion had been conducted by Orthodox rabbinic authorities, it might be held that, at the moment of her conversion, the woman was sincere about accepting "the yoke of the commandments." Even though she was subsequently nonobservant, the conversion would still be valid. In addition, Feinstein suggested that the woman simply may not have known enough about Jewish law at the time of her conversion to have voiced her demurral. In this event, it could be held that at the time she converted, she was sincere about observing the commandments, even though such sincerity stemmed from her ignorance. Again, it would be possible to hold that the conversion was valid.

36. Feinstein, *Igerot Moshe, Even Ha'ezer*, vol. 3, nos. 2 and 4.

37. Ibid., vol. 3, no. 2. Cf. also *Yoreh De'ah*, nos. 159–60, for similar views.

38. Cf. Hoffmann, *Melamed Leho'il, Even Ha'ezer*, no. 10, where he muses on what should happen if such instances were to become more common.

39. Feinstein, *Igerot Moshe, Yoreh De'ah*, no. 157.

40. In Hoffmann, *Melamed Leho'il, Yoreh De'ah*, no. 87, he says of a *safeik geir* (a person of dubious conversion): "Ideally, they should inform him of some of the commandments that he undoubtedly would want to perform, such as (prohibitions against) idolatry, incest, murder, the commandment of charity, respect for one's parents and loving one's fellow person, and then he should simply state that he accepts the commandments of the Jews, but none of this should imply any obstacle to his conversion." Similarly, in other cases in which Hoffmann rules, it was patently obvious that the convert would not be observant; after all, those Jews who had married their non-Jewish partners in civil ceremonies were obviously not

observant. Why, then, would it be reasonable to assume that their spouses would be observant after conversion?

41. It is not entirely clear, incidentally, what Feinstein's attitude toward Hoffmann was. Feinstein cites Hoffmann, *Melamed Leho'il*, in six responsa but only references the book, never actually mentioning Hoffmann by name. Cf. that Weinberg refers to Hoffmann as haGa'on, "the Great Sage" (in *Seridei Eish*, vol. 2, no. 19; in the new numbering, vol. 2, no. 40) and by name in numerous instances. Feinstein uses the appellation *haGa'on* in hundreds of instances but not in reference to Hoffmann. Weinberg succeeded Hoffmann five years after Hoffmann's death as head of the Hildesheimer rabbinical seminary. It could be that what we have is an internal Orthodox division between what sociologists label "modern Orthodox Judaism" and "traditionalist or enclavist Orthodoxy." See Heilman, *Sliding to the Right*, 2–5, on this division in the Orthodox world.

42. Cf., e.g., Hoffmann, *Melamed Leho'il*, *Even Ha'ezer*, nos. 22 and 51, where he refers to *rabanim mehadeshim* (innovating rabbis) or 3:29, where he refers to *harav shel hamehadeshim* (the rabbi of the innovators), using, in each case, the standard Hebrew word for "rabbi."

43. Cf., e.g., Weinberg, *Seridei Eish*, vol. 2, no. 95 and vol. 3, no. 28; in the new numbering, vol. 1, no. 93 and vol. 2, no. 60, respectively.

44. Cf., e.g., Feinstein, *Igerot Moshe*, *Even Ha'ezer*, vol. 1, no. 135; and vol. 3, no. 4.

45. Feinstein, *Igerot Moshe*, *Yoreh De'ah*, vol. 2, no. 125.

46. Levy's responsum is reported in Bernstein, *Challenge and Mission*, 43–44.

47. Levy's speech to the RCA is reported in "Rabbi Urges Leniency in Conversion Practices," *Jewish Post*, July 4, 1952, 1.

48. In a study conducted on the actual practice of American Orthodox rabbis regarding conversion and intermarriage in the 1960s, it appears that Levy was simply giving voice to the position in which countless community rabbis found themselves. See Ehrman and Fenster, "Conversion and American Orthodox Judaism," 53.

49. For a more detailed exploration of Illowy's religious attitudes in general and his stance on these issues in particular, see Ellenson, "Jewish Legal Decision by Rabbi Bernard Illowy of New Orleans and Its Discussion in Nineteenth-Century Europe," 101 ff.

50. Jack Simcha Cohen, "Conversion of Children Born to Gentile Mothers and Jewish Fathers."

51. Ibid., 21.

52. Ibid., 7.

53. Ibid., 22.

54. Ibid.

55. Another Los Angeles–based scholar, Rabbi Shmuel Hayim HaKohen Katz, a student of the Slobodka Yeshiva who was later ordained in Israel by Rabbi Isaac

Halevi Herzog and who in 1945 became rabbi of Congregation Ohev Shalom and *av beit din* of the RCA Rabbinical Court of Southern California, also ruled leniently on a matter of conversion, allowing a Jewish couple to adopt a Gentile baby in such fashion that the baby would not later have the right to reject the conversion. Katz's responsum is much more a legal analysis of the precedents that allow him to arrive at a defensible position that would ensure that the child could not reject the conversion upon reaching adulthood. Katz raises no sociological or interdenominational issues in the responsum. It is perhaps because of its exclusively halakhic nature that Katz receives a warm response from Feinstein, which is also included in Katz's volume. Cf. Katz, *Sefer Devar Shmuel*, sec. 1, 1–18.

56. Liberman, "Sephardic Ban on Converts," 49–50.

57. Quoted in ibid., 50–51.

58. Quoted in ibid., 51.

59. Quoted in Zemer, "Rabbinic Ban on Conversion in Argentina," 84.

60. Ibid., 93–96.

61. Cf. chapter 5 of this volume for a brief discussion of Rabbi Ben-Zion Uziel's support for those who sought to violate the ban.

62. Samuel Freedman, *Jew vs. Jew*, 91–92.

63. See the moving account in the introduction to the *Seridei Eish*, where Weinberg describes how Berkovits saved his responsa from destruction during the Holocaust and made their publication possible.

64. Samuel Freedman, *Jew vs. Jew*, 92. See also "Rabbinical Council Institutes New Programs to Equalize All Conversions," *Intermountain Jewish News* (February 10, 1978): 10.

65. Wertheimer, *People Divided*, 171–72.

66. Quoted in Samuel Freedman, *Jew vs. Jew*, 94.

67. Ibid., 110.

68. Quoted in Wertheimer, *People Divided*, 173.

69. Quoted in ibid.

Chapter 5

1. E.g., in *Alian (Hava) Pessaro (Goldstein) and the Movement for Reform Judaism in Israel v. the Minister of the Interior and the Director of Population Registry* (HCJ 1031/93), the Supreme Court refused to become involved in the question of whether a woman who had converted to Judaism in a Reform ceremony in Israel should be entitled to be registered as a Jew by virtue of the Law of Return. The court recognized that Israeli law does not employ a single definition of "Jewishness" across all areas of law and that a person might be regarded as a Jew in one situation (e.g., a civil law issue) but not in another (where a halakhic definition might be required). For a summary of this case, cf. Supreme Court of Israel, "Non-Orthodox Conversions in Israel."

2. For this reason, Israel's Supreme Court rulings, including those of 2005, which were quite significant, are not covered in this chapter.

3. Cf. extensive references to Liebman, "Extremism as a Religious Norm," in chapter 4 of this volume.

4. Kook, *Da'at Kohein*, no. 155, 281.

5. BT Mo'ed Katan 28a.

6. The Hebrew for "impudence" here is *she'at nefesh*, a paraphrase of Ezek. 36:5.

7. The phrase is taken from BT Gittin 17a, in which the original reference is to an argument that is simply not debatable.

8. Kook, *Da'at Kohein*, no. 147.

9. Ibid., 267. Kook reiterates this point in a defense of this responsum, *Da'at Kohein*, no. 148, 272.

10. Ibid., no. 149.

11. Ibid., no. 150, 275.

12. Sagi and Zohar note that Kook's corpus seems internally inconsistent. They suggest that *Da'at Kohein*, nos. 153 and 154, regarding whether the convert's inner thoughts are relevant even as he utters a statement to the effect that he will observe the commandments, actually disagree with each other. In *Da'at Kohein*, no. 153, Kook says that any internal thoughts are irrelevant; in no. 154, he argues that the convert's mind must conform to what he is saying publicly.

13. For a biography of Rabbi Uziel and an analysis of his teachings, see Angel, *Loving Truth and Peace*.

14. Cited in *Encyclopaedia Judaica*, 12:1527, s.v. "Ouziel."

15. According to Maimonides, in *Hilkhot Isurei Bi'ah*, 12:6, and Karo, *Shulḥan Arukh, Even Ha'ezer*, 17:2, Jews who have regular sexual relationships with Gentiles are subject to *kareit*. This punishment reflects the severity that the rabbis wished to accord intermarriage. Rabbi Uziel, like Rabbi David Hoffmann in his responsa, wanted the Jewish man to avoid this fate and hence urged that the non-Jewish partner be converted.

16. Uziel, *Piskei Uziel*, no. 65. See also Sagi and Zohar, *Transforming Identity*, 71 ff., for an instructive discussion of this responsum.

17. This metaphor is a rabbinic phrase suggesting that one trouble seems to draw another in its wake. For uses of the phrase in aggadic literature, cf., inter alia, Midrash Tanhuma (Warsaw edition), *Parashat Mikeitz*, par. 10, s.v. *ve'eil shadai*; Tanhuma (Warsaw), *Parashat vayigash*, par. 5, s.v. *vayigash*; and Yalkut Shimoni, *Parashat vayigash*, 150.

18. The reference to Israel and Jews as wayward sheep is ubiquitous in rabbinic literature. Its biblical roots are apparently Jer. 23:1 (Ah, shepherds who let the flock of My pasture stray and scatter!—declares the Lord) and Jer. 50:6 (My people were lost sheep: their shepherds led them astray). Note that in both instances, the verse ascribes the blame not to the people but to the shepherds. Uziel

apparently does not want to take action that, in his role as a leader of the Jewish community, would lead to his being counted among those shepherds.

19. Ezek. 34:4.

20. Feinstein, *Igerot Moshe, Yoreh De'ah*, no. 157.

21. Uziel, *Mishpetei Uziel, Yoreh De'ah*, vol. 1, no. 58. Also cited in Sagi and Zohar, *Transforming Identity*, 229.

22. Hoffmann, *Melamed Leho'il, Even Ha'ezer*, no. 8.

23. Uziel, *Piskei Uziel*, no. 63; also cited in Sagi and Zohar, *Transforming Identity*, 78.

24. The Malachi passage is not a legal verse and is from one of the books of the Prophets instead of the Pentateuch. Such prophetic passages are not commonly cited in support of a halakhic argument.

25. Cover, "Supreme Court, 1982 Term—Foreword: *Nomos* and Narrative," 4–5.

26. Dworkin, "Is Law a System of Rules?," 45 ff.

27. Hoffmann, *Melamed Leho'il, Even Ha'ezer*, no. 10.

28. Uziel cites the reference as Avraham Preiss, *Mishnat Avraham*, 7.

29. Uziel, *Piskei Uziel*, no. 75, 449 ff. Uziel does allow for one exception in this responsum. He says that when obviously observant Jews were married in civil courts because of fear of the government, there is reason to view such a marriage as having effect. But even this caveat does nothing to mitigate his generally dismissive attitude toward civil marriage.

30. This comment is made at the bottom of p. 433 of *Piskei Uziel*.

31. Uziel, *Piskei Uziel*, no. 59. The editors of the printed version of *Piskei Uziel* note that this responsum is also referenced as *Mishpetei Uziel*, vol. 1, *Yoreh De'ah*, no. 14.

32. Though unstated, Uziel is obviously assuming that the children already born would be converted.

33. Cf. our discussion of these sources in chapter 1 of this volume.

34. Uziel, *Mishpetei Uziel, Even Ha'ezer*, no. 20. This responsum is also cited in Sagi and Zohar, *Transforming Identity*, 229.

35. In another responsum, *Piskei Uziel*, no. 65, Rabbi Uziel matter-of-factly makes what seems the rather astonishing assertion that "stipulations about observing the commandments do not affect the validity of the conversion, even before the fact." It would be difficult to interpret Bekhorot 30b in this light.

36. Uziel, *Piskei Uziel*, no. 61. Cf. discussion of this ban in chapter 4 of this volume.

37. We first saw this argument in the famous responsum of Maimonides, in chapter 1 of this volume.

38. Uziel, *Piskei Uziel*, no. 64.

39. Ibid., no. 67. The petitioner had claimed that having non-Jewish wives come to Israel would increase incidences of *mamzeirut* (illegitimacy) in Israel.

However, Uziel points out that, according to Jewish law, the children of intermarriage are not considered illegitimate; they are simply non-Jews. Uziel correctly points out that to suggest that they are illegitimate is to err.

40. The reference is clearly to Judg. 11:10.

41. Two books that provide detailed discussions of the life and teachings of Rabbi Yosef have appeared in the past decade: Lau, *Mimaran ad maran*; and Picard, *Mishnato shel harav Ovadiah Yosef.*

42. For an anecdote that illustrates this point, see Lau, *Mimaran ad maran*, 11–12; see also Picard, *Mishnato shel harav Ovadiah Yosef*, 87–131, for a balanced discussion of the moderation that marks the rulings and informs the legal philosophy of Rabbi Yosef.

43. See Picard, *Mishnato shel harav Ovadiah Yosef*, 119–23.

44. Yosef, *Yabia Omer, Even Ha'ezer*, vol. 2, no. 3.

45. Ibid., no. 4.

46. Yosef discusses this case in his *"Bayot hagiyur bizmaneinu*—Problems of Conversion in Our Time," 21–32, esp. 29. Rabbi Yosef, after indicating that a candidate for conversion living on a nonreligious kibbutz should not be accepted into Judaism, justifies his decision by appealing to the "subjective principle"—*vehakol lefi re'ut hadayan*, "everything depends upon the judgment of the rabbi"—to bolster his case for rejection. This is the first time that we have seen this principle invoked for "stringency," not "leniency." Cited in Zemer, *Evolving Halakhah*, 125.

47. Yosef, *Yabia Omer, Yoreh De'ah*, vol. 8, no. 24.

48. This brief biographical sketch has been taken, with only minor emendation, from the biography of Rabbi Herzog provided on the Bar-Ilan University Responsa CD-ROM.

49. Herzog, *Heikhal Yitzhak, Even Ha'ezer*, vol. 1, no. 20.

50. Ibid., no. 21.

51. Herzog's response is found in Breisch's *Helkat Ya'akov*, no. 14.

52. Herzog, *Heikhal Yitzhak, Even Ha'ezer*, vol. 1, no. 19. The problem is raised because Jewish law does not allow a *kohein* to marry a convert or a divorced woman.

53. Ibid., no. 21.

54. This should not be construed to mean that Herzog took the same position as Hoffmann on civil marriage in every case or that Herzog had a generally positive outlook regarding civil marriage. In another responsum (*Heikhal Yitzhak, Even Ha'ezer*, vol. 2, no. 31), Herzog rules that a woman previously married to a Jew only by civil marriage is by no means considered to be married (p. 124). But here, too, we see the external motivation of the *posek* affecting his view of these social institutions. In our case, *Even Ha'ezer*, vol. 1, no. 21, Herzog's decision to give credence to civil marriage helps him permit a conversion. In *Even Ha'ezer*, vol. 2, no. 31, implicitly denying the significance of civil marriage allows him to permit a woman to remarry. Thus, despite the seemingly inconsistent natures of

his responses, it is the underlying principle or conception of what Jewish life is ultimately about (à la Robert Cover, above) that actually renders them entirely consistent.

55. Cf. *Piskei Uziel*, no. 67, where Uziel also addresses the problems of intermarried families coming to Israel, though he, unlike Rabbi Herzog, makes no far-reaching statements about the significance of the State in that responsum.

56. Unterman, "Hilkhot geirut vederekh bitzu'an," 17 ff. This article is cited at length in Finkelstein, *Hagiyur, halakhah uma'aseh*, 139n289.

57. For a biography of Goren, see Shalom Freedman, *Rabbi Shlomo Goren*.

58. As reported in the *Jewish Telegraph Agency*, November 5, 1980, on the occasion of Seidman's death.

59. Cf., e.g., Goren, *Torat haMedinah*, 168: "Reform conversion has nothing in common with conversion to Judaism as it has been accepted among the Jewish people for 3,233 years." Indeed, most of Goren's chapter on conversion in *Torat haMedinah* (esp. 168–71) is devoted to Reform conversion and how to ensure that neither the Israeli courts nor Israel's Ministry of the Interior grant it recognition.

60. J. David Bleich, "Conversion Crisis," 36–37.

61. Goren here is reported to have cited the views of Rabbi Isser Yehuda Unterman from the essay cited above in n. 57.

62. Goren, "Hagiyur ba'aretz uvahutz la'aretz," 186.

63. Ibid.

64. Ibid., 188.

65. Ibid., 189.

66. Halakhically, *mamzeirim* may only marry other *mamzeirim* and converts, not a very large pool from which to choose; the children of these unions are also *mamzeirim*, making such marriages undesirable options.

67. Washofsky, "Case of the Brother and Sister," vii.

68. Abramov, *Perpetual Dilemma*, 189, reports that Dayan threatened to demand the establishment of a system of civil marriage in Israel if a satisfactory solution was not found to the problem confronting the Langer brother and sister. Golda Meir, demanding that the chief rabbinate alleviate the plight of the Langer children, stated: "It is impossible to live in this country under the existing procedures of the chief rabbinate" (*Ma'ariv*, June 29, 1972, 3). On the political context and background for this case, see Washofsky, "Case of the Brother and the Sister," esp. the appendix "The Langer Case as Public Issue," 191–206, which provides a comprehensive and incisive description and analysis of this chapter in Israeli history.

69. Goren, *Pesak hadin be'inyan ha'ah veha'ahot*.

70. See Ellenson, "Retroactive Annulment of Conversion."

71. Discussed in chapter 4 of this volume.

72. "Israel's Conflict Within," *New York Times* editorial, November 26, 1997,

http://www.nytimes.com/1997/11/26/opinion/israel-s-conflict-within.html
(accessed July 8, 2011).

73. Quoted in Schmemann, "Accord on Conversion May Elude Netanyahu."

74. Ibid.

75. Schmemann, " 'Who's a Jew' Puzzle Gets More Tangled."

76. Even the non-Orthodox movements in Israel did not consider the Ne'eman Commission's proposed compromise very satisfying. Consider the statement issued by Rabbi Eric Yoffie, president of the Union for Reform Judaism:

> According to Ne'eman, the scenario will be as follows: Individual Orthodox rabbis will defy the Chief Rabbinate and will agree to work with Reform and Conservative rabbis in a Jewish studies institute; graduates of this institute will then be referred to newly created special Rabbinical Conversion Courts, to which the Chief Rabbis will appoint moderate judges; these Conversion Courts will then agree to convert most graduates of the Jewish studies institute, with the Chief Rabbis' implicit approval. The problem with this scenario is that it does not confer upon us the formal recognition provided by the original proposals of the Commission; at best, it gives us a very minor, totally unofficial role in the conversion process that would hardly justify the far-reaching concessions we have made. The heart of the Ne'eman recommendations was the willingness of the Chief Rabbinate to work with the Reform and Conservative movements in a joint studies institute leading to conversion, and this is precisely what is now omitted. Thus, what we gain from this proposal is nothing. Furthermore, even on this basis it is unlikely to occur because it ignores the fact that the Chief Rabbis have continued their nonstop attacks on the recommendations and on Reform and Conservative Judaism. To assume that they will now cooperate covertly in implementing these proposals, even in this form, is simply absurd. (http://urj.org/about/union/leadership/yoffie/archive/reptisrl, accessed July 8, 2011)

77. Finkelstein, *Hagiyur, halakhah uma'aseh.*

78. Finkelstein, "Conversion in the Age of Immigration," 47; emphasis in original.

79. Dr. Moshe Zilberg (b. 1900) became chief judge of the High Court of Jerusalem. A lecturer at the Hebrew University, he wrote numerous articles in the Jerusalem press on the justice system.

80. Quoted in Finkelstein, "Conversion in the Age of Immigration," 48.

81. Ibid., 49.

82. Ibid., 55.

83. Zohar and Sagi, *Giyur vezehut Yehudit.*

84. Schmelkes, *Beit Yitzhak*, vol. 2, no. 200.

85. BT Shabbat 31a.

86. Zohar, "For the Information of Those Who Are Strict in the Acceptance of Converts," 40.

87. Ibid., 41.

88. Ibid.

89. Ibid., 42.

90. Bin-Nun, "We Should Perform Mass, Centralized Conversion," 68–69.

91. Ariel, "Conversion of Immigrants from the Former Soviet Union."

92. Ibid., 82.

93. Ibid., 97.

94. Ibid., 89.

95. Ibid., 90.

96. Cf. ibid., 91.

97. The phrase *tinok shenishba bein hanokhrim*, "an infant who was kidnapped [from among Jews and raised] among Gentiles," appears twice in the Babylonian Talmud, both times in BT Shabbat 68b. A person who falls under this category is not considered liable for any sins that he commits.

98. Ariel, "Conversion of Immigrants from the Former Soviet Union," 94. In taking this stance, Ariel is obviously stretching Jewish law beyond its normal limits. After all, the category of *tinok shenishba* classically refers to persons born of Jewish mothers who are raised outside the framework of traditional Jewish practice. In the case of these Russian converts, the rabbinic court would be bringing people born outside the Jewish faith into Judaism. Thus, one might assume that the rabbinic court would be culpable for not informing the prospective convert of the punishments attached to nonobservance. The failure of Ariel to make this distinction explicit indicates how much his position is influenced by policy considerations and his desire to identify these people through conversion as "halakhic Jews."

99. Rosenfeld, " 'A Time to Act' in the Conversion of Mixed [Marriage] Families," 223 ff. The phrase "It is time to act," is taken from M. Berakhot 9:5 and BT Berakhot 54a, 63a, inter alia, where the ancient sages of the Talmud, writing on the phrase, " 'It is time to act on behalf of the Lord,' they have violated your Torah," play with the word "violate," reading it as an imperative, hence rendering the passage, " 'It is time to act on behalf of the Lord'; violate your Torah." This understanding has been employed by rabbis throughout the centuries to allow for unprecedented flexibility in Jewish law when confronting an emergency situation of grave consequence.

100. Ibid., 224.

101. Ibid., 225.

102. Cf., e.g., "Israeli Rabbis Nix Diaspora Conversion, Divorce," *Jewish Daily Forward*, May 26, 2006, http://www.forward.com/articles/1024 (accessed July 8, 2011).

103. See "Rabbi Moshe Feinstein and *Igerot Moshe*" in chapter 4 of this volume.

104. "Thousands 'Not Jewish' after Conversion Row," *Jewish Chronicle*, May 9, 2008.

105. Nahshoni, "Chief Rabbi Metzger Supports Conversions Annulment." "Fortifying the Walls of Conversion" was the name of the conference at which Metzger made his remarks.

106. Since there were no local rabbinic authorities in Brazil, the community turned to leaders of Eastern Europe with their questions. Throughout Jewish history, outlying small communities have often turned to geographically distant halakhic authorities renowned for their learning to render decisions on matters of Jewish legal import.

107. *Encyclopaedia Judaica*, 16:1183.

108. Nahshoni, "Conversion Bill to Face First Reading."

109. Quoted in Ain, "Israel Conversion Bill a Hard Sell to Jews."

110. Quoted in ibid.

111. Nadler, "Unwelcome Mat."

112. Ibid.

Conclusion

1. Hirsch, *Horeb*, 20.

2. Feinstein, *Igerot Moshe, Orah Hayim*, vol. 4, no. 49. Emphasis ours.

3. Halevi, *Aseh lekha rav*, vol. 7, no. 54. This translation of the Halevi responsum is taken from Walzer et al., *Jewish Political Tradition*, 295–97.

4. Ettlinger, *Binyan Tziyon*, no. 149.

5. Hoffmann, *Melamed Leho'il, Yoreh De'ah*, no. 85.

Bibliography

Primary Sources

Amsalem, Ḥayim. *Sefer zera Yisra'eil: Ḥikrei halakhah be'inyanei geirut vegiyur, uvedin goyim mizera Yisra'eil vetze'etza'eihem haba'im lehitgayer.* 2 vols. Jerusalem: Mekhon mekabetz nidḥe Yisra'eil, 2010.

Ariel, Yigal. "Conversion of Immigrants from the Former Soviet Union." (Hebrew.) *Teḥumin* 12 (1991): 81–97.

Aszod, Judah. *Yehudah Ya'aleh.* Brooklyn, N.Y.: Gevirtz, 2001.

Bamberger, Yitzhak Dov Halevi. *Yad Halevi.* Ed. Shelomoh Adler. 2 vols. Jerusalem: privately printed, 1965–72.

Bin-Nun, Yoel. "We Should Perform Mass, Centralized Conversion." *Eretz Acheret* 17 (Av–Elul 5763 [July–August 2003]): 68–69.

Breisch, Mordecai Yaakov. *Ḥelkat Ya'akov.* Bnei Brak: Eshel, 1968.

Chajes, Zvi Hirsch. *She'eilot uteshuvot.* Zolkiev, 1850.

Cohen, Jack Simcha. "The Conversion of Children Born to Gentile Mothers and Jewish Fathers." In Cohen, *Intermarriage and Conversion: A Halakhic Solution,* 3–40. Hoboken, N.J.: Ktav, 1987.

Eger, Akiva. *Teshuvot Rabbi Akiva Eger.* Vienna, 1889.

Ettlinger, Jacob. *Binyan Tziyon.* Altona, 1868.

Feinstein, Moshe. *Igerot Moshe.* 8 vols. New York: privately printed, 1959–96.

Goren, Shlomo. "Hagiyur ba'aretz uvahutz la'aretz" [Conversion in the Land of Israel and outside the Land of Israel]. In Goren, *Mishnat haMedinah,* 186–90. Jerusalem: Ha'idra rabbah, 1998–99.

———. *Mishnat haMedinah.* Jerusalem: Ha'idra rabbah, 1998–99.

———. *Pesak hadin be'inyan ha'aḥ veha'aḥot* [The ruling in the case of the brother and the sister]. Israeli Chief Rabbinate, 1972.

———. *Torat haMedinah.* Jerusalem: Ha'idra rabbah, 1995–96.

Guttmacher, Eliyahu. *Aderet Eliyahu.* Jerusalem: Mossad harav Kook, 1984.

Halevi, Ḥayim David. *Aseh lekha rav.* 9 vols. Tel Aviv: Hava'adah lehotza'at kitvei ha-g. R. Ḥ. D. Halevi, 1976–89.

Herzog, Isaac Halevi. *Heikhal Yitzḥak.* Jerusalem: Agudah lehotza'at kitvei harav Herzog, 1960–72.

Hildesheimer, Esriel. *She'eilot uteshuvot Rabbi Azriel.* 2 vols. Tel Aviv: Hafatzah biyede Ḥ. Gitler, 1969–76.

Hirsch, Samson Raphael. *Shemesh Marpe.* Brooklyn, N.Y.: Messorah, 1992.

Hoffmann, David Tzvi. *Melamed Leho'il.* 3 vols. in 1 bk. New York: Noble, 1954.

Horovitz, Marcus. *Mattei Levi.* Frankfurt, 1881.

Horowitz, David Halevi. *Imrei David.* Byelgora, 1933.

Karo, Joseph Ben-Ephraim. *Beit Yosef.* Included in standard editions of the *Arba'ah Turim.*

——. *Shulḥan Arukh.* Kraków, 1578–80.

Katz, Shmuel Ḥayim HaKohen. *Sefer Devar Shmuel.* Los Angeles: privately printed, 1986.

Kirschenbaum, Menachem Mendel. *Menaḥem Meishiv.* Ed. Efraim Fischel Klein. New York: Hamakhon leheker ba'ayot hayahadut haḥaredit, 1965.

Kook, Abraham Isaac. *Da'at Kohein.* Jerusalem: Mossad harav Kook, 1985.

Maimonides. *Mishneh Torah.*

——. *Responsa of Maimonides.* Ed. Yehoshua Blau. 4 vols. Jerusalem: Reuven Mass, 1986.

Rosenfeld, Shlomo. "'A Time to Act' in the Conversion of Mixed [Marriage] Families." (Hebrew.) *Teḥumin* 17 (1997): 177–232.

Schick, Maharam. *She'eilot uteshuvot Maharam Schick.* 3 vols. Munkács, 1880–81; Lemberg, 1884.

Schlesinger, Akiva Yosef. *Lev Ha'ivri.* Jerusalem, 1989.

Schmelkes, Yitzḥak. *Beit Yitzḥak.* Przemysl, 1901.

Sofer, Ḥatam [Moshe Schreiber]. *Derushim va'agadot Ḥatam Sofer.* Ed. Shlomoh Spitzer and Israel Stern. Jerusalem and London: E. Stern, 1997.

——. *She'eilot uteshuvot Ḥatam Sofer.* 3 vols. Bnei Brak: Sifrei Kodesh Mishor, 1990.

Tabak, Solomon. *She'eilot uteshuvot teshurat Shai.* 2nd ed. Sigal, 1897.

Unterman, Isser Yehuda. "Hilkhot geirut vederekh bitzu'an." *Toshba (Torah She-Ba'al Peh)* 13 (1971): 13 ff.

Uziel, Ben-Zion Meir. *Mishpetei Uziel.* 2nd ed. Jerusalem: Hava'ad lehotza'at kit-vei harav, z'l, 1994–95.

——. *Piskei Uziel bisheilot hazeman.* Jerusalem: Mossad harav Kook, 1977.

Weinberg, Yehiel Yaakov. *Seridei Eish.* 4 vols. in 2 bks. Jerusalem: Mossad harav Kook, 1977.

Yosef, Ovadiah. "*Bayot hagiyur bizmaneinu*—Problems of Conversion in Our Time." *Toshba (Torah She-Ba'al Peh)* 13 (1971): 21–32.

——. *Yabia Omer.* 10 vols. Jerusalem: Makhon me'or Yisra'eil, 1954–76.

Zohar, Zvi. "For the Information of Those Who Are Strict in the Acceptance of Converts." *Eretz Acheret*, no. 17 (Av–Elul 5763 [July–August 2003]): 38–43.

Other Sources

Bar-Ilan Responsa Project Database. Ramat-Gan: Bar-Ilan University, 1972–2008.
Encyclopaedia Judaica. Jerusalem: Keter, 1972.
Talmudic Encyclopedia. Jerusalem: Talmudic Encyclopedia Publications, 1965.

Secondary Sources

Abramov, S. Z. *Perpetual Dilemma: Jewish Religion in the Jewish State.* Cranbury, N.J.: Associated University Presses, 1976.
Ain, Stewart. "Israel Conversion Bill a Hard Sell to Jews." *Jewish Week*, April 27, 2010, http://www.thejewishweek.com/news/new york/israel_conversion _bill_hard_sell_us_jews (accessed July 8, 2011). Angel, Marc D. *Loving Truth and Peace: The Grand Religious Worldview of Rabbi Benzion Uziel.* Northvale, N.J.: Jason Aronson, 1999.
Baron, Salo W. "Aspects of the Jewish Communal Crisis in 1848." *Jewish Social Studies* 14, no. 2 (April 1952): 9–24.
Berger, Peter L. *The Heretical Imperative: Contemporary Possibilities of Religious Affirmation.* Garden City, N.Y.: Anchor, 1979.
Bernstein, Louis. *Challenge and Mission: The Emergence of the English-Speaking Orthodox Rabbinate.* New York: Sheingold, 1983.
Bleich, J. David. "The Conversion Crisis: A Halakhic Analysis." In *The Conversion Crisis: Essays from the Pages of Tradition*, ed. Emanuel Feldman and Joel Wolowelsky, 19–45. New York: Ktav, 1990.
Bleich, Judith. "Jacob Ettlinger: His Life and Works." Ph.D. diss., New York University, 1974.
Broyde, Michael, and Shmuel Kadosh. "Review Essay." *Tradition* 42, no. 1 (2009): 84–103.
Carlin, Jerome E., and Saul H. Mendlovitz. "The American Rabbi: A Religious Specialist Responds to Loss of Authority." In *Understanding American Judaism*, ed. Jacob Neusner, 1:165–214. New York: Ktav, 1975.
Cohen, Shaye J. D. "Conversion to Judaism in Historical Perspective: From Biblical History to Post-Biblical Judaism." *Conservative Judaism* 36, no. 4 (summer 1983): 31–45.
———. "From the Bible to the Talmud: The Prohibition of Intermarriage." *Hebrew Annual Review* 7 (1983): 23–39.
———. "The Origins of the Matrilineal Principle in Rabbinic Law." *AJS Review* 10, no. 1 (spring 1985): 19–53.
———. "The Rabbinic Conversion Ceremony." *Journal of Jewish Studies* 41, no. 2 (1990): 176–203.
Cohen, Stuart A. *Israel and Its Army: From Cohesion to Confusion.* London: Routledge, 2008.

———. "Relationships between Religiously Observant and Other Troops in the IDF: Vision Versus Reality." October 6, 2010, http://www.yutorah.org/lectures/lecture.cfm.749586/Rabbi%20Dr.%20Aharon%20Lichtenstein/Relationships%20Between%20Religiously%20Observant%20and%20Other%20Troops%20in%20the%20IDF:%20Vision%20Versus%20Reality (accessed July 8, 2011).

Cover, Robert M. "The Supreme Court, 1982 Term—Foreword: *Nomos* and Narrative." *Harvard Law Review* 97, no. 4 (1983): 4–68.

Daniszewski, John. "No Place to Bury Teen Bomb Victim." *Los Angeles Times*, August 5, 1997, A1.

Davis, Moshe. "Mixed Marriage in Western Jewry: Historical Background to the Jewish Response." *Jewish Journal of Sociology* 10, no. 2 (December 1968): 177–221.

Duckesz, E. "Zur Biographie des Chacham Jsaak Bernays." *Jahrbuch der Jüdisch-Literarischen Gesellschaft* 5 (1907): 321–22.

Dworkin, Ronald. "Is Law a System of Rules?" In *The Philosophy of Law*, ed. Dworkin, 38–65. Oxford: Oxford University Press, 1977.

Ehrman, Albert, and C. Abraham Fenster. "Conversion and American Orthodox Judaism: A Research Note." *Jewish Journal of Sociology* 10, no. 1 (June 1968): 47–53.

Eliav, Mordecai, ed. *Rabbiner Esriel Hildesheimer Briefe*. Jerusalem: R. Mass, 1965.

———. "*Torah im Derekh Eretz* in Hungary." (Hebrew.) *Sinai* 51, nos. 2–3 (Iyar–Sivan 5722 [1961]): 127–42.

Ellenson, David. *After Emancipation: Jewish Religious Responses to Modernity*. Cincinnati: Hebrew Union College Press, 2004.

———. "The Development of Orthodox Attitudes to Conversion in the Modern Period." In Ellenson, *Tradition in Transition: Orthodoxy, Halakhah, and the Boundaries of Modern Jewish Identity*, 61–80. Lanham, Md.: University Press of America, 1989.

———. "A Jewish Legal Decision by Rabbi Bernard Illowy of New Orleans and Its Discussion in Nineteenth-Century Europe." In Ellenson, *Tradition in Transition: Orthodoxy, Halakhah, and the Boundaries of Modern Jewish Identity*, 101–22. Lanham, Md.: University Press of America, 1989.

———. "Jewish Legal Interpretation: Literary, Scriptural, Social, and Ethical Perspectives." *Semeia* 34 (1985): 93–114.

———. "Retroactive Annulment of Conversion: A Survey of Representative Halakhic Sources." In *Conversion to Judaism in Jewish Law*, ed. Walter Jacob and Moshe Zemer, 49–66. Pittsburgh and Tel Aviv: Rodef Shalom Press, 1994.

Ferziger, Adam. *Exclusion and Hierarchy: Orthodoxy, Nonobservance, and the Emergence of Modern Jewish Identity*. Philadelphia: University of Pennsylvania Press, 2005.

Finkelstein, Menachem. "Conversion in the Age of Immigration." *Justice*, no.

19 (winter 1998): 47–49, 55, http://www.intjewishlawyers.org/main/files
/Justice%20No.19%20Winter1998.pdf (accessed July 8, 2011).

———. *Conversion: Halakhah and Practice,* trans. Edward Levin. Ramat-Gan:
Bar-Ilan University Press, 2006.

———. *Hagiyur, halakhah uma'aseh* [Proselytism, halakhah, and practice]. Ramat-
Gan: Bar-Ilan University Press, 1994.

Freedman, Samuel G. *Jew vs. Jew: The Struggle for the Soul of American Jewry.* New
York: Simon and Schuster, 2000.

Freedman, Shalom. *Rabbi Shlomo Goren: Torah Sage and General.* Jerusalem:
Urim, 2006.

Gordis, Daniel H. "David Zevi Hoffmann on Civil Marriage: Evidence of a Traditional Community under Siege." *Modern Judaism* 10, no. 1 (1990): 85–103.

Hamiel, Ḥaim. "The Ḥatam Sofer on Reform, Hebrew, and Israel's Fate among
the Nations." (Hebrew.) *Sinai* 44, no. 3 (Kislev 5725 [1964]): 164–66.

Hartman, Donniel. *The Boundaries of Judaism.* London: Continuum, 2007.

Heilman, Samuel. *Sliding to the Right: The Contest for the Future of American Jewish Orthodoxy.* Berkeley: University of California Press, 2006.

Hirsch, Samson Raphael. *Horeb: A Philosophy of Jewish Laws and Observances.*
Trans. I. Grunfeld. London: Soncino, 1962.

Horovitz, Marcus. *Frankfurter Rabbinen.* 4 vols. Frankfurt, 1882–85.

Hume, David. *Enquiry Concerning the Principles of Morals.* Ed. L. A. Selby-Bigge.
Oxford: Oxford University Press, 1975.

Illoway, Henry. *Sefer Milḥamot Elohim: The Controversial Letters and the Casuistic
Decisions of the Late Rabbi Dr. Bernard Illowy.* (Hebrew, German, and English.) Berlin: M. Poppelauer, 1914.

Katzberg, Nathaniel. "Hungarian Jewry's War for Equal Religious Rights in the
1890s." (Hebrew.) *Tziyon* 22, nos. 2–3 (5717 [1956/57]): 119–48.

Klein, Isaac. *A Guide to Jewish Religious Practice.* New York: Jewish Theological
Seminary, 1979.

Kramer, T. D. *From Emancipation to Catastrophe: The Rise and Holocaust of Hungarian Jewry.* Lanham, Md.: University Press of America, 2000.

Lau, Binyamin. *Mimaran ad maran: Mishnato hahilkhatit shel harav Ovadiah Yosef*
[From our master to our master: The halakhic philosophy of Rabbi Ovadiah Yosef]. Tel Aviv: Yediot Aḥaronot, 2005.

Levine, Robert N., and David H. Ellenson. "Jewish Tradition, Contemporary
Sensibilities, and Halacha: A Responsum by Rabbi David Zvi Hoffmann."
Journal of Reform Judaism 30, no. 1 (1983): 49–56.

Liberman, S. Zevulun. "A Sephardic Ban on Converts." In *The Conversion Crisis:
Essays from the Pages of Tradition,* ed. Emanuel Feldman and Joel B. Wolowelsky, 49–52. New York: Ktav, 1990.

Liebman, Charles S. "Extremism as a Religious Norm." *Journal for the Scientific
Study of Religion* 22, no. 1 (March 1983): 75–86.

Lowenstein, Steven M. "The 1840s and the Creation of the German-Jewish Religious Reform Movement." In *Revolution and Evolution: 1848 in German-Jewish History*, ed. Werner E. Mosse, Arnold Paucker, and Reinhard Rürup, 255–97. Tübingen: Mohr, 1981.

Marx, Alexander. *Essays in Jewish Biography*. Philadelphia: Jewish Publication Society, 1947.

Meiring, Kerstin. *Die christlich-jüdische Mischehe in Deutschland 1840–1933*. Hamburg: Dölling and Galitz, 1998.

Nadler, Allan. "The Unwelcome Mat." *Tablet*, April 16, 2010, http://www.tabletmag.com/news-and-politics/31038/nadler-on-conversion (accessed July 8, 2011).

Nahshoni, Kobi. "Chief Rabbi Metzger Supports Conversions Annulment." Ynetnews, June 17, 2009, http://www.ynetnews.com/articles/0,7340,L-3732780,00.html (accessed July 8, 2011).

———. "Conversion Bill to Face First Reading." Ynetnews, September 21, 2009, http://www.ynetnews.com/articles/0,7340,L-3777775,00.html (accessed July 8, 2011).

Picard, Ariel. *Mishnato shel harav Ovadiah Yosef be'idan shel temurot* [The philosophy of Rabbi Ovadiah Yosef in an age of transition]. Ramat-Gan: Bar-Ilan University Press, 2007.

"Rabbi Urges Leniency in Conversion Practices." *Jewish Post*, July 4, 1952, 1.

Riskin, Shlomo. "Conversion in Jewish Law." In *The Conversion Crisis: Essays from the Pages of Tradition*, ed. Emanuel Feldman and Joel B. Wolowelsky, 59–72. New York: Ktav, 1990.

Sagi, Avi, and Zvi Zohar. *Transforming Identity: The Ritual Transition from Gentile to Jew—Structure and Meaning*. London: Continuum, 2007.

———. "Transforming Identity." *Tradition* 42, no. 2 (2009): 107–14.

Schmemann, Serge. "Accord on Conversion May Elude Netanyahu." *New York Times*, January 24, 1998, http://www.nytimes.com/1998/01/24/world/accord-on-conversion-may-elude-netanyahu.html (accessed July 8, 2011).

———. "'Who's a Jew' Puzzle Gets More Tangled." *New York Times*, January 27, 1998, http://www.nytimes.com/1998/01/27/world/who-s-a-jew-puzzle-gets-more-tangled.html (accessed July 8, 2011).Shapiro, Marc B. *Between the Yeshiva World and Modern Orthodoxy: The Life and Works of Rabbi Jehiel Jacob Weinberg, 1884–1966*. London: Littman, 1998.

———. "Transforming Identity: The Ritual Transformation from Gentile to Jew—Structure and Meaning by Avi Sagi and Zvi Zohar." *Meorot: A Forum of Modern Orthodox Discourse* 8 (5771–2010): 2–14.

Shaviv, Yehudah. "Loved in Life [II Sam. 1:23]—and in Death?" (Hebrew.) *Tehumin* 14 (1993–94): 319–30.

Silber, Michael K. "The Emergence of Ultra-Orthodoxy: The Invention of a Tradition." In *The Uses of Tradition*, ed. Jack Wertheimer, 23–84. New York: Jewish Theological Seminary, 1992.

Supreme Court of Israel. "Non-Orthodox Conversions in Israel." *Justice*, no. 15 (December 1997): 43–48.

Walzer, Michael, Menachem Loberbaum, Noam J. Zohar, and Yair Loberbaum, eds. *The Jewish Political Tradition*. New Haven, Conn.: Yale University Press, 2000.

Washofsky, Mark E. "The Case of the Brother and the Sister: A Critical Analysis of the Decision of Rabbi Shelomo Goren in the Case of Hanokh and Miryam Langer." Rabbinical thesis, HUC-JIR, 1980.

Wertheimer, Jack. *A People Divided: Judaism in Contemporary America*. Waltham, Mass.: Brandeis University Press, 1997.

Zemer, Moshe. *Evolving Halakhah: A Progressive Approach to Traditional Jewish Law*. Woodstock, Vt.: Jewish Lights, 1999.

———. *Halakhah shefuyah*. Tel Aviv: Dvir, 1993.

———. "The Rabbinic Ban on Conversion in Argentina." *Judaism* 37, no. 1 (winter 1988): 84–96.

Zohar, Zvi, and Avraham Sagi. *Giyur vezehut Yehudit*: *Iyun bisodot hahalakhah* [Conversion to Judaism and the meaning of Jewish identity]. Jerusalem: Bialik Institute and Shalom Hartman Institute, 1994.

Zur, Yaakov. *Rabbi Dr. Jakob Hoffmann: The Man and His Era*. (Hebrew.) Jerusalem: Institute for Advanced Torah Studies, 1999.

Index

acculturation, 6, 82–84. *See also* assimilation

adjudication process, 8–9, 165–70. *See also* Jewish law and legal process/tradition; *posekim* (legal authorities/decisors)

Agudath Harabanim (Switzerland), 99, 139

Agudath Israel, 119, 159–60

Amalek. *See* Timna

Amar, Shlomo, 157–58

anusim [compelled ones], 80

Argentinian Jewish community. *See* Sephardim, Syrian

Ariel, Yigal, 155–56, 188n98

Arik, Meir, 101

Aseh lekha rav, 167

assimilation, 40–42, 115. *See also* acculturation

asufi (child of unknown lineage), 83

Aszod, Judah, 83–84

authorities, halakhic. See *posekim* (legal authorities/decisors)

Babylonian Talmud, 144–45. *See also under individual tractates*

Bamberger, Seligman Baer, 42–43

baraitot. See conversion and converts to Judaism: classical sources; Mishnah

Bayme, Steven, 162

beit din (rabbinic court), 40, 52–60; discretion/latitude of, 36, 58, 93, 97–98, 109, 167–68; limitations of, 132; responsibilities of, 188n98. See also *posekim* (legal authorities/decisors); rabbis and the rabbinate

Beit Yitzḥak, 64, 176–77n35

Beit Yosef, 35–36

Bekhorot (BT tractate), 21, 26, 62, 86

Benedikt, Moritz, 46

Berger, Peter, 5

Berkovits, Eliezer, 117, 182n63

Bernays, Isaac, 38

Bible, the: view of conversion and converts, 15–18, 23–24, 74; view of intermarriage, 40, 88

Bikurim (tractate), 23, 34–35

Bin-Nun, Yoel, 154–55

Bleich, J. David, 143

Borokovsky, 145–47

Borokovsky, Hava. *See* Langer, Hava (Borokovsky)

The Boundaries of Judaism, 10

boundary issues and maintenance, 41–42, 115, 119, 154, 163. See also *seyag leTorah* [fence around the Torah]

Braunschweig Rabbinical Conference of 1844, 39–40

Breisch, Mordecai Yaakov, 96–98, 139

Buenos Aires Jewish community. *See* Sephardim, Syrian

Burg, Avraham, 150

burial, Jewish, 94, 104–5, 172n5. *See also* Paschov, Lev

Cardon, E. Louis, 110

Chajes, Zvi Hirsch, 39–40

chief rabbis of Israel, 122; Goren, 142–48; Herzog, 136–42; Kook, 123–26,